· THE · GOURMET'S FREEZER

GLYNN CHRISTIAN
· SUE ROSS ·

SIMON & SCHUSTER

LONDON · SYDNEY · NEW YORK · TOKYO · TORONTO

Recipe Notes

Ingredients are given in both metric and imperial quantities. Use either set of quantities, but not a mixture of both, in any one recipe.

All spoon measurements are level unless otherwise stated:
1 tablespoon = one 15 ml spoon;
1 teaspoon = one 5 ml spoon.

Eggs are standard (size three) unless otherwise stated.

First published in Great Britain by Simon & Schuster Ltd in 1989

Simon & Schuster Ltd
West Garden Place
Kendal Street
London W2 2AQ

Simon & Schuster of Australia Pty Ltd
Sydney

British Library Cataloguing-in-Publication Data available

ISBN 0-671-65319-9

Design: Merchants!
Cover design: Clare Whiting
Typesetting: Goodfellow & Egan
Printed and bound by BPCC Wheatons Ltd, Exeter

GLYNN CHRISTIAN

Glynn Christian is best known as an entertaining and innovative television cook. During well over five hundred broadcasts he has been resident cook for four years on BBC TV's 'Breakfast Time' and now appears regularly on 'Daytime Live', 'Garden Party' and 'This Morning'.

A New Zealander by birth, Glynn has lived in Britain for over twenty years. His interest in food developed with his early career as a travel writer, followed by the opening of his own delicatessen on London's Portobello Road. A regular contributor to *Elle*, *Taste* and other magazines, he is the author of seventeen books, including *Fragile Paradise*, the only biography of Fletcher Christian, leader of the mutiny aboard *Bounty* and his great-great-great-great grandfather.

SUE ROSS

Sue Ross began her career with *Good Housekeeping* and since then she has contributed regularly to such publications as *Ideal Home, Good Housekeeping* and *Taste*. Her regular column for *A La Carte* on gourmet freezer food was highly popular and made her the ideal person to show how to freeze good food.

Sue has lived and worked in France and Africa and further travelling has given her a great interest in cuisines from around the world. She has written six books about food and one travel book.

CONTENTS

INTRODUCTION

The Gourmet's Freezer is a treasure trove of treats, ready when you are to convert plain fare into gourmet pleasure, quickly and excitingly. In it you'll find no bags of bulk basics. Instead you'll find that even the smallest gourmet freezer stores manageable amounts of imaginative ingredients and, if there's space, an exciting array of finished or partially finished dishes.

For country cooks a gourmet freezer stores supplies of specialist ingredients that are difficult to buy locally or a special harvest from the hedgerows; for city workers a gourmet freezer means never having to say sorry about serving plain food because there's always something enticing in the freezer to add zest, flavour and excitement to quickly prepared fresh food or prepared dishes you have bought.

The Gourmet's Freezer is the modern answer for everyone who is passionate about food and hospitality, but doesn't have the time to shop extensively every day. By combining today's style of once-weekly shopping with a constantly changing choice of unusual and exotic ingredients in your freezer, you'll always be able to thrill, amaze and satisfy without spending hours in the kitchen. Here you'll find advice on storing kaffir lime leaves to add exotic bite to a simple salad, a handful of autumn's wild mushrooms to serve with winter's game, rowanberries to add to a stuffing, or celeriac or kohlrabi purée to use in a soufflé. If you discover a fragrant summer rose we show you how to preserve the petals in butter to serve with hot scones on a winter afternoon, or how to save four perfect sardines or red mullets to grill with olive oil and herbs. Whatever your find – boneless breasts of corn-fed chickens, Kent cobs, perfect orange peppers, a single wild duck – you will find plenty of helpful advice and delicious recipes, in a style that is practical enough to add excitement to everyday eating, yet special enough for entertaining.

INFORMATION ON FREEZING

FREEZING AND FREEZERS

Freezing is the quickest and simplest way of preserving food so that it is at the peak of its quality. If correctly carried out it is perfectly safe, and it will keep food close to its original state for weeks, in some cases for months. To obtain the best results there are two basic principles to follow.

Firstly, the major component of most food is water, which crystallises when frozen. The faster the food is frozen, the smaller the crystals and the less damage to the cell walls of the food. Food that is frozen slowly tends to develop large crystals, which in many cases spoils the quality of the food.

Secondly, home freezers store food at a temperature of − 18°C. They are capable of freezing a specified quantity of fresh food (usually about ten per cent of the cabinet's total capacity) down to this temperature within twenty-four hours. If too much fresh food is packed into a freezer at one time,

the system will battle to freeze the food right through; this could affect the quality of the food and make it less safe. The same danger applies to cold, cooked food, which has a 'body' heat of its own called 'fresh warm'. If large quantities of this are put into a freezer the temperature is raised, and this may affect the condition of the food already in the freezer.

Therefore, fast-freezing food in fairly small quantities keeps the structure of the food as perfect as possible and keeps it, and the other food in the freezer, safe. Some freezers have a separate fast-freeze compartment with instructions as to the amount of fresh or 'fresh warm' food that can go in without affecting the temperature of the food already in the cabinet. Other models have a fast-freeze switch or control which lowers the temperature of the inside of the cabinet. If you have an older freezer with neither of these additions, it makes sense to put fresh food in the coldest part of the cabinet and, if possible, to move already frozen food away from it. In a chest freezer, arrange food against the walls. In an upright, stack fresh food on one shelf as near to the freezing coils as possible or, if there are no coils, against the walls of the cabinet.

A frozen food storage compartment inside older refrigerators will not freeze fresh food successfully and will only store already frozen food for short periods. The star rating system on some models indicates the length of time to keep frozen food safely. One star indicates keeping food frozen for up to one week, two stars for up to one month and three stars for three months. It is important to read the instructions that come with your freezer or to check with the manufacturers before trying to freeze any food in the freezer compartment of an older refrigerator.

When making up dishes to store in the freezer it is often perfectly possible to use ingredients that have already been frozen. Such ingredients include herbs, nuts, breadcrumbs, spices, flours and pastry, many of which can be used from frozen. However, it is best to use fresh meat in dishes that are to be frozen, particularly game and poultry, as the quality will be much better.

For good results high quality food should only be frozen for short periods. As a general rule of thumb, the shorter the freezing period of any finished or partially finished dish, the better the final result. Robustly flavoured soups, casseroles and breads can be frozen for long periods, but more delicately flavoured fish, vegetable dishes and desserts should be used within a couple of weeks of freezing.

PACKING AND SEALING

The purpose of careful packing and sealing is to protect food, to exclude as much air as possible (air causes oxidation which makes food look and taste unappetising), to protect delicate food from being crushed, to use the space available to its best advantage and to prevent cross flavouring. Any of the following methods can be used.

Plastic Bags Just about everything can be packed in heavy-duty plastic bags. Economising with 'thinner' bags is usually a waste of time as they tear or puncture so easily. Try to pack everything as squarely as you can so that the packages will stack neatly together. The easiest way is to line a rectangular plastic box or freezer container with a bag that is the same size or larger; then fill it up with the chosen food and freeze, unsealed, until it is hard. When it is frozen, remove the container and use it again; seal and label the filled bag with a chinagraph pencil, either on to the plastic bag itself or on self-sticking labels.

Rigid Containers Fragile items, particularly cakes and meringues, are best packed into rigid containers to prevent them becoming crushed.

Aluminium and Freezer-proof Microwave Dishes These are ideal for freezing precooked or made-up dishes, and they have the added advantage of taking up less space than casserole dishes.

Foil and Plastic Wrap These are ideal for separating individual items like crêpes, but they will need over-wrapping with a heavy-duty bag to prevent tearing.

Whichever way you wrap foods for the freezer, it is worth the extra five minutes it takes to seal and label each item properly.

FREEZING TECHNIQUES

Food that is to be frozen must be absolutely cold before freezing. Apart from freezing in containers or wrappers, the following methods of freezing work well for many items.

Open Freezing   This is often used for fresh fruit and blanched vegetables and it is also ideal for more delicate items such as small pastries. Arrange the food in a single layer on a foil lined tray and freeze it until it is firm before packing.

Purées   Fruit and vegetable purées are perfect for use in gourmet cooking, and fruit purées are particularly delicious if used as a basis for ice creams. Once puréed they may need to be sieved and fruit might need sweetening before freezing. When puréeing fruit that is likely to discolour, add ¼ teaspoon of ascorbic acid crystals or powder to each 250 ml (8 fl oz) of fruit purée.

Dry Sugar Packing   This can be used for fruit that will not discolour. It is not a method for healthy eaters or anyone watching their weight as it uses rather a lot of sugar, but it is useful if you like to serve the fruit with the syrup it produces on thawing. Allow 250 g (8 oz) of sugar to each 1 kg (2 lb) of fruit, toss the fruit and sugar well and freeze.

Sugar Syrup   This has long been favoured as a useful method for freezing fruits such as peaches that are likely to discolour. But if you prefer to freeze the fruit using less sugar, freeze it as a purée.

Ascorbic Acid Solution

Diabetics or slimmers may prefer to dip fruit into an ascorbic acid solution before freezing which avoids the need for sugar. Dissolve ¼ teaspoon of ascorbic acid in 150 ml (5 fl oz) of water, add 500 g (1 lb) of prepared fruit and leave for fifteen minutes before draining and packing. Or pack the fruit in a solution made with ¼ teaspoon of ascorbic acid and 500 ml (18 fl oz) of water.

Blanching   Vegetables that are to be frozen for longer than a week should be blanched. This destroys the enzymes or chemicals that affect their colour, flavour and texture. The vegetables need to be immersed in boiling water or steamed for an exact length of time: too little won't kill the enzymes and too much will spoil the flavour. Once blanched they must be drained quickly, plunged into iced water, drained again and frozen.

DEFROSTING AND MICROWAVE THAWING

Defrosting times, to be honest, are always approximate and depend on so many variables, from the amount to be thawed and the temperature of your refrigerator or kitchen, to the size and depth of dish you are using. Vegetables, on the other hand, are much nicer if cooked from frozen, and some fruits, particularly soft berries, are often nicer if they are still slightly frosted when eaten. We have indicated which ingredients can be used from frozen, other food should be thawed completely before use.

Thawing precooked food thoroughly shortens the time needed to recook or reheat. In order to prevent disappointment, allow plenty of time for thawing and reheating and do make sure that precooked dishes are, if necessary, completely heated through. A microwave cooker makes an amazing difference to thawing food more speedily and many of the newer ones have a defrosting control which is worth using to prevent spoilage. Special freezer-to-microwave dishes and containers make the process more foolproof for many made-up dishes. In general, thaw precooked foods, including pastries, for at least an hour at room temperature or for three to four hours in the refrigerator. Heat sauces gently and whisk hard to reconstitute them to a smooth consistency.

FURTHER READING

For more detailed information on freezing you should refer to a freezing handbook or any of the books listed below.
Mary Berry, *The Complete Book of Freezer Cooking*, Octopus
Marika Hanbury Tenison, *Deep Freeze Cookery*, Pan
Will it Freeze?, compiled by Joan Hood with additional research by Vivien Donald, Home & Freezer Digest

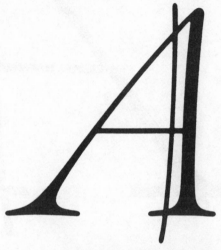

**THE GOURMET'S FREEZER
AN A–Z OF FABULOUS INGREDIENTS
AND RECIPES**

Almonds
Apples
Apricots
Artichokes
Asparagus
Aubergine
Avocado

A

ALMONDS

Indispensable for good cooking of every possible type and far more reliable and better value for being frozen. Buy them ready chopped, nibbed, flaked or ground, and from shops with a fast turnover, so they are as retail-fresh as possible. Pack them in useable quantities for freezing and use from frozen. Ground almonds are the most useful single choice. Used instead of breadcrumbs in stuffing or coatings, they perform the same task, adding rich, mysterious flavour which underpins what is there, rather than adding another. One of my favourite tricks is to coat whole skinned fish with a thick mixture of drained, grated courgettes, ground almonds, a little fresh thyme and an egg white or two for binding. Fillets and small soles, for instance, might gently be fried thus coated; whole coated fish (especially monkfish), steaks or boneless sides are best baked in the oven. Ground almonds wonderfully thicken sweet sauces: even something as simple as whipped cream is improved, especially with the addition of orange-flower water, which is the greatest culinary friend of almonds. I use them also to add bulk to mousses. But whatever I do I invariably toast them (yes, ground almonds) before I use them, for this concentrates the flavour and makes them more absorbent.

The smartest type of almond for freezing is the milky-fresh green almond, usually bought with a silken-furred soft shell. Freeze them as they are and use the slightly chewy kernel in salads later in summer, or strew them over fish. It would be sen-sational to serve them when you have used almond oil for a dressing. Finely chopped or minced and mixed with eggs, cream and perhaps the slightest touch of bitter almond essence, they make a voluptuous covered pie that I found in south-west France. More simply, you might serve them with dried fruits, or over that greatest of Moroccan ways to end a meal, thick slices of orange dusted with cinnamon.

CHOCOLATE ALMOND PETITS FOURS

150 g (5 oz) blanched almonds
125 g (4 oz) hazelnuts
50 g (2 oz) glacé cherries, chopped
50 g (2 oz) chopped mixed peel
75 g (3 oz) plain flour, sifted
2 tablespoons cocoa powder
1 teaspoon ground cinnamon
75 g (3 oz) sugar
125 ml (4 fl oz) clear honey
75 g (3 oz) plain chocolate, melted
1 sheet of rice paper
icing sugar, sifted, to serve

Makes 18

Spread the almonds and hazelnuts on a baking sheet and grill them, turning them occasionally, until they are lightly golden. Rub off any loose hazelnut skins and roughly chop the nuts. Mix the nuts, cherries, peel, flour, cocoa and cinnamon together.

Heat the sugar and honey in a saucepan over a low heat until the sugar has dissolved. Bring to the boil and boil steadily until the syrup reaches the soft ball stage, when a little dropped into a cup of cold water forms a ball if rolled between the fingers. This takes about 5 minutes. Add this syrup to the melted chocolate, stir in the nut mixture and spread into a 20 cm (8-inch) square cake tin lined with a sheet of rice paper.

see also
BUTTERS, FLAVOURED (page 40)
CREAM CHEESE (page 69)
KOHLRABI (page 115)
Amaretti Ice Cream
Sambuca (page 110)
Apricot Frangipane (page 16)
Berry Japonaise (page 123)
Chocolate Amaretti Figs (page 86)
Praline Japonaise (page 123)

Bake in a preheated oven at Gas Mark 3/160°C/325°F for 35 minutes.

Turn out the mixture and cool on a wire rack. Wrap in foil and leave for a day or two before cutting into bite-size diamonds. FREEZE or serve sprinkled with icing sugar. Serve with coffee.

To serve from frozen: Allow the petits fours to thaw at room temperature for at least 1 hour. Sprinkle them with sifted icing sugar before serving.

CHOCOLATE ALMOND CAKE

Cake
175 g (6 oz) good-quality plain chocolate, broken into pieces
5 large eggs (size 1 or 2), separated
150 g (5 oz) caster sugar
2 tablespoons hot water
oil for greasing
Filling
100 g (3½ oz) plain chocolate
284 ml (10 fl oz) carton of whipping cream
125 g (4 oz) almond flakes
25 g (1 oz) icing sugar
3–4 tablespoons brandy
Topping
125 g (4 oz) plain chocolate
2 tablespoons icing sugar

Serves 6

To make the cake, melt the chocolate in a bowl set over a saucepan of hot water. Remove from the heat. Whisk the egg yolks and sugar until pale and thick. Stir in the hot water and then fold the egg mixture into the melted chocolate. Whisk the egg whites until they are stiff and fold them thoroughly into the cake mixture.

Oil a 23 × 33 cm (9- × 13-inch) swiss roll tin and line it with non-stick baking paper. Spread the sponge mixture in the tin and bake in a preheated oven at Gas Mark 4/180°C/350°F for 15–20 minutes. Take out of the oven, cover with a clean tea towel and leave until cold. Turn the sponge on to a sheet of greaseproof paper and carefully peel away the baking paper. Trim the edges and cut the cake across the shortest width into four equal strips.

To make the filling, melt the chocolate, allow it to cool and then beat in the cream. Coarsely grind the nuts with the icing sugar and brandy. Spread the chocolate cream carefully over two of the strips of sponge. Top with the nut mixture and cover with a second layer of sponge.

To make the topping, melt the chocolate and spread it evenly over the top of the two strips of cake. When it is just beginning to set, use a sharp knife to cut each strip into three cakes. FREEZE or, using a sheet of thin card as a shield, dust half of each cake with the sifted icing sugar. Serve with extra cream if wished.

To serve from frozen: Thaw at room temperature for 2–3 hours and serve as above.

REDCURRANT AND ALMOND TARTLETS

Rich Pastry Tartlets
175 g (6 oz) plain flour
a pinch of salt
1 tablespoon icing sugar
140 g (4½ oz) butter, cut into small pieces
1 tablespoon iced water
Filling
2 tablespoons redcurrant jelly
125 g (4 oz) ground almonds
50 g (2 oz) caster sugar
50 g (2 oz) butter
1 egg
1 tablespoon plain flour
Topping
125 g (4 oz) almond flakes
175 ml (6 fl oz) whipping cream
150 g (5 oz) sugar
1 tablespoon Amaretto liqueur

Makes 12

A

To make the pastry, sift the flour, salt and icing sugar into a bowl. Add the butter and rub it into the flour until the mixture looks like fine breadcrumbs. Stir in the iced water and mix to a firm dough. Chill for 30 minutes; then press the pastry into twelve 9 cm (3½-inch) deep tartlet tins and chill again for 10 minutes. Bake the pastries blind in a preheated oven at Gas Mark 6/200°C/400°F for 10 minutes.

Spoon the redcurrant jelly into the pastry cases. Beat all the remaining filling ingredients together and divide between the pastry cases. Spread the tops flat and continue to bake at Gas Mark 5/190°C/375°F for 10 minutes.

For the topping, mix the almonds, cream and sugar together in a small, non-stick or heavy-based saucepan and, stirring all the time, boil briskly for 5 minutes or until thickened. Stir in the liqueur and leave to cool for 2 minutes; then spoon over the half-set almond filling and continue to bake for 10 minutes until golden. Remove the tarts from the tins while still warm. Cool and FREEZE or serve with cream or fromage frais.

To serve from frozen: Reheat the tarts from frozen in a preheated oven at Gas Mark 5/190°C/375°F for 8–10 minutes.

ANCHOVIES

see FISH

APPLES

It is only worth freezing apples if you can lay your hands on such rare varieties as the *d'Arcy Spice* or the violet-, pineapple-,

honey- or raspberry-flavoured varieties; they make spectacularly good pies which often don't need sugar. Otherwise you would do better to freeze whole crab apples, even if they do split. Shove them around or into poultry or game when roasting; then force the pulp and juices through a sieve to make a sauce. Serve the sauce with a couple of whole crab apples: excellent with wild duck and with guinea-fowl. Whole garlic cloves in their skins make a good garnish, and a dash of Calvados or greatly reduced cider from your frozen store (page 62) might be added towards the end of cooking.

Some store of frozen crab apple sauce made as above would be a very good thing to have, and a nice talking point, with a roasted duck or a piece of pork; as you have to cook them in their skins the sauce is often unexpectedly pink, and so much the better for that.

APRICOTS

A coulis of fresh apricots, or of some stewed ones, is good fare for the freezer. Apricots will freeze whole for up to a week, but if you want to freeze them for longer take out the stones and store them in sugar or syrup or as a purée.

Dried apricots are invariably much tastier and cut more of a culinary dash. They freeze perfectly as they are or cooked. Gently poach some sharp dried apricots – Turkish ones are a good bet – in orange juice, cider and wine or some other sensible combination; purée and strain. When defrosted, thin the purée and sweeten and spice it to flood pudding plates, instead of the ubiquitous raspberry;

see also
ELDERFLOWER (page 83)
PEARS (page 148)
PHYSALIS (page 153)
QUINCE (page 163)
SORBET (page 181)
Apple and Cinnamon Ice Cream (page 109)
Apple and Lime Rosti (page 159)
Duck with Apple and Green Peppercorn Sauce (page 79)

see also
CREAM CHEESE (page 69)
PUMPKIN (page 160)
SORBET (page 181)
Apricot and Orange Ice Cream (page 109)

black rum and/or orange-flower water are unexpected affinities for last-minute flavourings. Otherwise, stew gently with a little onion, garlic, bay and orange rind, and a piece of chilli pepper, to make a sharp hot or cold sauce for meat, fish and poultry; I would strain it, but you could also try leaving it lumpy and perhaps also add raisins or currants to make a fresh, lightly spiced, chutney-style sauce.

WINTER FRUIT COMPOTE WITH WHISKY

250 g (8 oz) dried apricots
250 g (8oz) dried peaches
125 g (4 oz) dried figs
cold black tea for soaking
500 ml (18 fl oz) fresh orange juice
3 tablespoons clear honey
150 ml (¼ pint) whisky
125 g (4 oz) fresh dates

Serves 6

Soak the apricots, peaches and figs in cold tea overnight. Drain.

Mix the orange juice, honey and whisky together in a pan and bring slowly to the boil. Simmer together for 2–3 minutes and then add all the fruit except the dates and simmer together for 30–40 minutes, or until the fruit is tender. Cool, stir in the dates and FREEZE, or serve with clotted cream or greek yogurt.

To serve from frozen: Thaw at room temperature for 2–3 hours before serving.

APRICOT FRANGIPANE

1 quantity of Rich Shortcrust Pastry (page 141)
Filling
150 g (5 oz) pre-soaked dried apricots
200 ml (7 fl oz) fresh orange juice
125 g (4 oz) butter
125 g (4 oż) caster sugar
2 large eggs (size 1 or 2), beaten lightly
75 g (3 oz) self-raising flour, sifted
40 g (1½ oz) ground almonds
125 g (4 oz) almonds, chopped finely
Decoration
2 tablespoons sieved apricot jam, warmed
284 ml (10 fl oz) carton of double cream, whipped
chocolate curls

Serves 6

Roll out the pastry and use it to line a 23 cm (9-inch) loose-based flan ring. Line the pastry case with foil, fill it with baking beans and bake blind in a preheated oven at Gas Mark 6/200°C/400°F for 15 minutes. Remove the baking beans and foil and continue to bake for a further 5–10 minutes until the pastry is crisp.

To make the filling, simmer the apricots in the orange juice until they are really tender and all the liquid has evaporated. When they are cool, chop them.

Cream together the butter and sugar. Beat in the eggs a little at a time. Fold in the sifted flour and ground almonds and then the chopped apricots and almonds.

Spoon the filling into the pastry case and bake in the oven at Gas Mark 4/180°C/350°F for 45–50 minutes until the filling is firm. When cool, lift the flan out of the tin. Leave until completely cold.

Glaze the top of the flan with the warm apricot jam. When the glaze is cold, pipe the top with the cream and decorate with chocolate curls. FREEZE or serve.

A

To serve from frozen: Thaw in the refrigerator for at least 4 hours before serving.

CARAMELISED APRICOT CREAMS

I like to cook dried apricot compote or fresh or frozen plums in the same way.

1 kg (2 lb) ripe apricots, halved and stoned
125 g (4 oz) soft brown sugar
284 ml (10 fl oz) carton of whipping cream
3 egg yolks
1 teaspoon plain flour
ground cinnamon for sprinkling

Serves 6

Toss the apricots with 25 g (1 oz) of the sugar in a basin and leave while making the custard.

Heat the cream. Beat the egg yolks until pale, stir in the flour and whisk in the hot cream. Return to the saucepan and reheat gently, without boiling, whisking all the time until the custard thickens enough to coat the back of a wooden spoon. Pour into a white china quiche dish or individual ovenproof dishes and arrange the drained apricots, cut side up, over the custard. FREEZE or chill overnight.

To serve, sprinkle the apricot custard with the rest of the sugar and cinnamon. Slide under a pre-heated grill and leave until the sugar is melted, bubbling and golden. Serve with brandy snaps or crisp almond biscuits.

To serve from frozen: Thaw the custard for 1–2 hours; then top with the sugar and cinnamon, and grill as above.

Globe artichokes: look specially for baby artichokes which can be eaten whole and freeze these either blanched or fully cooked. Naturally a glut of bigger globe artichokes suggests you would either blanch them whole before freezing or excavate, blanch and freeze the artichoke bottoms only, and very nice too; but as they are easily available in tins this may not be quite so necessary. The small ones are gorgeous sweated with garlic in olive oil and served warm, and can also be sliced as a superior addition to pasta dishes or salads, especially those containing shellfish or crustaceans; they also make pretty, if startling, additions to clear soups.

Jerusalem artichokes: these can be frozen whole once they have been blanched for a few minutes. But on boring days it is therapeutic to clean and cook piles of this knobbly root, and convert it into a thick, strained purée which can then be frozen. This can be the basis of a simple vegetable soufflé, or the greatest of all soups. When diluting the purée use lots of milk and a little chicken stock, or milk and stock cubes, to keep the colour light. The best serving suggestion for jerusalem artichoke soup I know, is to cook down strips of streaky bacon and then to add lots of coarsely chopped parsley, finely chopped garlic and some cubed, de-seeded and skinned tomato. Cook only long enough to brighten the colour of the parsley. Put a dollop of cold whipped cream on to the soup and then some of the warm dressing on the cream.

Chinese artichokes (Crosnes):

see also
FISH (page 86)
PASTA (page 134)
Cappelletti, Wild Mushroom and Artichoke Pie (page 137)
Potato and Celeriac Choux (page 45)
Strips of Veal with Artichokes in a Tomato Sauce (page 195)

these small pinkish vegetables did come from China but are also called *Crosnes* because that is the village in France where they were first grown in Europe. They have a nice flavour but are more impressive for their wonderful corkscrewed appearance; a really fun vegetable or salad ingredient on special occasions, and just the thing to add appeal to a stir-fry when little else interesting is available. Just blanch for a few minutes before freezing.

JERUSALEM ARTICHOKE AND CHERVIL PIE

Try this satisfying pie with sliced potatoes and herbs if you have no artichokes. Serve with roast or grilled meats, or serve as a dish on its own with green beans and almonds or broccoli.

500 g (1 lb) jerusalem artichokes
a little milk
500 g (1 lb) waxy potatoes, peeled and cut into thin, even slices
2 quantities (500 g/1 lb) of Puff Pastry (page 142)
2 garlic cloves, chopped finely
2 tablespoons freshly chopped chervil
2 tablespoons freshly chopped parsley
50 g (2 oz) butter
1 egg, beaten with a little milk
salt and freshly ground black pepper
Topping
142 ml (5 fl oz) carton of double cream
2 tablespoons freshly chopped chervil

Serves 6

Blanch the artichoke slices in milk for 7–8 minutes. Cook the potatoes in boiling, salted water for 4–5 minutes until just tender. Drain and rinse them thoroughly and drain again.

Divide the pastry into two and roll out one half to fit a round 25 cm (10-inch) cake tin. Line the tin with the rolled-out pastry. Arrange the potatoes and artichokes in layers in the tin, sprinkling each layer with the garlic, chopped herbs and seasoning and dotting the layers with the butter.

Brush the edges of the pastry with some of the beaten egg. Roll out the second piece of pastry and use this to cover the pie. Press the edges together to seal them firmly. Trim the pastry, make a hole in the centre and decorate the top with the trimmings if liked. Brush the top with the rest of the beaten egg and bake in a preheated oven at Gas Mark 7/220°C/425°F for 30 minutes until the pastry is golden-brown. If necessary, cover the pastry with foil to prevent it browning too much.

FREEZE the pie or heat together the cream and chervil and pour this mixture through the hole in the top of the pie.

To serve from frozen: Thaw the pie overnight in the refrigerator and reheat in a preheated oven at Gas Mark 4/180°C/350°F for 30 minutes. Prepare the cream topping and continue as above.

A

ARTICHOKE AND OYSTER CORONET

oil for greasing
125 g (4 oz) can of smoked oysters
1 chicken stock cube
1 large garlic clove
5 drops of Tabasco sauce
500 g (1 lb) jerusalem artichokes, peeled and cut into small pieces
milk if necessary
450 ml (¾ pint) tomato juice
juice of 1 large lemon
1 tablespoon chopped parsley
5 fl oz (142 ml) carton of double cream, whipped lightly
20 g (¾ oz) gelatine
salt

Serves 6

Chill an oiled 1.2-litre (2-pint) ring mould or soufflé dish.

Drain the smoked oysters and reserve them. Add the stock cube, garlic, Tabasco sauce and salt to the oil and juice from the can.

Place the artichoke pieces in a pan and pour over the oyster liquid, adding enough water so that the liquid just covers the artichoke pieces. Cook until tender and then purée and strain. You should have 450 ml (¾ pint) of purée. If not, add milk or reduce over a gentle heat until you have the right quantity. Add 300 ml (½ pint) of the tomato juice and leave to cool.

Cut the reserved oysters in half and drench them in the lemon juice. Toss them in the parsley and arrange them in the bottom of the prepared mould. Spread the lightly whipped cream evenly over them.

Dissolve the gelatine in the rest of the tomato juice over a gentle heat. Strain and stir in the artichoke purée. Pour enough of the mixture into the mould to cover the cream. Stir gently to create a marbled effect and then chill the mould until the mixture sets.

Pour the rest of the artichoke mixture into the mould and FREEZE, or chill for at least 4 hours before serving with parsley and brown bread.

To serve from frozen: Thaw the mould overnight in the refrigerator before serving.

© *Glynn Christian*

ASPARAGUS

In spite of advances being made in New Zealand with cryogenic freezing, asparagus fibre tends to break down and soften when frozen. Best therefore at glut time to make and freeze thick purées for sauces, soups and soufflés. Whizz some of it into a good vinaigrette to serve with hot or cold salmon in summer. Or steam it as a custard with eggs and cream in ramekins over the same fish, whole quails (the Romans did), chicken or turkey breast, or crisp-fatted slivers of duck or goose. To do this, make a custard with the purée mixed with cream, plus 1 egg yolk per 150 ml (¼ pint) of creamy purée.

AUBERGINE

You can save time for some future moussaka-party by freezing drained slices which have subsequently been fried in oil. Or store away blanched slices to use from frozen, thus avoiding the lengthy salting process. An aubergine purée, like the one following, is always useful to have at hand. But my favourite way is to buy the tiny spherical aubergines (which originally gave the vegetable its other name, egg-plant) freeze them

see also
COURGETTES (page 64)
SANDWICHES (page 171)
Aubergine and Chicken Liver Timbale (page 56)

whole, and serve them unexpectedly fried whole or halved in olive oil, with tomatoes and olives, chilli pepper and fresh coriander. Of course it would be no bad thing to have such a delicious mixture in the freezer to give colour and flavour to a simple piece of grilled fish or poultry.

AUBERGINE AND LIME SALAD WITH SUN-DRIED TOMATO

Strips of sun-dried tomato garnish make this Turkish speciality a really exciting first course or savoury. Serve it as a dip with strips of toasted pitta bread or as part of a buffet meal.

500 g (1 lb) aubergines
1 garlic clove, crushed
3−4 tablespoons walnut or olive oil
lime juice to taste
50 g (2 oz) sun-dried tomatoes, cut into thin strips
freshly chopped parsley
salt and freshly ground black pepper

Serves 6 as part of an hors-d'oeuvre

Put the unpeeled aubergines under a very hot grill, turning them once or twice, until the skins are blackened and beginning to blister. (You can bake them in a preheated oven at Gas Mark 6/200°C/400°F until they are soft, but they will lack the lovely smoky flavour of grilled aubergine.) Peel off the skins under running cold water; then put the aubergines into a sieve and press them down with a wooden spoon to squeeze out as much juice as possible.

Blend or liquidise the aubergine pulp with the garlic, at the same time adding half the oil drop by drop to make a smooth, thick

paste. Flavour with lime juice and salt and pepper. FREEZE or spoon into a serving dish, sprinkle with the remaining oil and top with a lattice of sun-dried tomato strips. Sprinkle with parsley and serve.

To serve from frozen: Thaw the purée for 3−4 hours at room temperature or overnight in the refrigerator and continue as above.

AUBERGINE AND RED PEPPER STRUDELS

These are good with a cucumber and yogurt salad, or serve them as part of a buffet meal.

6 tablespoons olive oil
250 g (8 oz) onion, chopped finely
2 garlic cloves, crushed
1 chilli, de-seeded and chopped
1 tablespoon ground coriander
750 g (1½ lb) aubergines, chopped finely
1 red pepper, de-seeded and chopped
397 g (14 oz) can of tomatoes
9 sheets of Filo Pastry or Strudel Pastry (page 143)
50 g (2 oz) butter, melted
grated parmesan cheese for sprinkling
salt and freshly ground black pepper

Makes 18

Heat half the oil in a large saucepan and sauté the onion and garlic until they are soft. Add the remaining oil, the chilli, coriander, aubergine and pepper, and stir well. Add the tomatoes and their liquid and simmer gently for 20 minutes, until the aubergine is tender and the liquid has evaporated. Cool, and check the seasoning.

Cut each sheet of pastry in half and stack the sheets one on top of the other. Brush the top sheet with a little of the melted butter,

A

fold the pastry in half and spoon a 6 cm (2½-inch) line of filling along one edge. Fold both edges of the pastry over the filling; then roll up the pastry to form a fat cigar. Lift the strudel on to a baking sheet while completing the remaining pastries.

Brush the pastries with the remaining butter, sprinkle the tops with grated parmesan cheese and bake them in a pre-heated oven at Gas Mark 5/190°C/375°F for 20–25 minutes until they are crisp and golden. FREEZE or serve.

To serve from frozen: Reheat the pastries in a preheated oven at Gas Mark 4/180°C/350°F for 30–35 minutes until piping hot.

TERRINES OF HOT AUBERGINE WITH TOMATO AND SHERRY SAUCE

The flavour of these individual aubergine terrines is equally delicious with Red Pepper Sauce (page 152). They make a good first course or an ideal side dish for grilled lamb.

1.5 kg (3½ lb) aubergines
125 ml (4 fl oz) oil
2 tablespoons plain flour
227 g (8 oz) carton of skimmed milk soft cheese
75 ml (3 fl oz) milk
3 large eggs (size 1), beaten
butter for greasing
salt and freshly ground black pepper
Tomato and Sherry Sauce
1 kg (2 lb) tomatoes, peeled, de-seeded and chopped
2 tablespoons dry sherry
125 ml (4 fl oz) tomato juice
a pinch of caster sugar
150 ml (¼ pint) chicken stock or water

Serves 6

Cut 500 g (1 lb) of the aubergines into 5 mm (¼-inch) slices and layer them in a colander, sprinkling each layer lightly with salt. Leave them for 15–20 minutes; then drain them and pat them dry. Sauté the aubergine slices in batches in a little of the oil until they are golden-brown on both sides and tender. Drain them well.

Carefully peel the remaining aubergines, dice the flesh and simmer in salted water for 5 minutes. Drain the aubergine dice; then stir fry them in 6 tablespoons of the oil until well coated. Stir in the flour and cook gently for 1 minute without browning. Take the aubergines off the heat and liquidise or blend them until smooth. Add the cheese, milk, beaten eggs and seasoning and blend again.

Arrange the slices of sautéed aubergine in six 150 ml (¼-pint) moulds. Fill with the creamed aubergine and cover the tops with sheets of buttered paper. Cook in a bain-marie in a preheated oven at Gas Mark 4/180°C/350°F for 20–25 minutes until the terrines are just firm and cooked through. Cool and FREEZE or leave them to stand for 2–3 minutes; then turn out on to individual plates.

To make the sauce, put all the ingredients into a saucepan and simmer them together for 25–30 minutes. Sieve or liquidise the sauce and check the seasoning. FREEZE or serve with the terrines.

To serve from frozen: Stand the aubergine terrines in a deep roasting tin of gently simmering water and reheat for 30–40 minutes until completely thawed and piping hot. Reheat the sauce over a gentle heat. Turn out the terrines and serve with the sauce.

AUBERGINE, TOMATO AND OLIVE SAUCE

This sauce is ideal to serve with lamb or pasta or buckwheat pancakes.

2 medium-size aubergines
2 garlic cloves, chopped finely
375 g (12 oz) ripe tomatoes, peeled, de-seeded and chopped
1 tablespoon Olivade (page 129)
1 teaspoon freshly chopped marjoram
salt and freshly ground black pepper

Serves 6

Put the aubergines under a very hot grill, turning them once or twice until the skins are black and beginning to blister. Cool and peel off the skins.

Chop the aubergine flesh and transfer it to a saucepan with the garlic, tomatoes, Olivade, marjoram and seasoning. Simmer gently together for 15–20 minutes; then liquidise if liked and FREEZE or reheat.

To serve from frozen: Reheat the sauce gently until piping hot.

No point freezing whole ones. But when there are plenty of softies about at a good price there are sorbets (page 184) and ice creams (page 112) to consider putting by for another day. Or store away the puréed flesh mixed with a little lemon juice and use it to make superb salad dressings. Just mix it with a little orange and lemon juice, ground almonds, olive oil, orange-flower water and salt and use instead of mayonnaise to dress cold meat and vegetables. Add a little yogurt or whipped cream for lightness or replace the orange juice with extra lemon juice, the orange-flower water with mint, add a little garlic and leave for a few hours to develop the flavours. Of course these can be frozen ready-made for up to a week if you want.

Please resist all recipes which call for avocado to be cooked, for it develops a bitter, grassy flavour. If gently warmed only, avocado retains its honesty, and thus that rich purée of ripe avocado also whisks wonderfully into such simple soups as a chicken or fish consommé (or that stock you've got hanging around) just before serving. Sadly for waistlines, cream soups are even more improved. If there are some good avocados about in the shops when you serve your soup, buy an extra one and sprinkle cubes of it, well bathed in lime juice, on top. Chopped dill, mint and parsley also like to be associated with warm cream of avocado. But don't boil the soup.

see also
Avocado and Cucumber Sorbet (page 184)
Avocado and Lime Ice Cream (page 112)

Smoked turkey makes an equally delicious alternative to chicken.

**1 tablespoon gelatine
200 ml (7 fl oz) chicken stock
2 small avocados, peeled, stoned and mashed
lemon juice to taste
Tabasco sauce to taste
100 ml (3½ fl oz) mayonnaise
200 ml (7 fl oz) double cream
375 g (12 oz) smoked chicken breast, sliced
salt and freshly ground black pepper**

Serves 6

Dissolve the gelatine in half the stock. When it is clear, add the remaining stock and mix well.

Season the mashed avocados with lemon juice, Tabasco and salt and pepper. Beat in the mayonnaise and then the gelatine mixture. Whip the cream until it forms stiff peaks and fold it into the avocado mousse.

Line a 750 ml (1¼-pint) loaf tin with plastic wrap and put a third of the chicken in the bottom. Cover with half the avocado mixture, another layer of chicken and the remaining avocado. Top with the remaining chicken slices. Freeze the terrine until hard and then double wrap and FREEZE, or freeze until firm, unmould and slice. Serve the slices with Melba toast or fresh wholewheat bread.

To serve from frozen: Thaw the terrine overnight in the refrigerator.

Bacon
Bamboo Shoots
Bananas
Beans
Bean Sprouts
Beef
Beetroot
Berries
Biscuits
Bread
Brioche
Buckwheat
Butters, flavoured

BACON

Crisp bits for salads, stuffing and likewise are worth putting into the freezer for a short time, if you cook more than you need. If you want to, fresh bacon rashers and joints, and cooked whole or sliced joints also freeze well for short periods.

see also
RICE (page 167)
Bacon Muffins (page 125)

BAMBOO SHOOTS

These are often available fresh at speciality Eastern suppliers and are not very expensive. When fresh they have an extra acidity and, well, bamboo flavour that the canned variety cannot match, but they don't keep at all well. If you see them it is thus worth putting them straight in the freezer once scrubbed, peeled and blanched. If you do find yourself with a partially used can of bamboo shoots for which you have no immediate use, freeze the contents either drained or in their liquid. Cook either kind straight from the freezer, but expect the freezing to break the fibres down somewhat.

BANANAS

Don't turn up your nose when you see really ripe, black-skinned or brown-spotted bananas. Only these *are* bananas, only these are ripe and sweet and flavoursome enough to eat, although the Great British public has this extraordinary ability to enjoy bananas that pull at the roof of the mouth with acidity and greenness of flavour. Mashed, really ripe bananas make the greatest of ice creams imaginable (page 109),

see also
Banana and Chocolate Muffins (page 125)
Banana Ice Cream (page 109)
Banana Muffins (page 125)

and cake-makers should make banana bread, banana muffins (page 125) or a banana cake, like the one following, for the freezer. One of the greatest tricks when eventually serving such goodies as a banana cake is to make the icing with mashed banana instead of or as well as butter; then to stir in masses of cocoa to give a rich chocolate flavour. The unexpectedness of the banana in the icing is memorable. Banana is always best frozen in such ready-made dishes, although a purée of banana, lemon juice and sugar can be frozen for later use.

Now, banana leaves. There are many thousands of banana trees grown in places far from the tropics — London office buildings and a conservatory I know of in Scotland, for instance. Fruit is unlikely, even a budding promise is far from the thoughts of their owners, yet the leaves, decorative as they might be, have further uses, as wrappings for steamed and baked food of Pacific or Oriental persuasion. Little flavour is given to the food, but the effect certainly helps conversation at a difficult table.

FRESH BANANA AND PINEAPPLE CAKE WITH CREAM CHEESE FROSTING

250 g (8 oz) self-raising flour
1 teaspoon baking powder
1 teaspoon ground cinnamon
250 g (8 oz) caster sugar
2 eggs, beaten
250 ml (8 fl oz) oil
175 g (6 oz) fresh pineapple,
chopped roughly
1 large ripe banana, mashed
butter for greasing
Icing:
50 g (2 oz) unsalted butter
125 g (4 oz) cream cheese
175 g (6 oz) icing sugar, sifted
a little milk if necessary
175 g (6 oz) fresh pineapple,
chopped finely, *or* 2 ripe bananas,
mashed (optional)

Makes one 20 cm (8-inch) cake

Sift the flour, baking powder and cinnamon into a large mixing bowl. Stir in the sugar. Add the eggs and oil and stir well, without beating, until all the ingredients are well mixed. Fold in the pineapple and banana and spoon into a base-lined, well-greased 20 cm (8-inch) spring-form deep cake tin. Bake in a preheated oven at Gas Mark 4/180°C/350°F for 45–50 minutes until the cake is firm. Cool in the tin for 10 minutes before turning out to cool completely.

To make the icing, blend together the butter and cream cheese. Add enough icing sugar to give the mixture a smooth spreading consistency, if necessary moistening the mixture with a little milk.

Once the cake is cold, spread with the finely chopped pineapple or mashed banana, if used, and top with the icing, marking the surface with the prongs of a fork. Leave for 1–2 hours for the flavours to blend. FREEZE or serve.

To serve from frozen: Thaw the cake at room temperature for 1–2 hours.

BEANS

see also
BUTTERS, FLAVOURED
(page 40)

Freezing home-grown beans is so time-consuming that you might be better-off buying good-quality commercial frozen beans. There are some special cases though.

Broad beans: smarties blanch and freeze the whole beans, pod and all, when they are very young, and serve them whole. Otherwise, if you have plenty of helpers, blanch the podded beans and then slip off the outer tough coating of each bean to reveal the vibrantly coloured inner bean. Defrost them for salads; they are gorgeous with really ripe tomatoes or with cubes of watermelon. Serve hot in a decent white sauce, perhaps just of reduced double cream, to which the frozen beans must only be added at the last minute; or simply as a casual, out-of-season pile. Summer savory, the *sariette* of Provence, is the best of herbs for broad beans (some would say the only one).

Butter beans: not the big dried ones, but the golden variety of so-called french beans. Grow them or find them at a pick-your-own, blanch quickly and freeze for gorgeous colour on hand just when you need it.

B

BEAN SPROUTS

These are excellent canned and don't freeze especially well raw. On the other hand they stand up well when frozen as part of a batch of home-made spring rolls, and these would be an excellent thing to keep in your freezer for cooking quickly from frozen.

SPRING PANCAKE ROLLS WITH CHINESE VEGETABLES

Delicious little parcels of savoury fillings which can be vegetarian or not, depending on your taste. Serve with spicy Tomato and Coriander Sauce (page 191) or a spicy plum sauce and lots of chinese noodles tossed in sesame seeds.

**6 tablespoons plain flour
4 tablespoons cornflour
2 tablespoons salad oil
approximately 300 ml (½ pint) water
oil for frying**
Filling
**1 teaspoon freshly chopped root ginger
1 garlic clove, crushed
1 tablespoon salad oil
1 bunch of spring onions, shredded finely
25 g (1 oz) mooli, shredded finely
1 red pepper, de-seeded and shredded
50 g (2 oz) mangetout, shredded finely
175 g (6 oz) bean sprouts
1 tablespoon black bean sauce
oil for deep-frying
salt and freshly ground black pepper**

Makes 14–15

Stir the flour, cornflour, oil and water together to make a thin, runny batter. To make the pancakes, spoon 2 tablespoons of batter into the centre of a hot, lightly oiled frying pan and swirl it around quickly to cover the entire bottom of the pan. Cook until the edges of the batter begin to shrink from the sides and the pancake is dry but not coloured. Transfer the pancake to a plate, cover it with a damp cloth and repeat the process until nearly all the batter is used up, making about 15 pancakes 16 cm (6½ inches) in diameter.

For the filling, stir-fry the ginger and garlic in the salad oil for 30 seconds. Add the shredded onions, mooli, red pepper and mangetout and stir-fry for 1 minute. Add the bean sprouts. Season with salt and pepper and stir in the bean sauce. Drain off any liquid.

Spread 1 tablespoon of the filling mixture evenly on the uncooked side of each pancake. Brush the edges of the pancakes with the remaining batter. Fold in the sides and roll up into cigar shaped parcels. FREEZE or fry in deep, hot oil over a low heat until they are golden in colour.

To serve from frozen: Deep-fry the pancake rolls in hot oil over a low heat for about 8 minutes until the filling is completely reheated.

BEEF

You might wish to keep some fillet steaks in the freezer. I do this only if I pass a butcher who has an end-piece which is rather blackened. This means that it has, at last, begun to age properly and might have some of the flavour for which you are paying. If cut thick, it is more useful for cleverness, especially for converting into 'carpetbag' steaks, which seem unfashionable now but are infinitely better than such horrors of seafood and steak as Surf and Turf (steak and lobster tails). In case you do not have the Australasian advantages I enjoy, a carpetbag steak is a thick piece of fillet which is pocketed, stuffed with raw oysters and then grilled or fried. Expensive restaurants further demonstrate their skills by wrapping bacon around the edge and thrusting all together with a series of truncated toothpicks. Naturally the frozen oysters from New Zealand would be the best bet.

BRAISED STEAK CASSEROLE

A rich and flavoursome beef casserole that makes the perfect basis for many variations (opposite). The stock can be replaced by red wine if wished. Any of these are perfect served with herb dumplings and buttery noodles tossed in poppy seeds.

1 kg (2 lb) lean braising steak
seasoned flour for coating
4 tablespoons oil
375 g (12 oz) onion, chopped
750 ml (1 ¼ pints) beef stock
2 tablespoons tomato purée
1 teaspoon dried thyme, marjoram or parsley
4 teaspoons cornflour
salt and freshly ground black pepper

Serves 6

Trim the steak, cut it into bite-size pieces and roll the meat in seasoned flour. Heat half the oil in a frying pan until smoking hot and seal the meat over a high heat until it is golden-brown. Transfer the beef to a casserole dish.

Add the remaining oil to the frying pan and soften the onion. Stir in a little of the stock. Bring the mixture to the boil and pour it over the beef. Add the remaining stock, tomato purée, seasoning and herbs. Cover the casserole and bake in a preheated oven at Gas Mark 2/150°C/300°F for 2 hours or until the meat is tender.

FREEZE the casserole, or blend the cornflour with a little water to make a thin paste and stir it into the casserole. Continue to bake for a further 30 minutes.

To serve from frozen: Thaw the casserole over a gentle heat in a saucepan until piping hot. Thicken with cornflour as above and simmer for a further 10 minutes.

B

Variations:

BURGUNDY STEAK CASSEROLE

Before softening the onion, sauté 4–6 rashers of back bacon until crisp, remove and chop. Add 2 sliced leeks and 2 large crushed garlic cloves to the onion and soften slowly in the oil and bacon fat. Add with the bacon to the beef and stir in equal quantities of stock and burgundy (or claret) plus 4 tablespoons of brandy. Fifteen minutes before serving, add 16 small cooked onions, 16 sautéed mushrooms and a dash of soy sauce if wished. Omit the cornflour. Serve sprinkled with chopped parsley and small *croûtons* of fried white bread.

STEAK, ALMOND AND OLIVE CASSEROLE

Toast 2 tablespoons of almond flakes until lightly golden and add to the beef with the stock. Sprinkle with a pinch of chilli powder and a tablespoon each of grated lemon and orange rind. Stir in 2 tablespoons of dark red plum jam and 125 g (4 oz) of stuffed green olives. Omit the cornflour. Serve sprinkled with chopped parsley.

STEAK, PEPPER AND CARAWAY CASSEROLE

Add 2 finely chopped garlic cloves and ¼ teaspoon of caraway seeds to the softened onion and stir well. Add 4 teaspoons of Hungarian paprika with the stock. While the casserole is cooking, grill 2 red peppers until the skin blisters. Cool and peel them; then halve, de-seed and slice. Add the slices to the casserole for the last 30 minutes of the cooking time. Omit the cornflour.

CHILLI STEAK, CHORIZO AND BEAN CASSEROLE

Add a 793 g (1 lb 12 oz) can of tomatoes, 2–3 tablespoons of chilli powder and 1 tablespoon of ground cumin to the browned beef. After an hour of the cooking time, mix in a 400 g (14 oz) can of drained red kidney beans and 250 g (8 oz) of thickly sliced chorizo sausage. Omit the cornflour.

STEAK, KIDNEY AND MUSHROOM CASSEROLE

Roll 175 g (6 oz) of trimmed, cored and quartered lamb's kidneys in seasoned flour and sauté them quickly after the beef. Add 250 g (8 oz) of button mushrooms to the softened onion and stir well. Add 300 ml (½ pint) of red wine to the stock and bubble the sauce over a high heat to reduce the sauce if necessary. Omit the cornflour. Serve sprinkled with parsley.

This can be covered with puff pastry if wished to make a traditional winter pie.

STEAK AND OYSTER PIES

These pies are best made in individual oval freezerproof pie or pâté dishes. Serve them with broccoli, courgettes or mangetout.

1 kg (2 lb) chuck steak
50 g (2 oz) beef dripping
250–300 g (8–10 oz) onion, chopped
1½–2 tablespoons plain flour
450 ml (¾ pint) beef stock
2 teaspoons Worcestershire sauce
1½ teaspoons dried thyme or marjoram
2 quantities (500 g/1 lb) of Puff Pastry (page 142)
1 egg, beaten
6 or 12 fresh oysters
salt and freshly ground black pepper

Serves 6

Cut the steak into bite-size cubes and briskly seal the meat in batches, in a little of the sizzling-hot dripping. Transfer the pieces to a casserole dish. Add the remaining fat and fry the onion until soft. Sprinkle with the flour and stir well for 30 seconds until the roux is light brown. Pour in the stock and Worcestershire sauce and bring to the boil, stirring constantly. Add the herbs, season well and pour over the steak.

Cover the meat mixture and bake in a preheated oven at Gas Mark 2/150°C/300°F for 1½ hours. Check the seasoning and divide the meat between six 300 ml (½-pint) individual pie dishes. Leave until cool.

Roll out the pastry and use to cover the pies. Flute the edges, decorate the tops of the pies and make a small hole in the centre of each one. FREEZE or brush the tops with the beaten egg and bake in a preheated oven at Gas Mark 7/220°C/425°F for 20–25 minutes until the lids are puffed and golden. Just before serving, lift the lids carefully and slip one or two fresh oysters into each pie.

To serve from frozen: Thaw the pastry-topped pies in the refrigerator for at least 1 hour. Brush the tops with the beaten egg and bake in a preheated oven at Gas Mark 7/220°C/425°F for 35–40 minutes until the filling is piping hot and the pastry is golden. Check the pies after 15 minutes of the cooking time and cover them with foil if the pastry seems to be browning too quickly. Add the oysters as above before serving.

FILLET OF BEEF WITH ROQUEFORT AND GARLIC BUTTER

For heartier appetites, allow two steaks per person. Delicious with rosti (page 159) and courgettes or broccoli.

2 tablespoons oil for frying
6 × 2.5 cm (1-inch) thick fillet steak each weighing about 125 g (4 oz)
50 g (2 oz) butter
1–2 garlic cloves, chopped finely
125 g (4 oz) Roquefort cheese
freshly ground black pepper

Serves 6

Heat a lightly oiled, heavy-based frying pan over a high heat until smoking hot and quickly seal each of the steaks on both sides. Transfer the steaks to a shallow ovenproof dish or to six squares of foil large enough to wrap each steak completely. Leave until cold.

Beat together the butter, garlic, cheese and pepper to taste; spread the mixture thickly over each steak and close the parcels if used. FREEZE or, just before serving, bake in a preheated oven at Gas Mark 6/200°C/400°F for 15–20 minutes without turning.

To serve from frozen: Thaw the steaks at room temperature for 30–45 minutes. Open the foil parcels, if used, and bake as above for 25–30 minutes.

FILLET EN CROÛTE WITH MORELS

A creamy celeriac purée will complement this dish perfectly; follow it with a green salad.

1 kg (2 lb) thick end of beef fillet in one piece
oil for frying
25 g (1 oz) butter
275 g (9 oz) morels
2 quantities (500 g/1 lb) of Puff Pastry (page 142)
1 egg, beaten lightly
salt and freshly ground black pepper
Burgundy Sauce
25 g (1 oz) butter
2 shallots, chopped
1 garlic clove, chopped finely
15 g (½ oz) plain flour
275 ml (9 fl oz) red burgundy
400 ml (14 fl oz) beef stock
1 bay leaf
a generous strip of orange rind
salt and freshly ground black pepper

Serves 6

Trim and cut the beef fillet into six thick steaks and brush them with oil. Heat a heavy-based frying pan until it is smoking hot. Add three of the steaks and sear them over a high heat on both sides for 1 minute, until they are golden-brown. Lift out the steaks and set them aside to cool. Wipe out the frying pan; then sear the remaining steaks. Heat the butter and add the morels. Cook the morels for 2–3 minutes until they are tender. Season and allow them to cool.

Roll out the pastry to a thin rectangle. Cut out six circles large enough to enclose the steaks. Place a steak in the centre of each circle and top with a spoonful of well-drained morels. Brush the edges of the pastry with some of the beaten egg and bring them up and over the top of the morels. Pinch the edges together. Cut six smaller circles of pastry, about 6 cm (2½ inches) in diameter, to fit over the top of each pastry bundle. Make four cuts, one at each quarter of the circle from the edge towards the centre, but leaving at least 1 cm (½ inch) in the centre of the pastry circle uncut. Arrange the cut circles on top of the pastry bundles and press the centre of the pastry firmly into place, sealing it to the bundle and making a deep hollow to hold a pastry rose decoration. Make six pastry roses* from the trimmings, brush the base of each rose with some of the egg glaze and press into place. FREEZE or glaze the pastries and bake in a preheated oven at Gas Mark 6/200°C/400°F for 20–25 minutes until the pastry is golden-brown.

For the sauce, melt the butter in a saucepan and sauté the shallots and garlic until they are soft. Sprinkle with the flour, stir well and slowly add the wine, stock, bay leaf and orange rind. Season the sauce and bring it to the boil, stirring constantly. Simmer for 10–15 minutes until the sauce is reduced by one-third. Strain, cool and FREEZE the sauce or strain and serve it with the pastries.

To serve from frozen: Thaw the pastry bundles in the refrigerator for at least 5 hours before glazing and baking them as above. Reheat the sauce gently and serve with the pastries.

* To make pastry roses, roll out the pastry trimmings and cut into strips about 2 cm (¾ inch) wide. Roll up each strip to make a simple rose.

CARPACCIO WITH OLIVADE AND PINE KERNELS

175 g (6 oz) fillet steak
To serve
1–2 teaspoons Olivade (page 129)
25 g (1 oz) pine kernels, toasted
1 garlic clove, chopped finely (optional)
a little olive oil
18 very thin slivers of fresh parmesan cheese
6 sprigs of flat-leaf parsley

Serves 6

Trim any fat from the fillet and put the meat into the freezer for 30 minutes until firm. Slice it very thinly and beat each slice into wafer thin sheets between two sheets of greaseproof or non-stick baking paper. FREEZE or arrange the pieces, slightly overlapping each other, on individual plates.

Garnish the steak slices with a very small spoonful of Olivade for each serving, sprinkle with the toasted pine kernels and chopped garlic, if liked, and drizzle with olive oil. Garnish with the slices of parmesan and sprigs of parsley. Serve with crusty french bread.

To serve from frozen: Thaw the sliced steak in the refrigerator for 5–10 minutes. Continue as above.

BEETROOT

It is infuriating to me how difficult it is to buy raw beetroot, for nothing is better as a baked or boiled vegetable. Cook, skin and freeze baby ones whole, whenever you see a supply. The golden variety is wonderful and very pretty but rarely seen commercially, which is all the more reason to have a store of them.

Beet leaves can be blanched and stored in just the same manner as spinach.

BERRIES

All of these are as good, if not better, converted into alcohol or stored in it – vodka, gin, cognac or brandy. It is not good sense to take freezer space with such common berries as raspberries or blackcurrants unless you grow them or have rotten local shops which do not stock them on your behalf. In which case open freeze unbruised ones before packing and storing in your freezer.

The soft ones – **blackberries**, **raspberries**, **strawberries**, **loganberries**, **tayberries**, **mulberries** and so on – take less space if sieved, sweetened if necessary and then stored as purées; if their flavour is enhanced with a suitable liqueur, they can be used simply to dress other whole fruits. Or store them in small quantities as whole berries to tumble together in small summer or winter puddings of mixed berries. Don't freeze any without tasting them seriously, for, as with apples or potatoes, there are varieties, some of which are good and some disgraceful. Strawberries, for instance, only deserve to be frozen if they are of the red-fleshed, probably autumnal varieties; only they taste like strawberries should. Pale raspberries (other than golden ones) are even worse. Even the gorgeously pungent alpine (or wild) strawberries cannot always be trusted, although surprisingly the golden ones, which you will have to grow yourself, seem better than the red. Even the best strawberries do not defrost well, but there are ways to make

see also
CAULIFLOWER (page 43)
CREAM CHEESE (page 69)
ELDERFLOWER (page 83)
WAFFLES (page 201)
YOGURT (page 205)
Basic Meringues (page 122)
Berry Japonaise (page 123)
Berry Muffins (page 125)
Brandy Basket Biscuits (page 36)
Chocolate Nests (page 60)
Fruit Ice Cream (page 110)
Médaillons of Hare with Cherries (page 101)
Nut Baskets (page 102)
Pork, Gammon and Cranberry Pie (page 156)
Port and Cranberry Sauce (page 46)
Raspberry Sauce (page 72)
Strawberry Sauce (page 133)

the most of them – as decoration while still slightly frosted or in fools, syllabubs and ice creams (page 110).

The most modern thing to do with these berries is to whizz them into a simple vinaigrette (no sugar please, but a little mustard to ensure the emulsification). The colour and flavour brilliantly finish simple dishes, especially, in my experience, those with fish and other seafood: grilled shark or tuna with a blackberry vinaigrette made with walnut oil; lightly cooked scallops on a *salade tiède* with a raspberry vinaigrette; grilled salmon on a pond of vinaigrette flavoured and coloured with the spicy tayberry. At the other end of the meal, the purées are the basis of excellent sorbets and granitas (page 181), and may indeed be stored as such, but can turn up unexpectedly usefully in such as my Raspberry Black Bottom Pie (page 34). If you still eat cream by the spoonful you might like to know that all soft berries make a syllabub of surpassing wonderfulness. Defrost them just covered with dry white wine, with a touch of cognac and a scraping of lemon or orange rind. After 3–4 hours at room temperature purée, strain, and then whip with about the same volume of double cream.

Blueberries are amongst the most disappointing of berries, especially if they are from the United States. But those grown in Dorset or imported from New Zealand are a superior variety with a definite spiciness, and well worth freezer space. Like raspberries and their relatives, blueberries defrost superbly and make something as simple as fresh peaches or a slice of fresh pineapple suddenly special.

Cranberries are something always to have in the freezer for making a fresh hot cranberry sauce in seconds, like the one on page 46 (follow Sue's advice and never add the sugar until after the berries have popped and you have removed them from the heat, or the skins toughen). For variety mix in blanched orange rind and toasted pecans before serving. I also love throwing them into stuffings of all kinds and try to make extra amounts so there are quantities of it for use at all times of the year. There is one other cranberry product worth making and freezing: an uncooked cranberry relish – but do let it sit for a week or so under refrigeration to allow the flavours to develop fully before freezing. To make it, process every 250 g (½ lb) with a de-pipped unpeeled orange and a cored unpeeled apple; add sugar to taste, a generous slurp of vodka, cognac or port and flavour with half a processed lemon (peel included), ground cinnamon, chopped celery or toasted nuts for variety.

Of the harder, usually bitter, hedgerow and native berries, **sloe**, **bullace**, **damson** and **rowanberries** are best known. The first three all make excellent alcoholic beverages simply by sitting in the relevant alcohol – gin, vodka, cognac or brandy. Bullaces need pricking first, but this can be made easier or avoided altogether by freezing the berries, in the hope that the skins will split. Sloes, which are usually stored in sweetened gin, are mostly taken out at Christmas time, although they can be left very much longer. It is more important to take a deep breath and remember that the red liquid improves for seven years if left to itself.

Rowans make wonderful jellies, with or without apple, for their bitterness and flavour prevail in a way that those of redcurrants do not. It is worth keeping some whole rowans, for using in sauces and stuffings for game; they have the reputation of being poisonous but this is not so, at least for humans (they are thought to induce hallucinations and associated ungainless in birds that overindulge).

Currants are found in many freezers, and rightly so, although I would tend to have fewer black and more red or white. The latter are both less useful in the kitchen other than for jelly making, because of their large pips. But as accents in mixed berry puddings, in stuffings, or with apples and pears in crumbles, pies, sponges and steamed puddings, they more than earn their keep.

RASPBERRY BLACK BOTTOM PIE

Black Bottom Pie — an American speciality — traditionally consists of a layer of rich chocolate custard topped with a light, cognac-flavoured chiffon. Combining the chocolate layer with raspberry purée and flavouring the top with rosewater, framboise or cognac gives it an extra freshness and fascination.

oil for greasing
1 large Brioche loaf, sliced (page 37), *or* 300 g (10 oz) boudoir biscuits
5 tablespoons cognac
4 tablespoons water
200 g (7 oz) bar of plain chocolate
3 eggs, separated
20 g (¾ oz) cornflour
600 ml (1 pint) milk
2 × 10 g (½ oz) sachet of gelatine
75 g (3 oz) unsalted butter
300 ml (½ pint) unsweetened raspberry purée
2 teaspoons caster sugar (optional)
1 tablespoon rose-water, framboise or cognac
Decoration
chocolate curls
750 g (1½ lb) raspberries
rose-water, framboise or cognac to taste
a little single cream

Serves 12

Lightly oil a 25 cm (10-inch) springform tin and, if using the brioche, lay some of the slices evenly over the base, standing the rest around the edges to make a crust. If using the sponge fingers, line the edges of the tin with them, keeping the sugared sides facing outwards; cut the tops level with the top of the tin. Cover the base with the remaining pieces. Mix together the cognac and water, sprinkle this over the bottom layer and allow it to soak in. Melt 50 g (2 oz) of the chocolate in a bowl over a pan of hot water and drizzle it over the biscuits in the base.

Mix together the egg yolks and the cornflour. Heat the milk to simmering point, pour on to the cornflour, whisking continuously, and then cook over a gentle heat until it has thickened. Cook over a low heat for 5 more minutes, stirring. Sprinkle the gelatine on the top and, when melted, whisk it into the custard. Remove the custard from the heat and divide it into two portions. Cover one portion and leave at room temperature to cool, but do not let it set. Cut up the remaining chocolate and the butter and stir them into the second portion of custard. Let them melt into the custard, stirring regularly.

Once the chocolate custard is cool, but before it has set, stir in the raspberry purée, taste and add some of the sugar if liked. Ladle it carefully on to the prepared base and leave to set in the refrigerator.

Flavour the remaining custard, which should be sloppy, with the rose-water, framboise or cognac and sweeten slightly with a little of the sugar if you must. Whisk the egg whites and fold them into the mixture; then ladle it evenly over the set chocolate and raspberry layer. FREEZE or chill for at least 4 hours, overnight if you can.

To serve, decorate the top of the pie with chocolate curls and 250 g (8 oz) of the raspberries. Purée the rest of the raspberries and flavour with rose-water, framboise or cognac. Serve the pie on a pool of the raspberry purée, using the tip of a teaspoon to dribble circles of single cream on to the purée and drawing lines from the pie to the edges of the plate to create a cobweb effect.

To serve from frozen: Thaw the pie in the refrigerator for 5–6 hours or at room temperature for 2–3 hours. Decorate and serve as above.

© Glynn Christian

Speciality biscuits can make or break a meal, especially puddings. Provided they have no fillings, most bought biscuits freeze excellently, although some will need a little crisping in the oven before serving. This is a particularly good plan when you are in France for the day or so, for the army of *pâtissiers* all offer terrific speciality biscuits, especially of an almond or spiced persuasion to serve with coffee, fruits or frozen or iced puddings.

If you are a baker you will probably know that uncooked biscuit mixtures are perfect freezer fodder. Firm mixtures are simply rolled neatly in foil and sliced when partially thawed after thirty to forty minutes. Soft mixtures should be piped on to a baking tray or shaped before freezing. Bake straight from frozen.

see also
Nut Baskets (page 102)

BRANDY BASKET
BISCUITS

Lacy baskets make ideal containers for scoops of ice cream or mousse. The same biscuit mixture can be shaped into cornets which can be half-filled with whipped cream, topped up with fresh berries and laid on their sides on individual dessert plates filled with a pool of crème anglaise or fresh fruit purée.

50 g (2 oz) unsalted butter
50 g (2 oz) caster sugar
2 tablespoons golden syrup
50 g (2 oz) plain flour
½ teaspoon ground ginger
1 teaspoon brandy

Makes 6 large or 12 small baskets

Gently melt the butter, sugar and syrup in a saucepan and stir until smooth. Sift the flour and ginger together and add to the syrup mixture with the brandy. Mix well and leave to cool for 2 minutes.

Drop 2–3 heaped teaspoons of the mixture on to a baking tray lined with non-stick baking paper, leaving space for the biscuits to spread as they bake. Bake in a preheated oven at Gas Mark 4/180°C/350°F for 5–6 minutes until golden and bubbling. Leave to cool for a minute, and, using a palette knife, either lift them on to a wire cooling rack and leave them until hard before FREEZING or drape the biscuits over upturned glasses or teacups so that the edges fall in gentle folds. When hard, remove and repeat with the remaining biscuits. FREEZE or fill.

To serve from frozen: For the unshaped biscuits, place them on a baking tray lined with non-stick baking paper. Reheat in a preheated oven at Gas Mark 4/180°C/350°F for 1 minute

until they are pliable and then shape as above. For the shaped biscuits, thaw them at room temperature for about 1 hour.

BLACKBERRIES

see BERRIES

BLUEBERRIES

see BERRIES

BREAD

Space dictates what you do. Now freezer space is used more intelligently, I presume you will not have the slightest inclination to waste it on such as the sliced white loaf unless you are really isolated, and then you should be making your own once a week anyway and using freezer space for fresh yeast (page 205).

Such speciality breads as a French-style walnut loaf for serving with good cheese or salad are much more the type of thing to squirrel away, and I do. Like all breads these can be quickly reheated from frozen if you don't want to wait for them to thaw. Otherwise, look for partly-cooked loaves and rolls sold specifically for you to freeze, which seem universally worthwhile if only because they smell exactly as though you have been baking rather than reheating, thus offering fairly safe grounds for swank.

Bread a little past its prime is probably best made up into the wickedness of spice and raisin-rich bread pudding on the model of Sue's Brandied Raisin Brioche Pudding (page 38), to be served warm with custard on

see also
BRIOCHE (page 37)
BUTTERS, FLAVOURED (page 40)
PITTA (page 154)

B

a cold and miserable day. Soaked in really rich milk or thinned greek yogurt, the same old bread might be baked into a large or individual bread and butter puddings. If you can't or won't plan so far ahead, simply slice some and grate the rest into crumbs for future use. Or rub slices with crushed garlic or chopped herbs and cut into half-moon-, heart-, cube- or diamond-shaped *croûtons*, which once fried can be reheated quickly from frozen in a hot oven.

Slices of French or Italian loaves should soak up olive oil whilst defrosting and then be toasted and served as *crostini*, a voluptuously rich hot base for piquant topping – as simple as a scraping of anchovy for serving with a fish lasagne, some herby chicken liver pâté to accompany roasted or boiled chicken, or just slices of decent lightly chilled tomatoes as a rustic snack or first course.

Breadcrumbs are best used from frozen to sprinkle authentically on *gratins* with a scatter of parmesan, rather than the modern plague of grated Cheddar, which is far too overpowering for most food.

BRIOCHE

It's well worth freezing good bought or home-made brioche to use in a variety of ways. Reheat it as you would do breakfast croissants, or try it in my Raspberry Black Bottom Pie (page 34) or similar.

Uncooked brioche dough can be frozen after the knocking-back stage – once thawed it can be shaped in a variety of ways for baking. Small ones are a great alternative to ordinary rolls to accompany

*see also
SMOKED FISH (page 174)
Raspberry Black Bottom Pie (page 34)*

soups and starters. A large loaf sliced and toasted is delicious for tea or to serve with snacks. Or wrap the dough around pork sausages before baking – a heavenly treat.

BRIOCHE DOUGH

Brioche is delicious served straight from the oven with egg dishes like a soufflé or roulade, or use it as a base for scrambled or soft-boiled eggs or kidneys.

**2 teaspoons dried yeast
1 teaspoon sugar
2 tablespoons warm water
275 g (9 oz) plain flour, plus extra
for kneading
a pinch of salt
150 g (5 oz) unsalted butter, melted,
plus extra for greasing
3 eggs, beaten
4 tablespoons milk, *or* beaten egg
mixed with a pinch of salt, to glaze**

*Makes 8 individual loaves or
1 large loaf*

Stir the yeast and sugar into the warm water and leave until frothy. Sift the flour and salt into a large bowl. Add the melted butter, beaten eggs and activated yeast and mix to a sticky dough. Turn on to a lightly floured surface and knead for 5 minutes. Shape the dough into a ball, put it into a clean bowl, cover and leave in a warm place until the dough has doubled in size. Turn out, knead for 2 minutes; then use to make eight individual brioches or one large brioche.

Butter 8 small brioche pans or a 25 cm (9-inch) round cake tin. Knead the dough lightly and place it in the cake tin or divide it into eight pieces. Pinch off one-third of each piece of dough and shape both large and small pieces into balls. Set the large balls in the base of each buttered brioche pan, cut a deep cross in the top of each one and crown it with the smaller ball. FREEZE or chill the brioche(s) for at least 12 hours or leave to rise slowly in a cool place.

Let the brioche(s) rise at room temperature until the pans are almost full, brush with the milk or beaten egg and bake in a preheated oven at Gas Mark 7/220°C/425°F for 15–20 minutes for the rolls or 40–45 minutes for the loaf until well browned and hollow-sounding when tapped on the bottom. FREEZE or cool and use.

To serve from frozen: For the dough, thaw in the refrigerator for 2 hours and then continue as above. For the brioche(s), thaw at room temperature for 1 hour and then reheat in a preheated oven at Gas Mark 7/220°C/ 425°F for 20 minutes.

BRANDIED RAISIN BRIOCHE PUDDING

**50 g (2 oz) raisins
4 tablespoons brandy
125 g (4 oz) unsalted butter, plus extra for greasing
3 tablespoons clear honey
10 slices of Brioche loaf (above)
4 eggs plus 1 extra egg yolk
142 ml (5 fl oz) carton of double or whipping cream
400 ml (14 fl oz) milk
3 tablespoons brown sugar
ground cinnamon for sprinkling**

Serves 6

Soak the raisins in the brandy for 1 hour.

Melt the butter and honey together and spread over each slice of brioche. Cut the bread into 2 cm (1-inch) cubes and arrange both the bread and the raisins in a buttered baking dish. Beat together the eggs, egg yolk, cream and milk with any remaining brandy and pour over the bread. Leave to stand for 30 minutes.

Sprinkle the pudding with the sugar and cinnamon. FREEZE or bake in a preheated oven at Gas Mark 3/160°C/325°F for 45 minutes until set.

To serve from frozen: Thaw the uncooked pudding at room temperature for at least 1 hour; then bake as above.

BROAD BEANS

see BEANS

BUCKWHEAT

see also
CRÊPES (page 71)

The nutty warm flavour of buckwheat is a must in my kitchen. The grains themselves last well, but buckwheat flour benefits from being frozen to keep it fresh. As it contains no gluten, buckwheat flour is very difficult, if not impossible, to use by itself. Thus it is best to pack it into small amounts – say of 50 g (2 oz) – for mixing into other flours for pancakes, blinis, pasta dough (page 135) and the like. The really well organised would use it to make proper yeast-raised blinis, like the ones in the following recipe, and freeze those; small pancakes lightly raised with baking powder are just as appreciated, and imagine the effect when you are able to serve a gift of caviare with warm buckwheat blinis within minutes. The thick buckwheat pancakes, traditionally served as a breakfast dish with hot syrup, are also worth storing. If you keep the sweetening down they are magical served warm with a topping of sliced chilled tomatoes of excelling redness

B

and ripeness, herbs, and lightly warmed walnut oil.

BUCKWHEAT BLINIS

Small, cocktail-size blinis measuring 4–5 cm (1½–2 inches) in diameter make an excellent hors-d'oeuvre, topped with fresh soured cream and dill, caviare, smoked trout or smoked salmon. The batter can be made with a mixture of plain and buckwheat flours and flavoured with herbs and seeds if liked.

**15 g (½ oz) dried yeast
1 teaspoon sugar
500 ml (18 fl oz) warm milk *or* a mixture of warm milk and water, plus extra if necessary
250 g (8 oz) buckwheat flour
a pinch of salt
2 tablespoons freshly chopped dill (optional)
1 egg, separated
25 g (1 oz) butter, melted
butter or oil for frying**

Makes about 40

Stir the yeast, sugar and 125 ml (4 fl oz) of the warm milk or milk and water together and allow to stand until the mixture bubbles. Stir together the flour, salt and herbs if used. Whisk in the remaining milk or milk and water to make a smooth batter. Whisk in the activated yeast mixture, egg yolk and melted butter. The batter should have the consistency of thick cream – add a little more liquid if necessary. Cover the batter and leave it in a warm place to rise for about 1 hour.

Whisk the egg white until stiff and fold this into the batter. Cover the batter again and leave it to rise for a further 30 minutes.

Heat a heavy-based frying pan and brush it with butter or oil. Cook three blinis at a time, allowing about ½ tablespoon of batter for each one. When the undersides of the blinis are lightly browned, turn them and cook them briefly on the other side. Cool and FREEZE or keep warm on a hot platter covered with foil.

To serve from frozen: Flip the frozen blinis in a lightly oiled pan over a high heat until piping hot, or thaw, wrap them six to a parcel in foil and reheat in a preheated oven at Gas Mark 4/180°C/350°F for 20–25 minutes.

see also
CHESTNUTS (page 51)

BUCKWHEAT FLAT CAKES WITH ALMOND KASHA

The French fill their buckwheat pancakes with a fried egg and grated cheese or apple sauce and black pudding; this vegetarian topping of buckwheat with almonds and red peppers is really delicious with a spoonful of greek yogurt.

see also
Aubergine, Tomato and
Olive Sauce (page 22)

Pancakes
**75 g (3 oz) buckwheat flour
50 g (2 oz) plain flour
a large pinch of salt
3 eggs
75 g (3 oz) butter, melted, plus extra for frying
300 ml (½ pint) milk *or* a mixture of half milk and half water, plus extra if necessary**
Filling
**50 g (2 oz) almond flakes
4 tablespoons olive oil
1 garlic clove, chopped finely
75 g (3 oz) onion, chopped finely
1 small red pepper, de-seeded and chopped
250 g (8 oz) untoasted buckwheat
500 ml (18 fl oz) chicken stock**
To serve
150 ml (¼ pint) greek yogurt

Serves 6 (makes 24 pancakes)

Start by making the pancake batter. Stir the flours and salt together and make a hollow in the centre. Break the eggs into this hollow. Whisk together the melted butter and the milk or milk and water and beat it gradually into the flour and eggs to make a batter of good pouring consistency. Add a little more liquid if the mixture is too thick. Leave to stand while making the filling.

To make the filling, sauté the almonds in the oil until they are lightly golden. Lift them out and set aside. Add the garlic, onion and red pepper to the pan and cook over a gentle heat until the onion is soft and lightly golden. Add the buckwheat and stock. Mix well, turn into a casserole and bake in a preheated oven at Gas Mark 3/160°C/325°F for 30 minutes. Stir in the almonds and bake for a further 15 minutes until the buckwheat is tender and the liquid has been absorbed. FREEZE or keep warm while cooking the pancakes.

Cook the pancakes in a 20 cm (8-inch) heavy-based frying pan brushed with a trace of melted butter for 1–2 minutes on each side. FREEZE or cover with foil and keep the cakes hot on a plate in a warm oven. When all the batter is cooked, spoon some filling on to each pancake and roll them up. Serve with the greek yogurt.

To serve from frozen: Flip the frozen cakes in a hot frying pan until heated through. Keep them warm as above until all the cakes are thawed. Stir-fry the filling in a lightly oiled frying pan over a gentle heat until piping hot; then continue as above.

BULLACE

see BERRIES

BUTTER BEANS

see BEANS

BUTTERS, FLAVOURED

If you don't fancy yourself as a saucemaker yet feel that some foods should be moistened, flavoured butters are your saviours. Simply made, using left-overs of butter and flavourings, they can be stored in the freezer and brought out in an emergency. Try beans with a red pepper butter, or poached fish with an olive and olive oil butter, ham sandwiches with a seed mustard butter, salmon with a dill and lemon butter, and almost anything with a vodka butter!

All the following flavourings are given in quantities sufficient for 125 g (4 oz) of butter. Use a good quality unsalted or slightly salted butter, and soften but *do not* melt it before beating in the other ingredients. Spoon the flavoured butter on to a sheet of foil and roll into a sausage shape before freezing. This is easily sliced and used from frozen.

Anchovy Mix into the butter 4 teaspoons of anchovy essence and a pinch of Cayenne pepper. Great with finely chopped tomatoes and olives for serving with pasta.

Currants and Cumin Seed Heat 1 tablespoon of cumin seeds in a small non-stick pan until they turn a light golden-brown. Cool before beating into the butter with 2 tablespoons of chopped

see also
CRÊPES (page 71)
FISH (page 86)
FLOWERS (page 92)
SANDWICHES (page 171)
SNAILS (page 180)
Fillet of Beef with Roquefort and Garlic Butter (page 30)

B

currants. Marvellous on most vegetables but especially on cabbage and carrots.

Curry and Lemon Stir in 1 heaped tablespoon of curry paste with 1 tablespoon of finely grated lemon rind. Don't use curry powder, or the butter will have an unpleasant floury taste. This is good on poached fish, or as a sandwich spread with cold chicken or salmon.

Green Olive and Orange Chop 2 tablespoons of green olives very finely and beat into the butter with 2 teaspoons of finely grated orange rind. Great on fish.

Green Peppercorn and Walnut Mix 1 tablespoon of crushed green peppercorns with 2 tablespoons of chopped walnuts and beat into the butter. This is wonderful with all poultry and game – either for roasting the meat or for making sandwiches with the cold meat.

Ground Almonds Toast 50 g (2 oz) of flaked almonds and grind them in a food processor. Beat the almonds into the butter with ½ teaspoon of grated lemon rind. Particularly good on green beans and broccoli.

Hazelnut Grind 2 tablespoons of toasted hazelnuts in a food processor. Add ½ teaspoon of finely grated orange rind. Especially good on green beans and cauliflower.

Olive Oil and Black Peppercorn Mix 3 tablespoons of good olive oil into the butter with 1 teaspoon of roughly ground black peppercorns. Have your pepper-mill on its coarsest setting, or use a pestle and mortar to crush the peppercorns. This is excellent on poached or grilled fish, in tomato sandwiches or on braised endive or celeriac.

Orange and Coriander Seeds Beat into the butter 1 tablespoon of finely grated orange rind, 1 teaspoon of lemon juice, 1 teaspoon of orange juice and 2 tablespoons of crushed coriander seeds. Try it in ham sandwiches, or on hot rolls to serve with chilli-con-carne or vegetable soup.

Red Pepper and Garlic Roughly chop 125 g (4 oz) of red pepper and plunge into fast-boiling water. Bring back to the boil; then drain in a colander and run cold water through until cold. Chop very finely, mince or process before beating into the butter with a crushed garlic clove.

Seed Mustard Toast 2 teaspoons of mustard seeds by putting them into a small non-stick pan and heating until you hear the seeds popping. Cool before mixing with 1 heaped tablespoon of Dijon mustard and beating into the butter. You can use 1 tablespoon of seed mustard instead of the toasted mustard seeds, if you wish.

Tomato, Garlic and Olives Beat into the butter 2 teaspoons of tomato purée, 2 teaspoons of crushed garlic, and 4 black Calamata olives, stoned and minced or very finely chopped. This is excellent on poached cod, or on hot toast or cold biscuits as a drinks snack.

Vodka Honestly, you can't believe how good this is. Put 2 tablespoons of vodka and the softened butter into a food processor or blender and whizz until emulsified. Add a little salt to taste.

If ever you get bored, add chopped walnuts or toasted hazelnuts, crushed green or black peppercorns, fresh tarragon leaves, mint leaves, grated orange rind or red lumpfish caviare. All these combinations are wonderful on everything!

Cashew Nuts   Coconut
Cauliflower   Coffee
Celeriac   Courgettes
Celery   Crab
Cheese   Cream
Cheesecakes   Cream Cheese
Cherries   Crêpes
Chestnuts   Croissants
Chicken   Custard
Chick-peas
Chicory
Chillies
Chocolate
Cider
Citrus Fruits

C

CARP

see FISH

CASHEW NUTS

Rarely found untoasted; thus found they are much more worth having, so you can freeze them unsalted or toast them without salt for freezing for short periods. A brilliantly popular addition to stir-fried vegetables, and common with green beans; once they are ground they can be used in the same way as ground almonds. Specially good in your favourite chocolate mousse, or in a chocolate icing if toasted. Yellow tomatoes, lightly-toasted cashew nuts, halved hard-boiled quail's eggs and fresh coriander leaf is a ravishing salad combination. Use your store straight from the freezer.

CAULIFLOWER

Though not usually thought of as 'gourmet', puréed cauliflower is amazingly good if you have not overcooked it; defrost it for soups, sauces and soufflés. Or add it to your cooking from frozen. Lightly blanched florets have a startling affinity with prawns; one works well as a garnish for a soup of the other or both might be whisked up *en famille*. Blanched florets dipped into raspberry vinegar (who would have thought it?) are an arresting snack. Perhaps you don't need to freeze anything I have said so far; but you might want to be clever with florets of the green Romanesco cauliflower. It grows in a spiral of pagoda turrets and unlike, say,

see also
BUTTERS, FLAVOURED (page 40)
Spinach Soufflé(s) with Blue Cheese and Walnuts (page 186)

purple broccoli, keeps its colour when blanched.

43

CAULIFLOWER AND PARMESAN CREAMS

Serve this lovely light cauliflower cream with roast or grilled meats. The marigold petal garnish is delightful.

1 large or 2 small cauliflowers, trimmed and broken into florets
50 g (2 oz) butter, plus extra for greasing
200 ml (7 fl oz) milk
4 large eggs (size 1 or 2), beaten
75 g (3 oz) grated parmesan cheese
75 g (3 oz) fine white breadcrumbs
Sauce
75 g (3 oz) butter
50 g (2 oz) plain flour
300 ml (½ pint) milk
salt and freshly ground black pepper
Decoration
fresh marigold petals (optional)

Serves 6

Cook the cauliflower florets in boiling, salted water for 5 minutes. Drain well and dry. Heat the butter in a saucepan and sauté the partially cooked florets until just beginning to colour. Slowly add the milk and simmer for 5–6 minutes. Roughly mash the cauliflower.

Make a basic white sauce from the butter, flour and milk. Bring it slowly to the boil, whisking all the time until it thickens. Season well. Stir in half the cauliflower and liquidise to a purée with the eggs and half the cheese. Fold in the remaining mashed cauliflower.

Liberally butter and base-line six individual ring moulds or soufflé dishes. Mix together the remaining parmesan cheese and the breadcrumbs and use to coat the insides of the moulds or dishes before filling with the cauliflower mixture. FREEZE or cover with a sheet of greaseproof paper and cook in a bain-marie in a preheated oven at Gas Mark 5/190°C/375°F for about 35 minutes until just firm. Peel off the greaseproof paper, unmould and serve strewn with fresh marigold petals, if wished.

To serve from frozen: Thaw the moulds completely; then bake as above.

CELERIAC

see also
BUTTERS, FLAVOURED
(page 40)
Scallop and Celeriac
Soufflés (page 173)

Unquestionably one of the most important vegetables in the repertoire – used raw in salads or grated into stuffings it is a clean and refreshing part of eating from autumn to spring. Defrost 250 g (½ lb) of your grated celeriac over a gentle heat in butter and 5 or 6 tablespoons of single cream; fold into 175 g (6 oz) of curd cheese with a tablespoon of lemon juice and a little seasoning, adding garlic and chopped parsley for flavour and colour – marvellous as a stuffing for poultry. In winter its celery flavour in hot purées, sauces and different styles of stuffing perfectly balances the fattier, fuller flavours of game, red meats and stews. A stuffing need only consist of grated celeriac flavoured with lemon juice, crushed garlic and Dijon mustard – simple, effective and perfect with lamb.

Store celeriac in blanched slices or cubes, and use from frozen as you would potato, especially mixed with other vegetables; indeed it is often at its best combined *with* potato. Cubes of celeriac explode in the mouth if you have buried them in a creamy purée of mashed potato; stir in garlic and coarsely chopped parsley just before serving.

Celeriac retains its essential virtues through several cookings and reheatings, and thus your frozen store is well used as a purée for the basis of individual soufflés.

CELERIAC AND HAZELNUT SOUP

50 g (2 oz) butter
1 tablespoon oil
625 g (1¼ lb) celeriac, peeled and sliced thinly
275 g (9 oz) leeks, sliced
125 g (4 oz) cooking apples, peeled and chopped roughly
1.5 litres (2½ pints) chicken stock
200 ml (7 fl oz) dry white wine
142 ml (5 fl oz) carton of double cream
salt and freshly ground black pepper
Garnish
25 g (1 oz) hazelnuts, toasted and sliced thinly

Serves 6

Heat the butter and oil in a large saucepan, add the celeriac, leeks and apple and stir well. Cover and sauté gently for 10–12 minutes until the vegetables are soft. Pour in the stock and wine and add seasoning. Bring to the boil, cover and simmer gently for 30 minutes.

Cool the soup slightly, and purée until smooth. Sieve and reheat, adjusting the seasoning as necessary. Stir in the cream. FREEZE or reheat and sprinkle with the toasted hazelnuts. Serve with Melba toast or *croûtons*.

To serve from frozen: Thaw the soup over a gentle heat until piping hot. Garnish and serve.

BUTTERNUT, CRAB AND CELERIAC SOUP

Serve this soup chilled in summer or piping hot during cooler months.

25 g (1 oz) butter
1 garlic clove, crushed
1 teaspoon freshly chopped root
ginger
875 g (1¾ lb) butternut squash,
peeled, de-seeded and cut into small
cubes
375 g (12 oz) celeriac, peeled and
cut into small cubes
1.2 litres (2 pints) chicken stock
250 ml (8 fl oz) dry white wine
142 ml (5 fl oz) carton of double or
whipping cream
250 g (8 oz) white crab meat, flaked
roughly
salt and freshly ground black pepper

Serves 6

Melt the butter in a pan and lightly sauté the garlic and ginger for 30 seconds. Add the squash and celeriac and stir well. Pour in the stock and wine, bring to the boil and simmer for 25–30 minutes until the vegetables are tender.

Sieve or liquidise the soup and season to taste. Stir in the cream and crab meat and FREEZE, or reheat or chill before serving.

To serve from frozen: To serve chilled, thaw the soup over a gentle heat and then chill, or thaw overnight in the refrigerator. To serve hot, thaw over a gentle heat until piping hot.

POTATO AND CELERIAC CHOUX

These crisp curls of vegetable choux can be made with just potato or equal quantities of potato and jerusalem artichoke purée, but this mixture of potato with celeriac gives a wonderful flavour that is perfect with rich meat or game dishes, as well as making a delicious starter or vegetarian dish. Serve them with a red pepper or tomato sauce.

75 g (3 oz) butter
125 ml (4 fl oz) water
75 g (3 oz) plain flour, sifted with a
pinch of salt
2 eggs
250 g (8 oz) potatoes, peeled and
sliced thinly
250 g (8 oz) celeriac, peeled and
sliced thinly
oil for deep-frying
salt and freshly ground black pepper

Serves 6

Bring 50 g (2 oz) of the butter and the water slowly to the boil in a small saucepan. When the butter has melted, add the flour and beat hard until the mixture leaves the sides of the saucepan and forms a smooth, glossy ball. Cool slightly; then beat in the eggs, one at a time, to make a smooth paste.

Cook the potatoes and celeriac in separate saucepans of salted water until really tender. Drain and mash them with the remaining butter and seasoning to taste. Beat them into the choux paste.

Spoon the mixture into a piping bag fitted with a large plain or fluted nozzle. Pipe the mixture into 4–5 cm (1½–2-inch) rings on to waxed paper or non-stick baking trays (or make small drops of the mixture with two teaspoons). Freeze until firm; then pack into containers and FREEZE, or fry four or five potato rings at a time in deep, hot oil until they are puffed and golden yet soft in the middle. Lift the rings out and drain them well while frying further batches.

To serve from frozen: Thaw the rings or drops for 25–30 minutes before frying as above.

CELERY

It is easy to forget how useful the green tops of celery can be for soups and stuffings and

see also
CREAM CHEESE (page 69)
OXTAIL (page 129)
POTATOES (page 158)

sauces, or how badly celery behaves when it is an ingredient of a frozen dish: it dominates very quickly. You will get more pleasure from keeping a small bag of celery greens frozen, and stirring them into dishes which might otherwise have required celery when you cooked or finished them. Or freeze them chopped in stock or water: these flavoured ice cubes can be added to dishes as they are.

CHANTERELLES

see WILD MUSHROOMS

CHEESE

The general rule for cheese, like cream, is that the higher the fat content, the better it will freeze. But remember that frozen cheese is 'dead' cheese, and so it must be eaten as soon as it has defrosted.

The best cheeses to store are the creamy ones like Camembert and Brie – choose them when perfectly ripe and ready for eating and cut them into sensible portions so that they can be eaten quickly once thawed. Next best are the hard and blue cheeses although they do have a tendency to crumble on thawing, so you might find these better for cooking. Of course, cooked dishes containing cheese are among the tastiest standbys for the freezer.

DOLCELATTE NUT PUFFS WITH PORT AND CRANBERRY SAUCE

1 quantity of Savoury Choux Pastry
(page 141)
a little beaten egg
grated parmesan cheese
Filling
175 g (6 oz) dolcelatte cheese
3 tablespoons single cream
25 g (1 oz) macadamia nuts, chopped roughly
Port and Cranberry Sauce
500 g (1 lb) cranberries
100 ml (3½ fl oz) red wine
3 tablespoons fresh orange juice
4 tablespoons ruby port
a pinch of sugar

Serves 6

Turn the choux pastry mixture into a piping bag fitted with a 1 cm (½-inch) plain nozzle. Pipe 30 small balls of choux pastry on to a dampened baking tray, leaving space between them for the pastries to swell. Brush the top of each ball with a little beaten egg and dust with parmesan cheese. Bake in a preheated oven at Gas Mark 6/200°C/400°F for 15–16 minutes until they are firm and golden. Cut a small slit in the side of each puff; then pop them back into the oven for a further 2 minutes to dry out the centres. Cool and FREEZE or set aside for filling.

For the filling, trim any crusts from the cheese and mash the remainder with enough cream to make a stiff piping consistency. Fold in the nuts. FREEZE or set aside to fill the choux puffs.

To make the sauce, simmer the cranberries with the wine and orange juice and, after 30 seconds, remove 18 whole berries for the garnish. Simmer the rest for 3–4 minutes until tender. Sieve and FREEZE or stir in the port and sugar to taste and reheat gently, adding a little water if necessary to make a sauce of the consistency of cream.

To serve, pipe the cheese filling into the hot puffs and, for each person, arrange five puffs on a bed of cranberry sauce. Sprinkle the sauce with the whole cranberries.

To serve from frozen: Thaw the cheese mixture and beat it well. Reheat the puffs in a preheated oven at Gas Mark 6/200°C/400°F for 6—8 minutes and fill with the cheese mixture. Reheat the sauce over a gentle heat, add the port and sugar to taste, and serve as above.

POTTED CHEESES WITH BRANDY

This is something between a pâté and a spread and is perfect for serving as a starter with hot toast and a herb salad or on hot croûtons of French baguette to accompany a creamy leek soup.

**50 g (2 oz) butter
125 g (4 oz) cream cheese
3 tablespoons brandy
a pinch of ground mace
50 g (2 oz) walnuts, chopped roughly
300 g (10 oz) Stilton cheese, crumbled roughly
2 tablespoons freshly chopped flat-leaf parsley
freshly ground black pepper**

Serves 6

Beat the butter, cream cheese and brandy together with a pinch of ground mace. Stir in the walnuts, Stilton and parsley and season with pepper. Pack into a dish and FREEZE or chill.

To serve from frozen: Thaw at room temperature for 2—3 hours or overnight in the refrigerator before serving.

LEEK AND BRIE PIE

This is a delicious accompaniment for roast meats; or serve it as a main course with plenty of green vegetables.

**175 g (6 oz) butter
1 tablespoon olive oil
750 g (1½ lb) trimmed leeks, sliced thinly
5 sheets of Filo Pastry (page 143)
50 g (2 oz) goat's cheese, grated
125 g (4 oz) blue Brie cheese
1 large egg (size 1 or 2)
salt and freshly ground black pepper**

Serves 6 as a starter or side dish or 2 as a main dish

Heat 50 g (2 oz) of the butter and the oil in a pan and soften the leeks. Season well with salt and pepper.

Butter a 20 cm (8-inch) shallow pie or *gratin* dish with a little of the butter and melt the rest. Lay one sheet of pastry in the dish, allowing the ends to overlap the edges of the dish. Brush with a little of the melted butter. Repeat the process until you have used all five sheets of pastry.

Beat the cheeses and egg together and stir in the leeks. Spoon the mixture into the pastry-lined dish. Fold each overlapping layer of pastry over the filling, covering the pie completely. Pinch the last sheet of pastry into a twist on top of the pie. Brush with the rest of the melted butter and bake in a preheated oven at Gas Mark 4/180°C/350°F for 25–30 minutes until the top is crisp and golden. FREEZE or serve.

To serve from frozen: Thaw overnight in the refrigerator and reheat in a preheated oven at Gas Mark 4/180°C/350°F for 15–20 minutes.

GORGONZOLA AND FETA MOUSSE

150 ml (¼ pint) aspic jelly
6 sprigs of flat-leaf parsley
2 eggs, separated
142 ml (5 fl oz) carton of double cream
1 teaspoon gelatine, dissolved in 2 tablespoons water
75 g (3 oz) gorgonzola cheese, crumbled
75 g (3 oz) feta cheese, crumbled
salt and freshly ground black pepper
Herb Sauce
150 g (5 oz) Boursin *or* garlic and herb cream cheese
100 ml (3½ fl oz) single cream
2 tablespoons freshly chopped basil or fennel

Serves 6

Spoon a little of the aspic into the base of six individual moulds. Add a sprig of parsley to each one and leave until the jelly has set. Cover with a second layer of the remaining aspic and leave until set.

Whisk the egg yolks with 3 tablespoons of the cream in a bowl over a saucepan of gently simmering water until the mixture becomes pale and creamy. Take off the heat, add the dissolved gelatine and crumbled cheeses and beat well. Taste and season if necessary. Lightly whip the remaining cream. Whisk the egg whites until stiff and fold them into the cheese mixture with the lightly whipped cream. Divide the mixture between the aspic-lined moulds and chill until set. FREEZE or turn out.

To serve at once, make the sauce. Beat the cheese and cream together and fold in the herbs. Serve with the mousse (do not freeze), with water biscuits, Melba toast or toasted pitta bread triangles.

To serve from frozen: Thaw the cheese creams in the refrigerator for 2–3 hours. Make the sauce as above.

CHEESECAKES

see also
CREAM CHEESE (page 69)

Thin slices of chilled cheesecake served on beautiful plates are the perfect accompaniment to fruit and elderflower wine. Likewise elderflower itself gives an exquisite flavour to cheesecakes. One of my favourites (below) originated in the court of Richard II – cheesecakes were a popular feature of medieval banquets.

Surprisingly, savoury cheesecakes are less common than sweet ones. Yet they can make a light, refreshing and often visually stunning first course.

Whether baked or unbaked, sweet or savoury, you will find that all cheesecakes freeze well, as long as any fruit toppings or cream are added after thawing.

FRAGRANT CHEESECAKE

Orange-flower and rose petals are equally delicious in this cheesecake.

175 g (6 oz) fresh elderflowers
142 ml (5 fl oz) carton of double cream
125 g (4 oz) caster sugar
1 kg (2 lb) curd or cream cheese
50 g (2 oz) fresh white breadcrumbs
6 egg whites
a 25 cm (10-inch) Rich Shortcrust Pastry case (page 141), baked blind

Serves 10

Soak the fresh elderflowers in the cream until they are well moistened. Add the sugar and stir until it dissolves.

Mash or sieve the cheese until it is smooth and add the breadcrumbs. Stir in the elderflower cream.

C

Beat the egg whites until they are stiff but not dry and fold lightly into the cheese mixture. Gently spoon it into the pastry case and bake in a preheated oven at Gas Mark 5/190°C/375°F for 50 minutes or until set and firm. Turn off the heat and leave the cheesecake to cool in the oven with the door open for at least 15 minutes. Cool and FREEZE or serve just warm.

To serve from frozen: Thaw in the refrigerator for 3–4 hours or at room temperature for about 2 hours before serving.

© *Glynn Christian*

MARBLED CHOCOLATE AND GINGER CHEESECAKES

Base
250 g (8 oz) ginger snap biscuits, crushed finely
50 g (2 oz) almonds, toasted and chopped
150 g (5 oz) butter, melted
Filling
2 eggs
50 g (2 oz) caster sugar
250 g (8 oz) full-fat soft cheese
100 ml (3½ fl oz) soured cream
50 g (2 oz) plain chocolate, melted
50 g (2 oz) white chocolate, melted
Decoration
chocolate curls made from plain and white chocolate

Serves 6

Mix the crushed biscuits, nuts and melted butter together and press into six 11 cm (4½-inch) round loose-based individual quiche tins. Line with foil, add baking beans and bake blind in a preheated oven at Gas Mark 4/180°C/350°F for 12 minutes. Remove the foil and baking beans and continue to cook the biscuit bases for another 5 minutes. Leave them to cool.

For the filling, beat together the eggs, sugar, cheese and soured cream. Transfer half the mixture to a second bowl. Stir the plain chocolate into one half of the mixture and the white chocolate into the other half. Divide the plain chocolate mixture between the biscuit cases. Add the white mixture and gently swirl the two together. Bake at Gas Mark 2/150°C/300°F for 20 minutes or until the filling is just set. Cool the cheesecakes and remove them from the tins. FREEZE or top with chocolate curls before serving.

To serve from frozen: Thaw the cheesecakes at room temperature for 2–3 hours before decorating.

WATERCRESS AND CORIANDER CHEESECAKE

1 quantity of Rich Shortcrust Pastry (page 141)
25 g (1 oz) butter
1 small bunch of spring onions, chopped finely
1 large bunch of watercress weighing about 125 g (4 oz), coarse stems removed and the remainder chopped
2 tablespoons freshly chopped coriander leaves
250 g (8 oz) cream or curd cheese
2 eggs
50 g (2 oz) mature Cheddar cheese, grated
284 ml (10 fl oz) carton of soured cream
salt and freshly ground black pepper

Serves 6

Line a 25 cm (10-inch) loose-based tart or quiche tin with the pastry. Chill until firm. Line with foil, fill with baking beans and bake blind in a preheated oven at Gas Mark 4/180°C/350°F for 15 minutes. Remove the beans and foil and bake for a further 5 minutes until the pastry is firm.

For the filling, melt the butter in a saucepan and stir-cook the onion, watercress and coriander in the melted butter for 1–2 minutes. Sprinkle this mixture over the pastry. Beat the cream or curd cheese, eggs, Cheddar cheese and seasoning together and pour over the filling. Bake in the oven at Gas Mark 3/160°C/325°F for 15–20 minutes until just set. FREEZE or spread the top with the soured cream and continue to bake for a further 15 minutes. Serve with a crisp green salad.

To serve from frozen: Thaw the cheesecake at room temperature for 1 hour. Spread the top with the soured cream and bake for 15 minutes as above.

CHERRIES

see also
Black Cherry Sauce
(page 123)
Médaillons of Hare with
Cherries (page 101)

A great and wonderful thing to rely upon, especially for sweet or savoury sauces like the one following. Use them from the freezer for cooking. The sour cherries are perhaps more worth keeping than the sweet ones, and perhaps you would want to cook them down into a basic sauce first, to be sweetened, spiced or given alcoholic content later.

A sauce of puréed and sieved black cherries laced with black rum makes dinner party fare of chocolate profiteroles (which freeze and defrost rather well). Rather simpler but more effective is to distribute a few stoned cherries, still slightly frozen, on the base of six ramekins, to pour in both rum and cream and to top that with a simple vanilla soufflé mixture. The latter is made by blending a tablespoon of cornflour, 4 of caster sugar and 3 egg yolks with 300 ml (½ pint) of hot milk, to which, once cooked and smooth, you add a tablespoon of butter, a couple of teaspoons of vanilla essence and 4 stiffly beaten, but not dry, egg whites. Place in a moderately hot oven; by the time they have cooked through, the cherries are defrosted and warm, and the cream and rum gives the runny bottom expected of a *baveuse* (runny) soufflé.

SPICY CHERRY SAUCE

Best served warm, this is good with chicken and turkey, ham and tongue or pork tenderloin.

**450 ml (¾ pint) red wine *or* a
mixture of red wine and port
1 cinnamon stick
1–2 whole cloves
1 teaspoon grated orange rind
1 bay leaf
2 tablespoons cornflour
3–4 tablespoons water
500 g (1 lb) red cherries, stoned
a little sugar or redcurrant jelly or
orange or lemon juice to taste
3 tablespoons dark rum or cognac
a knob of butter**

Makes about 600 ml (1 pint)

Place the wine or wine mixture, spices, grated orange rind and bay leaf in a pan, cover and simmer for 5 minutes. Cool; then strain into a clean pan.

Mix the cornflour to a paste with the water, stir into the spicy wine and heat, stirring, until it thickens. Add the cherries and heat through. Taste and sweeten it with a little sugar or redcurrant jelly, or sharpen with a little citrus juice. Add the rum or cognac and beat in the butter. FREEZE or serve.

To serve from frozen: Thaw the sauce over a gentle heat and serve warm.

© *Glynn Christian*

CHESTNUTS

I freeze chestnut flour, which helps to keep its sweetness. It is not easy to use, for many find the flavour difficult, which I cannot understand. Best sources of ideas are southern Italian and southern and south-western French recipes, and, best of all, Corsican.

It is difficult to bake with chestnut flour by itself, for like buckwheat and cornflour it contains no gluten, and so its traditional use is in rather porridgy things or mixed with other flours in breads and batters. I would use it instead of buckwheat and in the same proportions for any recipes featuring that warm flavour, especially in pancakes large and sweet, or in small and savoury blinis to serve with roasted game. Otherwise, use it to make Castanaccio, a recipe of impeccably ancient origin, which may be eaten hot or cold and adapted as, how and when it moves you.

To make this, soak 125 g (4 oz) of sultanas in boiling water until they are warm, and then leave to dry. Add a good pinch of salt to 500 g (1 lb) of chestnut flour and mix it to a soft, rather scone-like paste (although it won't be as spongy) with water. Pour into an oiled or buttered baking tray and sprinkle with the soaked sultanas, a little fennel seed and some pine kernels. Drip on some good olive oil and bake at almost any heat that suits you until a crust has formed. Need I tell you that brown sugars, rum, cognac, butter and other dried fruits all offer an end result of advanced sophistication?

Whole chestnuts freeze well, in or out of their shells, and can be used from the freezer. They

BUCKWHEAT (page 38)
Iced Marron and Ginger Cream (page 111)
Marron Meringues with Black Cherry Sauce (page 123)
Sweetbreads with Chestnuts and Mushrooms (page 188)

make a wonderful addition to baked risotto or red cabbage dishes, and a perfect foil for rich winter stews. They particularly complement pigeon and pork dishes, and, of course, brussels sprouts (the latter especially if mixed with a cream-based onion purée first). If you want to freeze them minus their skins, pierce them and boil for a few minutes before peeling; then continue to cook until just tender. Chestnut purée – either painstakingly home-made by further cooking or bought leftovers – has a concentrated flavour and rich colour which is useful to have at hand for soups; and either whole or puréed chestnuts are excellent additions for stuffings.

CHESTNUT AND ONION TARTLETS

Serve as a side dish with roast or grilled meats, or as a vegetarian dish with sautéed mushrooms and green vegetables.

**1 kg (2 lb) chopped onion
25 g (1 oz) butter
175 g (6 oz) Italian long-grain rice
1½ litres (2½ pints) chicken stock, plus extra if necessary
100 ml (3½ fl oz) double cream
500 g (1 lb) chestnuts, skinned
6 baked Pastry Tartlets (page 89)
salt, freshly ground black pepper and freshly grated nutmeg**

Serves 6

Sauté the onion gently in the butter for 1 minute. Stir in the rice. Add 1 litre (1¾ pints) of the stock, season with salt, pepper and nutmeg and simmer, covered, for about 30 minutes, until the rice is very tender. Purée and sieve the rice mixture and then reheat with enough cream to make a thick purée. FREEZE or keep warm.

Meanwhile, place the chestnuts in the remaining stock, season and simmer for about 30 minutes until they are really tender. Drain and FREEZE or keep warm.

To serve, reheat the pastry cases in a preheated oven at Gas Mark 4/180°C/350°F for 10 minutes. Spoon the onion purée between the pastry cases and sprinkle with the chestnuts.

To serve from frozen: Reheat the pastry cases as above, reheat the purée over a gentle heat and reheat the chestnuts in a little extra chicken stock over a gentle heat. Assemble as above and serve.

CHESTNUT POLENTA

This can be adapted to serve with any game bird or meat by varying the flavouring liquid. Orange liqueurs are good, black rum goes well with goose or you could try brandy or a sharp eau-de-vie. Serve it with the gravy or cooking juice of the accompanying dish.

**250 g (8 oz) can of unsweetened chestnut purée
2 tablespoons fruit juice, liqueur, vinegar, brandy or black rum
grated orange or lemon rind (optional)
2 teaspoons cornflour or arrowroot
2 large eggs (size 1 or 2)
butter for greasing**

Serves 4–6

Mash the chestnut purée with the flavouring liquid and add a little grated citrus rind if using orange or lemon juice. Ensure that the liquid blends with, rather than dominates, the chestnut flavour. Beat in the cornflour or arrowroot and then the eggs.

Butter a small ovenproof dish. Cover the base with the polenta, ensuring that it is no more than 2 cm (¾ inch) thick. Pattern the top with the prongs of a fork and FREEZE, or bake in a preheated oven at Gas Mark 4/180°C/350°F for about 30 minutes or until firm. Serve sliced and warm.

To serve from frozen: Thaw the polenta for 1–2 hours at room temperature; then bake as above until firm.

© *Glynn Christian*

CHICKEN

A good freezer should always contain some good chickens: free-range, perhaps a corn-fed one, or the black-legged *poulet noir* which has a definite gamy flavour. The small spring chickens are less likely to be as interesting in flavour but are a perfect greedy meal for one at the end of a long day, given a microwave.

A more useful thing to have in the freezer is a reduced stock made from the bones of such chickens, for although many people affect not to notice the difference in flavour between the above types and the typical frozen or fresh chicken, the difference in taste in a stock made from their bones and leftovers is unmistakable, and makes the higher prices paid justifiable. If stock-making seems old-fashioned to you, remember that like bread-making, you can do other things while it's happening. But if you aren't even home that long, go the whole old-fashioned way and make your stocks quickly in a pressure cooker; you can with care make them concentrated enough to freeze as they are, as soon as they have cooled.

The most important piece of a chicken always to have in the freezer is the supreme or boneless breast. Microwaved in minutes so it keeps its lovely whiteness, it is the basis of as many gourmet dishes, hot or cold, as your imagination allows. Without the bother of skin and bones it slips under any sauce and slices into any stir-fry. Or you might enjoy its whiteness as it is. If you have frozen poached strips of mixed red, green and yellow peppers, reheat these as the chicken sits to rest. Then combine their juices and those the chicken is bound to have expressed, perhaps adding a little white wine or dry vermouth. Whilst those juices are hot, stir in herb- and garlic-flavoured soft cheese to make a sauce as thick or thin as you like. Scatter the peppers all over the plate to make a carpet, place the chicken centrally and pour the sauce on to the chicken only, so the peppers make a technicolour frame for its whiteness.

It's amazing how many people enjoy chicken livers as a snack, simply fried quickly in butter and served on toast or *crostini* (page 37). They can be used half-frozen – much easier for slicing – and they make simple pâté in minutes; if they are well flavoured this is quite the best sort of pâté for coating a beef fillet you are planning to bake in pastry. About which some advice – never wrap a potential Beef Wellington thickly in pastry and always cut very big vents which have no chance of joining up again. With these precautions you just might get pastry which is cooked and meat which is baked rather than steamed, both a worthwhile objective if you have ever dared compute the cost of offering beef this way.

FILO CHICKEN PIE

Baby beans, courgettes or a ratatouille all make good accompaniments to this pie.

125 g (4 oz) butter, melted
10 sheets of Filo Pastry (page 143)
Filling
40 g (1½ oz) butter
4 teaspoons oil
500 g (1 lb) chicken breast fillets
175–250 g (6–8 oz) onion,
chopped finely
250 g (8 oz) button mushrooms,
sliced thinly
2 tablespoons plain flour
300 ml (½ pint) milk or chicken
stock
1 egg, beaten
salt, freshly ground black pepper
and grated nutmeg

Serves 6

To make the filling, heat a teaspoon of the butter and half the oil in a heavy-based frying pan and, when smoking hot, seal the chicken breasts over a high heat until both sides are golden-brown. Lift out the chicken breasts, cool them and cut them into slivers. Meanwhile, wipe out the frying pan, add a teaspoon of the butter and the remaining oil and gently sauté the onion until soft. Add the mushrooms and stir-fry over a high heat for 1 minute; then add the chicken.

Make a thick white sauce from the rest of the butter, the flour and the milk or stock. Season it well with salt, pepper and grated nutmeg and beat in the egg. Stir in the chicken and vegetable mixture.

Brush a 30 cm (12-inch) round pie dish with some of the melted butter. Unroll the pastry and cover with a cloth. Take one sheet of pastry, butter it and fold it in half to make a square. Place this in the bottom of the dish and butter the top. Brush another sheet with the butter and, without folding, place it in the dish so that it covers the bottom and extends well over the sides. Continue with six more sheets of pastry, buttering each one in turn and placing them in the dish at an angle to the last one so that the corners project like the spokes of a wheel. Fill the case with the chicken mixture. Fold the overlapping sheets into the centre to cover the filling. Brush the two remaining sheets of pastry with more of the butter, fold them in half and place them over the pie, tucking them in around the edges. FREEZE or brush the top with more of the melted butter and bake in a preheated oven at Gas Mark 6/200°C/400°F for 20 minutes untill the top is crisp and golden. Remove from the oven, loosen the edges and invert the pie on to a buttered baking sheet. Brush with the rest of the butter and continue to bake for a further 12 minutes.

To serve from frozen: Thaw the pie for 2–3 hours at room temperature or overnight in the refrigerator; then bake as above.

C

VEGETABLE BROTH WITH WONTON CHICKEN

1 tablespoon oil
3 or 4 spring onions, chopped finely
1 garlic clove, chopped finely
1½ teaspoons fresh root ginger, shredded finely
150 g (5 oz) chicken fillet, cut into very small dice
3–4 teaspoons soy sauce
24 wonton wrappers
1 tablespoon plain flour, blended with 2 tablespoons water
1 medium-size carrot
1 small leek
1 small celery stick
1.5 litres (2½ pints) good chicken stock
salt and freshly ground black pepper

Serves 6

Heat the oil in a frying pan and stir-fry the spring onions in the oil for 30 seconds. Add the garlic and ginger and continue to stir-fry for a further 30 seconds; then add the chicken. Take off the heat, stir well and add 1 teaspoon of the soy sauce and a little seasoning. Allow the mixture to cool.

Place about 1 teaspoon of the chicken mixture on to each of the wonton wrappers. Paint the edges with some of the flour mixture and fold the wrappers over to form triangles. Paint the two points of the triangles that are farthest apart with the rest of the flour mixture and then paste them together to make a bishop's hat shape. FREEZE or set aside.

Cut the vegetables into fine julienne strips and blanch them in boiling water for 1 minute. Drain them and plunge them into iced water. Drain them again and dry them. FREEZE them or set aside.

To make the soup at once, bring a large saucepanful of salted water to a gentle simmer, add the wonton dumplings and blanched vegetables and cook the dumplings for 2 minutes and the vegetables until they are tender. Bring the chicken stock and the remaining soy sauce to the boil and spoon into six soup plates. Add the vegetables and dumplings and serve.

To serve from frozen: Poach the dumplings and vegetables julienne from frozen and assemble the soup as above.

FRICASSEE OF CHICKEN, ALMONDS AND BROCCOLI

This is also delicious made with turkey instead of the chicken.

425 g (14 oz) broccoli, trimmed and cooked lightly
4 tablespoons freshly grated parmesan cheese
875 g (1¾ lb) chicken breast fillets
15 g (½ oz) butter
2 tablespoons oil
75 g (3 oz) almond flakes, toasted
Sauce
50 g (2 oz) butter
4 tablespoons plain flour
300 ml (½ pint) chicken stock
200 ml (7 fl oz) dry white wine
1 tablespoon Dijon mustard
284 ml (10 fl oz) carton of double cream
2 egg yolks
salt and freshly ground black pepper

Serves 6

Arrange the broccoli in the base of a shallow *gratin* dish. Sprinkle with 1 tablespoon of the grated parmesan cheese. Trim the chicken breast fillets of any sinew and sauté them in the butter and oil until lightly golden on both sides. Cool and cut into thin slices. Arrange them on top of the broccoli and sprinkle with the almonds.

To make the sauce, melt the butter in a saucepan, stir in the flour and cook for 30 seconds without browning. Slowly add the stock and bring to the boil, stirring constantly to make a smooth sauce. Whisk in the wine, seasoning and mustard and simmer together for 5 minutes. Whisk together the cream and the egg yolks. Whisk in a little of the hot sauce and return this mixture to the rest of the sauce, whisking constantly to keep it smooth.

Pour the sauce over the chicken and broccoli and sprinkle with the remaining parmesan cheese. FREEZE or bake in a preheated oven at Gas Mark 4/180°C/350°F for 30 minutes until crisp and bubbling.

To serve from frozen: Thaw the dish for 1 hour at room temperature and bake as above for 45–55 minutes until piping hot.

AUBERGINE AND CHICKEN LIVER TIMBALE

Aubergine gives a delicious succulence to this wonderfully Baroque Sicilian dish of pasta. Serve it with a fresh green salad.

4 large aubergines
175 ml (6 fl oz) olive oil
175 g (6 oz) chicken breast fillets
200 g (7 oz) chicken livers, trimmed and halved
2 garlic cloves, crushed
1 kg (2 lb) tomatoes, peeled, de-seeded and chopped
1 tablespoon freshly chopped basil leaves
500 g (1 lb) penne
125 g (4 oz) mozzarella cheese, diced
75 g (3 oz) freshly grated parmesan cheese
salt and freshly ground black pepper

Serves 6

Cut the aubergines into 5 mm (¼-inch) slices and layer them in a colander, sprinkling each layer lightly with salt. Leave them to drain for 15–20 minutes; then dry the slices well. Reserve 3 tablespoons of the oil, and sauté the aubergine slices in the remainder until they are lightly golden on both sides and tender.

Heat 1 tablespoon of the reserved oil in a frying pan and sauté the chicken breasts until golden on both sides and cooked right through. This will take about 8 minutes. Lift them out of the frying pan and allow them to cool; then cut them into slivers. Wipe out the frying pan and add another 1 tablespoon of the oil. When it is sizzling, sauté the chicken livers over a high heat for 2–3 minutes. Remove the chicken livers and wipe out the frying pan.

Heat the remaining oil in the

C

frying pan, add the garlic and sauté for 10 seconds. Add the tomatoes and the basil. Season, bring to the boil, cover and simner for 20–30 minutes, stirring from time to time.

Cook the pasta in plenty of boiling, salted water until *al dente*, and drain well.

Stir the mozzarella, half the aubergine slices, the chicken, the chicken livers and half the tomato sauce into the pasta. Liquidise and sieve the remaining tomato sauce and FREEZE the sauce or set aside.

Use the remaining aubergine slices to line the base and sides of a 3-litre (5½-pint) straight-sided, deep, ovenproof dish. Fill the centre with the pasta mixture, sprinkle the top with the parmesan cheese and press down firmly. Bake in a preheated oven at Gas Mark 5/190°C/375°F for 20 minutes.

Remove the pasta dish from the oven, cool and FREEZE or cool for 4 minutes, slide a palette knife around the edge of the dish and turn out the pasta mould on to a warmed platter. Reheat the reserved tomato sauce and serve with the pasta dish.

To serve from frozen: Thaw the pasta dish and the tomato sauce for 2–3 hours at room temperature and reheat the pasta dish in a preheated oven at Gas Mark 5/190°C/375°F for 20–30 minutes until piping hot. Reheat the tomato sauce and serve separately.

If you are cooking some, it's well worth doing a double quantity for the freezer. Look for the larger ones which tend to cook more quickly and are generally more tender. After soaking them for up to forty-eight hours, cook them in plenty of water with an onion, garlic clove and *bouquet garni* for one-and-a-half hours until tender (a pressure cooker will cut this down to about twenty minutes). Salt them and freeze whole or blend to a purée beforehand. Add them frozen to casseroles or use them in hummus, which many people think is best made with home-cooked, not canned, chick-peas.

LIME HUMMUS WITH FETA AND ALMONDS

Try making your own chick-pea pâté. It's inexpensive, easy to make and far less 'processed' than bought hummus, and it freezes well for later use as a dip or salad or as part of an hors-d'oeuvre or buffet meal.

250 g (8 oz) chick-peas *or*
2 × 400 g (13 oz) can of chick-peas
juice of 2 limes
2–3 tablespoons tahini paste (sesame seed paste)
salt and freshly ground black pepper
Garnish
1 tablespoon olive oil
75 g (3 oz) feta cheese, crumbled
50 g (2 oz) almond flakes, toasted
sprigs of parsley

Serves 6

If using dried chick-peas, soak the chick-peas overnight. The next day, drain the chick-peas and cover them with fresh water. Boil for about 1½ hours or until they are soft.

Drain the cooked or canned chick-peas and reserve about half of the cooking liquid or the liquor from one of the cans. Set aside a quarter of the chick-peas to use later as a garnish. Put the rest of the peas, the lime juice, tahini and some seasoning into a food processor and blend, in short bursts, to a thick purée, adding a little of the reserved liquid to keep the purée from becoming too solid. Taste and adjust the seasoning.

FREEZE the hummus and whole chick-peas or serve spread on a shallow platter, sprinkled with the whole chick-peas, the oil, crumbled cheese and almond flakes and sprigs of parsley.

To serve from frozen: Thaw the hummus and cooked chick-peas at room temperature for 5–6 hours. Check the seasoning, spread on to a plate and garnish as above.

CHICORY

I'm talking here about 'witloof', with long, pointed, green-tipped leaves, not the curly salad ingredient often called the same name. No point in freezing these raw, but they are a beguilingly good vegetable when braised, good enough to serve as a first or separate course if you are being French. (Remember that all braised vegetables freeze beautifully.) The effort would be even better repaid if you used the brand-new variety of red chicory (*not* radicchio) and braised them as normal, with a touch of red wine and a knob of butter. A serving of braised chicory, of either colour, seems especially to like guinea-fowl, game or roast rib of beef, so it's really worthwhile to buy the new chicory in season in summer and braise and freeze it for the game season.

CHICORY AND CHÈVRE SOUP

500 g (1 lb) chicory
2 lettuces
50 g (2 oz) butter
200 g (7 oz) potato, cooked and diced
1.75 litres (3 pints) chicken stock
175 g (6 oz) log of *chèvre* or *crottin* cheese, grated
142 ml (5 fl oz) carton of single cream
salt and freshly ground black pepper
Garnish
finely chopped parsley
miniature *croûtons*

Serves 6

Wash the chicory and lettuces and cut them into strips. Melt the butter in a saucepan and stir in the chicory and lettuce. Cook over a gentle heat until softened. Add the potato, stir well and add the stock. Bring to the boil, add seasoning, and cover and simmer for 25–30 minutes until the vegetables are tender.

Liquidise and sieve the soup. Add the cheese and cream and reheat gently. FREEZE or serve sprinkled with chopped parsley and miniature *croûtons*, accompanied by hot Muffins (page 125) or Melba toast.

To serve from frozen: Reheat very gently to prevent 'threads' of cheese forming. Garnish as above.

CHICORY AND GRUYÈRE TART

A spinach, mushroom and walnut salad sprinkled with crisply grilled bacon complements this dish well. It can also be served as a first course.

200 g (7 oz) Rich Shortcrust Pastry (page 141)
250–375 g (8–12 oz) chicory
25 g (1 oz) butter
a squeeze of lemon juice
75 g (3 oz) Gruyère cheese, grated
3 eggs
142 ml (5 fl oz) carton of single cream
a pinch of Cayenne pepper
salt and freshly ground black pepper

Serves 6

Line a loose-bottomed 23 cm (9-inch) tart tin with a thin layer of pastry. Bake the pastry case blind in a preheated oven at Gas Mark 6/200°C/400°F for 15 minutes; then allow it to cool.

Wash and thickly slice the chicory, discarding the thick stalk ends. Melt the butter in a saucepan, add a squeeze of lemon juice and soften the chicory. Season the cooked chicory with salt and pepper and arrange it in the bottom of the half-baked pastry case. Sprinkle with the cheese.

Beat the eggs and cream together and season with salt and a pinch of Cayenne pepper. Pour the mixture over the chicory and bake at Gas Mark 4/180°C/350°F for about 30 minutes until the custard has set. FREEZE or serve.

To serve from frozen: Thaw the tart at room temperature for 1–2 hours; then reheat in a preheated oven at Gas Mark 4/180°C/350°F for 20–25 minutes.

Note that the red or green fruit that others grow and you eat are spelt with two 'l's; when these are used in a dish, the dish becomes a *chili*, with but one of the letter 'l's. Although becoming available pretty much all of the year, it might be interesting to have some pouches of different blanched chillies on hand for using straight from the freezer. There are dozens in the world, hundreds perhaps. All you need to know is that the smaller they are, the hotter they will be, even allowing for the fact that if you remove the seeds of chillies of any size this will reduce their heat. The very smallest are those most beloved by the Thais.

Chocolate is supposed never to be frozen, but if you do not have anywhere cool and you have brought back some of that really dark chocolate from the continent for cooking, you are much better advised to freeze it to use from the freezer. The shiny bloom will go, but this will not be seen if you are merely grating it over a cake or on to coffee, or making mousses.

It's such a good idea to have the wickedness of chocolate truffles available in the freezer. They will lose their chocolate bloom if made with a crisp outer coating, so go for those with cocoa dustings or something of that ilk. If ever you ruin truffles by letting them melt in the car or kitchen, here's what you do – whisk them into hot creamy milk or milky coffee, or stir them into slightly softened ice cream to refreeze or to serve in a pastry case as truffled ice cream pie. Mistakes worth making.

see also
CASHEW NUTS (page 43)
CREAM CHEESE (page 69)
CROISSANTS (page 73)
Banana and Chocolate Muffins (page 125)
Chocolate Almond Cake (page 14)
Chocolate Almond Petits Fours (page 13)
Chocolate Amaretti Figs (page 86)
Chocolate Hazelnut Tortoni (page 103)
Chocolate Ice Cream (page 108, 109)
Marbled Chocolate and Ginger Cheesecakes (page 49)
Raspberry Black Bottom Pie (page 34)

CHOCOLATE NESTS

There are many variations on these delicate chocolate containers. Try 'nests' made in paper cases, 'cups' made in ramekins, 'saucers' made in foil-lined bun trays or 'lacy baskets' made by drizzling melted chocolate into plastic wrap-lined ring moulds. Fill them with lemon mousse, ice cream or fresh berries and cream.

**150 g (5 oz) plain chocolate
oil for greasing (if necessary)**

Makes 6

Break the chocolate into pieces and melt it in a bowl standing over a saucepan of hot water. Drizzle a little of the chocolate into a paper cake case or into a ramekin lined with oiled foil and roughly spread around the base and sides to make a 'nest' shape. Fill a further five cases or lined ramekins with chocolate and chill until hard. Peel off the paper cases or foil, and FREEZE or use.

To serve from frozen: Thaw the nests in a cool place for about 1 hour.

CHOCOLATE BRANDY SAUCE

The perfect topping for ice cream, crêpes or choux pastries!

250 g (8 oz) plain chocolate
50 g (2 oz) unsalted butter
150 ml (¼ pint) water
4 tablespoons brandy

Serves 6

Melt the chocolate and butter with the water in a small, heavy-based saucepan over a gentle heat, stirring constantly. Do not allow to boil. Add the brandy and FREEZE, or serve warm or cold.

To serve from frozen: Reheat the sauce gently in a double boiler.

WHITE AND DARK TRUFFLES

250 g (8 oz) best-quality plain chocolate
2 tablespoons double cream
1 tablespoon Armagnac
175 g (6 oz) chopped dates
50 g (2 oz) pecan nuts, chopped
50 g (2 oz) preserved ginger, drained and chopped
50 g (2 oz) icing sugar, sifted
125 g (4 oz) white chocolate
12–16 pecan halves, to decorate
cocoa powder for dusting

see also
Basic Ice Cream (page 109)

Makes 12–16

Melt half the plain chocolate in a bowl over a pan of hot water. Take off the heat and beat in the cream and Armagnac. Stir in the dates, nuts, ginger and icing sugar and chill until the mixture is firm.

Roll the mixture into small barrel-shaped truffles. Melt the remaining plain chocolate and use it to coat the truffles. Chill until it is firm.

Melt the white chocolate and, when firm enough, spoon a little on top of each truffle. Top each truffle with a pecan half and FREEZE or chill before serving.

To serve from frozen: Thaw at room temperature for 1½ hours. Dust with cocoa powder before serving.

CIDER

see also
APPLES (page 15)
Rabbit in Cider (page 167)

The proper thing to do with cider is to pour bottles of it into a large saucepan and reduce the liquid over heat by at least three-quarters, and then freeze that in 300 ml (½ pint) amounts to use from frozen. The reason? The flavour of cider is extremely fugitive in cooking and is rarely worth the expense of using unless you underpin it with apple cores, apple skins and a slug of Calvados before the dish is served. By using it concentrated when you are stewing – something I learned from the Shakers of the USA, and which is thus probably British in origin – you get the apple flavour right through. Keep some back to stir in shortly before serving, refreshing the flavour as you would do with a wine sauce or wine-based stew.

CITRUS FRUITS

see also
ALMONDS (page 13)
BUTTERS, FLAVOURED (page 40)
CREAM CHEESE (page 69)
CRÊPES (page 71)
CUSTARD (page 74)
KAFFIR LIME LEAVES (page 115)
KOHLRABI (page 115)
PASTRY (page 140)
Cream of Pumpkin and Orange Soup (page 161)
Duckling with Cointreau (page 80)
Fresh Fig and Orange Gratinée (page 85)
Glazed Duckling with Ginger and Mandarin (page 81)
Lemon Cream Torte with Fresh Guava and Ginger (page 98)
Peppered Venison with Orange (page 197)
Raspberry and Lemon Souffle Crêpes (page 72)
Tomato and Orange Sorbet (page 184)

All citrus fruits are good freezers, but obviously it doesn't make good sense to take up space with such things as whole oranges and lemons. Instead freeze the flesh for use in watercress salad or similar, or store slices of lemon and lime to use straight from the freezer in drinks and to decorate citrus-flavoured cheesecakes and sponges. Grated citrus rind to hand is always good for adding flavour to almost anything. Useful combinations are lime or lemon with lamb and fish; orange or lemon with pork; and strips of mandarin skin with oxtail and beef casseroles, like Daube de Boeuf.

It is worth storing away a good amount of kumquats when you see them. These tiny members of the citrus family, which smell of Earl Grey's tea if you think about it, soften when frozen, and are then ideal for adding to dishes straight from the freezer, and thus it is even quicker to make a simple sauce with them to serve with all poultry, game, pork, veal and lamb. Just cook each 125 g (4 oz) with 125 ml (4 fl oz) of orange juice and one tablespoon of caster sugar until a little transparent and syrupy. If you follow my advice and cut the kumquats into segments rather than slices you will find it much easier to perform the essential task of removing the pips, and your sauce will look as though you meant it, rather than like a dwarf marmalade.

BAKED GAMMON STEAKS WITH ORANGE AND BRANDY SAUCE

These are delicious served with steamed potatoes and a watercress salad, or try them with a pumpkin and potato purée and mangetout.

**6 lean gammon steaks about 1 cm (½ inch) thick
6 tablespoons oil
125–175 g (4–6 oz) onion, chopped
1 celery stick, chopped
3 carrots, chopped
600 ml (1 pint) chicken stock
2 teaspoons Dijon mustard
slivered rind of ½ and trimmed segments of 3 oranges
150 ml (¼ pint) concentrated orange juice
4 tablespoons brandy
salt and freshly ground black pepper**

Serves 6

Snip the fat at regular intervals around the gammon steaks.

C

Lightly oil a frying pan and sauté the steaks one at a time, until they are golden on both sides. Remove and set them aside. Add the remaining oil to the frying pan and soften the vegetables over a gentle heat, stirring frequently.

Sprinkle the vegetables over the base of a shallow *gratin* dish and lay the gammon steaks on top. Mix the stock with the mustard and pour over the gammon and vegetables. Cover and simmer or bake in a preheated oven at Gas Mark 4/180°C/350°F for 30 minutes. FREEZE or set aside.

Blanch the orange rind in boiling water for 5 minutes, drain it and set it aside. Lift the gammon on to a serving dish and keep it warm.

Liquidise the vegetables and stock. Add the orange juice and simmer hard to make a rich sauce. Add the brandy and bring the sauce to the boil. Stir in the orange segments and seasoning with the blanched orange rind. Serve with the gammon.

To serve from frozen: Thaw the gammon in its sauce for 2–3 hours in the refrigerator. Cover and simmer or bake in a preheated oven at Gas Mark 4/180°C/350°F for 35–40 minutes. Lift out the gammon and keep warm; make the sauce as above.

KUMQUAT AND CURAÇAO BABAS

15 g (½ oz) fresh yeast
125 ml (4 fl oz) warm milk and water mixed
200 g (7 oz) plain flour
a pinch of salt
2 eggs, beaten
1 tablespoon clear honey
50 g (2 oz) butter, softened, plus extra for greasing
Syrup
250 g (8 oz) clear honey
250 ml (8 fl oz) water
6 tablespoons brandy
3 tablespoons Curaçao
Decoration
250 g (8 oz) kumquats
284 ml (10 fl oz) carton of double cream, whipped

Makes 6–8

Dissolve the yeast in the warm milk and water and leave for 5–10 minutes until the mixture is frothy.

Sift the flour and salt into a warm mixing bowl. Beat together the eggs and honey. Add the yeast mixture to the flour; then add the egg mixture, a little at a time, mixing the sticky dough lightly with your hand. Dot the dough with small flakes of the butter, cover with a clean cloth and leave in a warm place to rise for 45 minutes to 1 hour (but no longer than this).

Knock back the dough, knead it lightly and shape it to fit six to eight 7 cm (3-inch) well-buttered ring moulds, so that each is about one-third full. Cover and leave the dough to rise to the top of the moulds, which will take about 10 minutes.

Bake the babas in a preheated oven at Gas Mark 6/200°C/400°F for 10–15 minutes until golden. Cool a little; then loosen them, turn them out and leave for 5 minutes before returning them to the moulds.

To make the syrup, dissolve the

honey in the water. Stir in the brandy and Curaçao.

Poach the whole kumquats in half the syrup until they are tender. Leave them to cool in the syrup and then slice them. FREEZE or set aside.

Meanwhile, prick the babas all over with a fork and spoon the remaining hot syrup over them before they cool completely. Keep spooning on the syrup until most of it has been absorbed. Turn out the babas and FREEZE, or serve with the whipped cream and kumquat slices.

To serve from frozen: Allow the babas to thaw in the refrigerator overnight. Thaw the sliced kumquats and use to top the babas, with the whipped cream.

COCONUT

Chips, chunks or thin slivers of fresh coconut cut with a vegetable peeler all freeze very well and make an unusual and usually welcome snack with drinks, an unexpected late addition to curries, or a background to the other fruits of a tropical fruit salad. Store it fresh, moistened with a little of its own milk, or toasted, and use from frozen. Don't keep it longer than a month as its high fat content will make it tend towards rancidity.

Coconut milk is especially good for finishing the curries of southern India, or as the basis for many Thai soups that are flavoured with lemon grass, ginger and chillies. Although it is available in cans and bottles, made easily by soaking desiccated coconut or by diluting those invaluable blocks of coconut cream, freezing fresh coconut milk will ensure that what you have is closest to the real thing, and you can buy it like that too.

see also
CHOCOLATE (page 60)
SORBET (page 181)
Mocha Ice Cream (page 109)
Mocha Rice Creams (page 168)

see also
Coconut Pasta with Orange-almond Syrup (page 140)
Toasted Coconut and Ginger Ice Cream (page 110)

see also
Herb Roulade (page 104)

COFFEE

There's no question about it, freezing roasted coffee beans is an excellent idea. Oxidation of the essential oils is prevented and you get what you have so expensively paid for. But do pack and freeze in amounts that suit your lifestyle, and which will be used, when defrosted, within a day or two. Decanted fresh coffee also keeps far fresher in the freezer. Use it straight from the freezer for absolutely fresh coffee.

If you make too much coffee, freeze it in ice blocks. Use them to cool iced coffee, or to make mocha-flavoured iced chocolate milk. When the kids are away, pour vodka and a coffee liqueur over your coffee rocks, before, after or instead of supper.

COURGETTES

These will freeze but have a tendency to go floppy on thawing. Much better is to blanch or sauté slices of courgette in olive oil and butter beforehand. Better still is to use them in ratatouille-type mixtures which can be frozen ready for use straight from the freezer. One of the more unusual of these is an all-yellow ratatouille. A useful quantity for storing is made by adding to 500 g (1 lb) of yellow courgettes the same quantity both of white aubergines and of yellow peppers, all cut into fairly large pieces. Add 500 g – 1 kg (1–2 lb) of yellow cherry tomatoes and cook everything gently in plenty of good olive oil, together with whole unpeeled garlic cloves. If you want to use onion, only add a small amount,

C

finely chopped. Season and flavour with basil or thyme on thawing.

The delicate, yellow flowers of courgettes and marrows are wasted by frying in batter but are perfect for poaching, stuffed with cooked, spicy rice. But they don't freeze well as they are, so pick them just before you intend to use them.

COURGETTE AND BASIL SOUP

Serve this with Parmesan Muffins (page 125) or crisp Melba toast.

75 g (3 oz) butter
125–175 g (4–6 oz) onion, chopped
750 g (1½ lb) golden courgettes, diced
1 tablespoon plain flour
2.25 litres (4 pints) light stock
2 eggs, separated
142 ml (5 fl oz) carton of double cream
1 tablespoon freshly shredded basil
salt, freshly ground black pepper and freshly grated nutmeg

Serves 6

Heat the butter in a large saucepan. Add the onion and allow it to soften gently in the butter. Stir in the courgettes, cover and cook for 5 minutes, without browning the vegetables. Sprinkle over the flour; then stir in half the stock and simmer until the courgettes are tender.

Purée the courgette mixture and add the remaining stock to make a thin soup. Season and add nutmeg to taste. Beat the egg yolks and cream together; then slowly pour in a ladleful of soup, stirring constantly. Pour this back into the pan and stir over a low heat for a few minutes. FREEZE or keep warm.

Whisk the egg whites with a pinch of salt until they stand in stiff peaks. Fold in the shredded basil leaves and poach large spoonfuls of this mixture in a shallow frying pan of lightly salted, simmering water, turning once during poaching. Once they are firm – after about 5 minutes – remove them, drain them well and FREEZE, or serve floating on each serving of soup.

To serve from frozen: Thaw the soup over a gentle heat and whisk it well. Thaw the egg white garnish for 25–30 minutes at room temperature and serve on top of the piping hot soup.

HOT COURGETTE TERRINE WITH RED PEPPER MARMALADE

This creamy, custard-based terrine with its layer of courgette makes an attractive starter or vegetarian main dish. It is equally delicious served with Tomato Coulis (page 191) and baby vegetables.

300 g (10 oz) courgettes, grated
50 g (2 oz) butter, softened
250 g (8 oz) full-fat soft cheese
5 eggs, beaten
200 ml (7 fl oz) milk
salt and freshly ground black pepper
Red Pepper Marmalade
6 red peppers, de-seeded and the ribs removed
2 large tomatoes, de-seeded
175–250 g (6–8 oz) onion
3 garlic cloves
4 tablespoons red wine vinegar
1 teaspoon sugar
salt and freshly ground black pepper

Serves 6

Sauté the grated courgettes in about one-third of the butter for 1 minute. Remove from the heat and set aside. Mix together the cheese and the rest of the butter.

Beat in the eggs and then the milk. Add the courgettes and seasoning.

Line a 1-litre (1¾-pint) non-stick oblong mould with grease-proof paper and pour in the courgette mixture. Stand the mould in a bain-marie and bake in a pre-heated oven at Gas Mark 3/160°C/325°F for 1 hour or until the custard has set. FREEZE or leave it to stand for 5–10 minutes before unmoulding.

Meanwhile, make the sauce. Put the vegetables into a baking dish with the garlic, cover them with foil and bake in the oven with the terrine for 1 hour or until they are completely soft. Purée them in a blender; then sieve and season to taste with the vinegar, sugar and salt and pepper. FREEZE or serve with the terrine.

To serve from frozen: Thaw both the terrine and sauce at room temperature for about 3 hours. Reheat the terrine in a bain-marie in a preheated oven at Gas Mark 3/160°C/325°F for 30 minutes or until piping hot. Reheat the sauce over a gentle heat.

TWICE-BAKED COURGETTE AND DILL SOUFFLÉ

The secret of this soufflé is that it is bound with vegetables: this helps to keep it light and firm after the first baking and enables it magically to mop up most of the cream sauce and so to swell at the second baking. Serve it as a first course, or serve with baby beans or spinach and plenty of crusty bread.

500 g (1 lb) courgettes, grated
75 g (3 oz) butter, plus extra for greasing
40 g (1½ oz) plain flour
175 ml (6 fl oz) milk
3 large eggs (size 1 or 2), separated
salt, freshly ground black pepper and freshly grated nutmeg
Topping
1 tablespoon freshly chopped dill
284 ml (10 fl oz) carton of double cream
50 g (2 oz) grated Gruyère or parmesan cheese

Serves 6

Sprinkle the grated courgettes with 1–2 teaspoons of salt and leave for 30 minutes in a sieve.

Squeeze the courgettes thoroughly to remove as much liquid as possible. Melt 25 g (1 oz) of the butter in a heavy-based frying pan and stir-fry the courgettes over a medium heat for 5 minutes until they are lightly golden and well dried.

Make a thick white sauce from the remaining butter, the flour, milk and seasoning. Cool for a minute; then beat in the egg yolks, more seasoning if necessary and the drained courgettes. Whisk the egg whites until they stand in stiff peaks and carefully fold them into the soufflé.

Turn the soufflé mixture into a well-buttered 1-litre (1¾-pint) ring mould. Give the mould a gentle tap to break up any large pockets of air. Stand it in a dish of hot water and bake in a pre-heated oven at Gas Mark 4/180°C/350°F for 25–30 minutes until firm. Take the dish out of the pan of water and leave it to cool for at least 15 minutes. FREEZE or unmould the soufflé on to a large, shallow heatproof serving dish or platter.

About 20 minutes before serving, heat the dill and cream until just beginning to simmer. Coat the soufflé with the sauce. Sprinkle with the cheese and bake in a preheated oven at Gas Mark 6/200°C/400°F for 20 minutes, until richly golden.

To serve from frozen: Thaw the soufflé for 2–3 hours at room temperature or in the refrigerator. Turn it out, coat with the sauce and continue as above.

once they have defrosted and bake and brown them under a grill.

A store of crab meat gives greater pleasure than buying it in, no matter how wonderful the Alaskan or Russian variety you find. It is cheaper, for a start, and a much better talking point.

Soup-makers of an oriental persuasion know how good the meat is stirred into bowls at the last moment. Crab makes an interesting alternative or addition to seafood cocktails and stuffings: crab and prawn in half a papaya is infinitely preferable to prawns and avocado, and very much more colourful. And one of my favourite first courses from the deep freeze is lightly spiced crab in small pillow-folded crêpes, gently browned and warmed in sesame oil and served on a bed of salad sprinkled with toasted sesame seeds.

CRAB

see also
Butternut, Crab and Celeriac Soup (page 44)
Ravioli with Crab and Armagnac (page 136)

Whole boiled crabs bought from Portobello Market or, even better, over a fence in Lulworth Cove, are amongst my favourite lunches. Provided they are very fresh – either cooked yourself or from a very reliable supplier – cooked crabs freeze very well for a few weeks and make a welcome sight in the expensive off season. It is a more efficient use of storage space to pick the crab and store the white and brown meats separately. A half-way measure is to dress each crab properly, including the picking of the leg and claw meat, and to stuff it into the back shell in the prescribed manner. They may then be returned to a temperature no more nor less than a light chill and served as they are, or you can cover them with a sauce

CRAB CAKES WITH SHERRY SAUCE

75 g (3 oz) butter
4 shallots, chopped finely
3 tablespoons plain flour
350 ml (12 fl oz) milk
1 large egg (size 1 or 2), beaten
1 tablespoon Dijon mustard
3 tablespoons freshly grated
parmesan cheese
500 g (1 lb) crab meat, flaked
roughly
175 g (6 oz) fine dry white
breadcrumbs
oil for deep-frying
salt and freshly ground black pepper
Sherry Sauce
15 g (½ oz) butter
3 shallots, chopped finely
1 teaspoon plain flour
250 ml (8 fl oz) dry white wine
250 ml (8 fl oz) fish stock
3 tablespoons dry sherry
142 ml (5 fl oz) carton of double or
whipping cream

Serves 6

Heat the butter in a saucepan and gently sauté the shallots until soft. Stir in the flour and cook for 30 seconds before gradually adding the milk. Bring slowly to the boil, stirring constantly to make a smooth, very thick sauce. Cool the sauce slightly and beat in the egg. Season with the mustard, cheese, and salt and pepper. Fold in the crab meat and chill for at least 2 hours.

Shape the mixture into small cakes and dip each cake into the breadcrumbs. Chill the crab cakes for 30 minutes.

Fry the crab cakes quite fast in deep, hot oil until they are golden-brown. Lift them out of the oil with a slotted spoon and drain them well. FREEZE or serve.

To make the sauce, heat the butter in a pan and sauté the shallots until soft. Stir in the flour; then gradually add the white wine and stock and boil to reduce the liquid by half. Add the sherry and cream and FREEZE, or reheat gently and serve with the crab cakes.

To serve from frozen: Heat the crab cakes in a preheated oven at Gas Mark 6/200°C/400°F for 25–30 minutes until piping hot. Reheat the sauce and whisk it well before serving.

CRAB AND SORREL SOUFFLÉ WITH PARMESAN CREAM

The sorrel gives an interesting flavour and a lovely speckled green colour to the soufflé. If you have none, try using mint.

25 g (1 oz) butter, plus extra for
greasing
2 heaped tablespoons plain flour
200 ml (7 fl oz) milk
250 g (8 oz) crab meat, flaked
2 tablespoons grated parmesan
cheese
2 tablespoons double cream
3 large egg yolks (size 1 or 2),
beaten
50 g (2 oz) sorrel leaves, chopped
finely
50 g (2 oz) fine dry breadcrumbs
2 teaspoons brandy
4 egg whites
salt, freshly ground black pepper
and Cayenne pepper
Parmesan Cream
10 g (¼ oz) unsalted butter
1 teaspoon plain flour
90 ml (3 fl oz) dry white wine
284 ml (10 fl oz) carton of single
cream
2 tablespoons grated parmesan
cheese
salt and freshly ground black pepper

Serves 2

Make a white sauce with the butter, flour, milk and seasoning. Add the flaked crab meat, cheese, cream and beaten egg yolks, with the sorrel, breadcrumbs and brandy.

Whisk the egg whites until stiff but not dry. Fold them into the crab mixture and turn the mixture into a buttered 1.2–1.5-litre (2–2½-pint) soufflé dish.

C

FREEZE or bake in a preheated oven at Gas Mark 6/200°C/400°F for 35–40 minutes until risen and golden.

To make the sauce, melt the butter in a pan, stir in the flour and gradually add the wine. Bring to the boil and stir in the cream, seasoning and cheese. Reheat, strain and FREEZE or serve with the soufflé.

To serve from frozen: Thaw the soufflé for about 20 minutes at room temperature; then bake as above. Thaw the sauce over a very gentle heat, whisk well and serve with the soufflé.

CRANBERRIES

see BERRIES

CREAM

Like cheese, creams with a butterfat content of thirty-five per cent or more make good fare for the freezer. Naturally, clotted cream – the richest and most heavenly of all – freezes beautifully; this is absolutely essential for a traditional cream tea. Double cream also deserves freezer space. This is the cream that does everything; it can even be made to go further when diluted with milk. Freeze it semi-whipped and slightly sweetened if wished (as you should whipping cream) and stir or whip it well on thawing. Use it, unsweetened, to make the simplest rich sauce of all – gently simmer until it is reduced by half and then flavour with herbs or a vegetable purée.

Unpasteurised double cream from accredited herds is certainly worth keeping. This is quite delicious, particularly if it is from Jersey cows: its thick, rich, slightly acid taste makes it quite the best accompaniment for soft fruit or chocolate cake.

Don't bother with single cream as this has a tendency to separate on thawing. Soured cream and *crème fraîche* might also separate or thin slightly, but you may find them useful to have at hand for using in sauces.

CREAM CHEESE

The richer cream cheeses are certainly worth freezing for a short time to preserve their freshness, however you choose to use them eventually. But if you are going to give cheese space you might consider giving it flavour first by mixing with things perfumed, spiced or herby and letting them permeate before the freezing: rose petals and a touch of rosewater, for instance, frozen in empty *petits suisse* containers, for serving with fresh fruits.

Although sweet and light ricotta is not strictly a cheese, (it is not made from solidified casein but by boiling up whey) and is certainly not creamy, this is the soft white cheese I would be most likely to freeze: it is harder to find than cream and curd cheeses proper, and more delicate because of its high moisture content. I mix it with a little single or double cream and ground almonds until the texture is like that of whipped cream, and then make it savoury or sweet to fill blind-baked pastry. As a savoury filling I might add toasted flaked almonds and thick generous strands of cooked chicken, or both a purée and chunks of cooked salmon and *petits pois*. Well-flavoured herb and garlic mayonnaise is also an excellent addition. The ground almonds

see also
BERRIES (page 32)
ELDERFLOWER (page 83)
FLOWERS (page 92)
ICE CREAM (page 107)
PASTA (page 134)

see also
CHEESECAKES (page 48)
CROISSANTS (page 73)

gradually thicken the mixture, and it takes twenty-four hours for the flavours to blend fully. If you wish to serve your savoury cheesecake immediately, you might add some celery greens too.

The best sweet version starts the same way – with cream and ground almonds – and is then sweetened lightly and perfumed with three flavours of orange: cubes of glacé orange peel, orange-flower water and grated orange rind. There is nothing as seductive as an accompaniment to summer's soft berries, and you might also scatter the top with grated chocolate or cocoa powder, or both.

Ricotta is the proper basis of Sicilian or Corsican cassata, not always a frozen dessert although it can be. Layers of sponge, which have been sprinkled with an orange liqueur, are stuck together with ricotta that has been sweetened and stiffened with glacé fruits and finely chopped or grated chocolate. I also add dried apricots for their sharpness, although this is not traditional.

The only other reason for keeping a supply of cream, curd, cottage or ricotta cheese is to use for baked cheesecakes, like the ones on page 48–9, which themselves freeze excellently. I am pleased to note a big move back to this original style of cheesecake from the modern gelatine-set versions.

CONFETTI PIE

A real treat to eat: the topping is one of the lightest and most delicious you will ever have eaten.

1 quantity of Rich Shortcrust Pastry (page 141)
4 eggs plus 1 extra egg white
4 tablespoons grated parmesan cheese
2 × 400 g (15 oz) can of beans, drained, e.g. kidney beans, chick-peas, butter beans, etc.
2 tablespoons olive oil
25 g (1 oz) freshly chopped mint or parsley
½ teaspoon grated lemon rind
1 garlic clove, crushed (optional)
500 g (1 lb) ricotta cheese
250 g (8 oz) strained greek yogurt
salt and freshly ground white pepper

Serves 8 as a starter or 4 as a main dish

Use the pastry to line a 25 cm (10-inch) pie dish at least 5 cm (2 inches) deep. Chill until firm; then line the pastry with foil, fill with baking beans and bake in a pre-heated oven at Gas Mark 6/200°C/400°F for 10 minutes. Remove the beans and foil, paint the hot pastry with the extra egg white and sprinkle on half the grated parmesan. Return to the oven and bake for just long enough to set the egg white.

Toss the beans in the olive oil, chopped mint or parsley, lemon rind and garlic if used. Season to taste and spread the mixture evenly over the pastry.

Mix the ricotta cheese with the yogurt, season and stir in the eggs. Ladle this on to the bean mixture in the pastry case and sprinkle with the rest of the grated parmesan. Bake in the oven at Gas Mark 4/180°C/350°F for 40–45 minutes until well risen and set. Cool and FREEZE or cool to lukewarm before serving.

C

To serve from frozen: Thaw the pie at room temperature for 2–3 hours. Reheat in a preheated oven at Gas Mark 4/180°C/350°F for 30 minutes and serve as above.

© *Glynn Christian*

CRÊPES

Crêpes are a classic freezer standby. But, as you are going to all the necessary trouble to interleave them with waxed paper, vary the size and make some bigger and thicker, to make the effort worthwhile. I make a distinction between crêpes and pancakes: to me crêpes are very thin and either quite big for rolling or no bigger than a small saucer for folding into triangles, as you do for Crêpes Suzette. (Pressed into a sieve and then deep-fried they are also a delightfully pretty way of serving food.) Pancakes are not only thicker and bigger, but seem much nicer for being lightened by the use of self-raising flour or baking powder. The added advantage is that they absorb juices and syrups more readily and lusciously. And whilst you are about it, consider using some of the buckwheat you have already stored to make buckwheat versions of both crêpes and pancakes.

Provided you are certain you know you will use them, it is a cinch to store pudding crêpes ready-folded and filled with flavoured butters or fruit. Orange of course for Crêpes Suzette (except that I think lime is even better than that), using teaspoons of butter flavoured with grated orange rind and sweetened with sugar for each crêpe. Passion-fruit is my favourite: use the sweetened pulp of four fruits for every twelve crêpes. Pineapple might be yours: use the drained, crushed fruit from a 425 g (15 oz) can for every six crêpes. After an hour or so of defrosting, finish the process in the pan or oven in the usual mixture of butter, juices and alcohol before serving with whipped cream. Start by caramelising butter and sugar and add fruit juice and alcohol as appropriate: orange and lemon juice, cognac and orange liqueur for Crêpes Suzette; orange and lemon juice and passion-fruit pulp for passion-fruit crêpes; pineapple juice and gin for pineapple crêpes.

I'm also a great admirer of the Breton way with their outsize pancakes, 'galettes'. Savoury versions are always made with buckwheat, sweet ones are plain. To make the filling and the eating of them more interesting, Bretons fold the pancakes into a neat square parcel rather than rolling them. Much simpler to store, far more fun to eat. Be careful about which side you leave exposed (the knobbly, spotted surface should be wrapped inside), and don't brown them too much, so leaving yourself some leeway when grilling, frying or baking them. They reheat excellently in a microwave, but you will be foregoing the pleasure of crispy bits.

see also
BUCKWHEAT (page 38)
CHESTNUTS (page 51)
CRAB (page 67)
Buckwheat Flat Cakes with Almond Kasha (page 39)
Chocolate Brandy Sauce (page 61)

BASIC CRÊPES

125 g (4 oz) flour, sifted with a
pinch of salt
3 eggs
250 ml (8 fl oz) milk *or* a mixture of
milk and water, plus extra if
necessary
75 g (3 oz) butter, melted, plus extra
for greasing
2 tablespoons cognac

Serves 6 (makes 18)

Whisk the flour, eggs and milk or
milk and water together to make a
smooth batter. Stir in the melted
butter and cognac.

Lightly brush a 20 cm (8-inch)
omelette pan with melted butter
and cook the first crêpe as a trial,
adding more liquid to the batter if
necessary. Once the consistency
of the batter is correct, continue
to make about 18 crêpes. (The
pan should need no further buttering as there is fat in the mixture.) FREEZE or fill.

To serve from frozen: Thaw the
crêpes for 1–2 hours at room
temperature or overnight in the
refrigerator before filling.

RASPBERRY AND LEMON
SOUFFLÉ CRÊPES

juice and finely chopped rind of 6
lemons
300 g (10 oz) caster sugar
4 eggs, separated
3 tablespoons plain flour
350 ml (12 fl oz) milk
1 quantity of Crêpes batter (above),
made into 18 crêpes
butter for greasing
Raspberry Sauce
500 g (1 lb) raspberries
icing sugar to taste
1 tablespoon Kirsch

Serves 6

Heat the lemon juice and rind
with 200 g (7 oz) of the sugar in a
pan until the sugar has dissolved.
Cook, stirring constantly, for
20–25 minutes until the mixture
is thick but still falls from the
spoon. Be very careful not to let
the mixture turn dark brown and
bitter.

Beat the egg yolks with the
remaining sugar until the mixture
is pale and fluffy. Stir in the flour
and enough of the milk to make a
smooth paste. In a pan, bring the
rest of the milk to the boil and
whisk it into the egg mixture to
make a smooth sauce. Continue
to whisk the sauce over a gentle
heat until it is just boiling. Simmer
for 2 minutes, whisking continuously. Beat in the lemon con-
serve and leave the soufflé
mixture to cool slightly.

Whisk the egg whites until they
are very stiff and fold them into
the lemon soufflé mixture. Put 2
tablespoons of the mixture on to
one half of each crêpe. Fold over
the top half of each one and lay
the crêpes side by side on a flat,
buttered dish or tray. FREEZE or
bake in a preheated oven at Gas
Mark 6/200°C/400°F for 10–12
minutes until the crêpes are well
puffed.

To make the sauce, press the
raspberries through a sieve, and
add icing sugar and the liqueur to
taste. FREEZE or serve with the
hot crêpes.

To serve from frozen: Thaw the
sauce at room temperature. Thaw
the filled crêpes at room
temperature for 30–40 minutes,
and bake them in a preheated oven
at Gas Mark 6/200°C/400°F for
20–25 minutes until they are well
puffed. Serve immediately, with
the sauce.

C

GRUYÈRE SOUFFLÉ CRÊPES

Serve these crêpes with a tomato sauce or Red Pepper Sauce (page 152).

**75 g (3 oz) unsalted butter, plus extra for greasing
125 g (4 oz) plain flour
450 ml (¾ pint) milk, warmed
75 g (3 oz) grated parmesan cheese
200 g (7 oz) Gruyère cheese, cut into small dice
9 eggs, separated
1 quantity of Crêpes batter (opposite), made into 18 crêpes
salt and freshly ground black pepper**

Makes 18

Melt the butter in a saucepan, stir in the flour and cook over a low heat for 1–2 minutes. Blend in the warm milk and bring slowly to the boil, stirring constantly to make a smooth, thick sauce. Stir in half the parmesan and all the Gruyère cheese. Season and beat in the egg yolks. Whisk the egg whites with the salt until stiff and fold them into the cheese mixture.

Put 2 tablespoons of the soufflé mixture on to one half of each crêpe and fold over the top. Arrange the crêpes side-by-side on a flat, buttered baking dish or tray and sprinkle with the remaining parmesan cheese. FREEZE or bake in a preheated oven at Gas Mark 6/200°C/400°F for 12–15 minutes until the filling has puffed up.

To serve from frozen: Thaw the crêpes at room temperature for 30–40 minutes; then bake as above for 20–30 minutes until the pancakes have puffed up.

CROISSANTS

If you can't easily buy them, freezing a supply when you spot them is an excellent idea. You can also freeze unbaked croissants or croissant dough. But don't bother unless they have been made with butter. Look specially for miniature versions and try to discover, whatever the size, how sweet they are. Those with only a little sweetening can be used far more interestingly than merely to sop up coffee of a morning. Smoked salmon pâté (page 144), rare roast beef, and other expensive fillings look and taste far more exotic in croissants than in bread.

If you do make your own croissant dough, roll the croissant with smoked salmon, smoked ham or a good spread of a flavoured cream cheese. Even more interesting is to make miniature croissants and this, of course, is when you might include a goodly chunk of that bitter dark chocolate you have been saving, thus making superior *petits pains au chocolat.*

CURRANTS

see BERRIES

CUSTARD

I know this sounds mundane, but honestly once you know you have some decent custard of one sort or another, like the following, in the freezer, your pudding horizons will expand dramatically. We are, of course, speaking of egg custards, and the action of freezing would split them if you didn't also use a little cornflour or arrowroot; you can still call it a *crème anglaise* quite properly.

My favourite dinner party way to use custard is to thin it with double cream which has been simmered until reduced by a third or more (opposite). Its resultant richness and texture means you can add a liqueur without losing the throat-stroke of the cream. Personally I think this is far better served cold than hot.

You cannot beat the simplicity of such a sauce when it is flavoured with real almond essence and topped with chilled, thick slices of navel or blood orange. I would sprinkle the orange with orange-flower water and cinnamon, but I would, wouldn't I? This extra creamy but thin custard is, incidentally, a far better sauce for Christmas pudding than brandy or rum butter; these should, in fact, only be served on crackers.

see also
Praline Japonaise (page 123)

Crème pâtissière is what the French and clever dick British put into chocolate éclairs instead of cream, without telling you. *Quelle* swizz. It is properly and better used as the basis for their delicious fresh fruit flans, layered and filled cakes (what some would call gâteaux) and associated goodies. Because *crème pâtissière* relies on egg rather than starch to thicken it, or should do so, it is almost bound to go wrong if you attempt it on the day of a dinner party. Make it well in advance, using a starch so it does not split during freezing, and store it in useful amounts. Thinned with cream and perfumed with something alcoholic or floral it makes a much better cold sauce upon which to sit fruits, fruit puddings, pastries and cakes than it does as a stuffing for them.

CUSTARD SAUCE

Flavour the custard with a teaspoon of vanilla essence (the most common flavouring), or any spirit such as brandy, whisky or rum, or any liqueur. Other good flavourings are very strong black coffee, orange-flower water or rose-water. Or follow the variations below.

4–5 egg yolks
75 g (3 oz) caster sugar
1 teaspoon cornflour
450 ml (¾ pint) full cream milk

Serves 4–6

Beat the egg yolks and sugar well until pale and creamy; then beat in the cornflour. Heat the milk to boiling point and pour it on to the egg mixture in a stream, beating all the time. Return the mixture to the pan and stir continuously over a medium to low heat until the mixture is thick enough to coat the back of a spoon. Don't let the mixture bubble at all in case it burns or turns to scrambled egg on the base. Leave it to cool and thicken until it is lukewarm; then strain it through a sieve and flavour it lightly. FREEZE or serve lukewarm.

To serve from frozen: Thaw the custard in a double boiler, whisk it well and sieve if necessary before serving.

Variations:

BAY CUSTARD

Bay is a wonderful, old-fashioned way of flavouring custard; it is particularly good with baked apples. Macerate 1–2 bay leaves in the milk until it is flavoured, and then remove before using.

C

FOAMY CUSTARD

Another old-fashioned custard and a charming change in texture from the usual. Make the custard using 2 egg yolks, 2 tablespoons of cornflour and 600 ml (1 pint) of milk. Flavour it in your favourite way and cool; then whisk up 2 egg whites and fold them into the warm custard.

RICH CUSTARD SAUCE

This is the richer version that I recommend serving with Christmas pudding; it is also good cold with fresh fruit. Make the custard using 2 egg yolks, 1 or 2 tablespoons of sugar, 1 tablespoon of cornflour and 300 ml (½ pint) of milk. Once it has thickened, remove from the heat and add 300 ml (½ pint) of double cream that has been reduced to half its original volume. Stir in a little rum, cognac or orange liqueur.

© Glynn Christian

CUTTLEFISH

see SQUID

Danish Pastries
Dates
Dim Sum
Duck

DAMSONS

see BERRIES

DANISH PASTRIES

Hardly the sort of thing to find yourself making for the deep freeze, unless you have been snowed in for a week with a supply of suitable ingredients, which should, incidentally, include ground cardamom. As with croissants it is worth keeping a supply if you find a decent maker. The best to store are the miniature ones, often sold by the pound. Served slightly warm they make a delicious change for tea time. Make sure you have extra apricot ones if I am to be invited.

DATES

Fresh dates usually arrive frozen in Britain. Check when your green grocer is expecting them and squirrel some away before they defrost. They are of course the most perfect addition to fresh fruit salads, and I think it is best to take the time to take off the skins, slit them and remove the stones.

see also
TURNIPS (page 193)

Some would stuff fresh dates with flavoured cream cheese, which is something I have never understood. An ancient Moorish use is to make a voluptuous stuffing of dates and almond-flavoured rice for whole fish, to which Oliver Cromwell was more than partial during Lent. But the best way I have found to use them is as an alternative to sorbets as punctuation in a long or heavy meal, especially the Christmas blowout. Once they have been skinned and stoned, dribble just a little vodka and a tiny amount of demerara sugar on each and leave in the refrigerator for a day, so the sugar dissolves and mixes with the vodka and the dates' natural sugars, to make a glisten of golden syrup. If you don't fancy adding even this small amount of alcohol to your guests' intake, use even less orange-flower water. Serve the flavoured dates very cold, a few per person, on exquisite plates.

DIM SUM

These must rate as my greatest recent discovery in commercial deep freezers. They are, as I expect you have no need of reminding, the ingredients of the greatest of all Chinese culinary inventions, the Tea Lunch. In cavernous temples of food in Hong Kong, San Francisco, London, Manchester, Melbourne, Seattle and China itself I have feasted well on the procession of bite-size pieces of food offered in bamboo baskets. Some are steamed, some fried. Ducks' tongues and ducks' feet are revealed for you to indicate acceptance or otherwise. So too might be a snake soup with chrysanthemum petals, five-spiced chicken claws, snowy pork buns, prawns wrapped in translucent sheets of rice flour dough – it is always hard to leave room for the wickedness of a hot, sweet custard tart in crumbly pork-lard pastry.

Much of the more arcane does not appear in the commercially deep-frozen range, but there is a choice of a dozen or more. As well as a perfect lunch served with bowls of tea – Oolongs are better than Jasmine ones – dim sum make a stunning and fast first course or impromptu snack straight from the freezer, for the variety of flavour, colour and texture is extraordinarily great. Most universally popular are *char sui*, the white mounds of steamed dough stuffed with sliced roasted pork in a rich sauce. Dim sum have a guaranteed place in my freezer and it is well worth your chatting to any Chinese restaurant which does dim sum, or a Chinese supermarket, to obtain a regular supply.

This is an appropriate place to insert a word about steaming. It is utterly wrong to steam food of any kind directly above the water, i.e. on a perforated tray of some kind, on the slats of a bamboo steamer, on the base of a colander or, worst of all, in one of those silly folding things from the French which are recommended for vegetables. Steaming must be done with the food sitting on a plate or other impermeable surface, or the moisture dissolves the salts and minerals in exactly the same way as boiling in water would do – just look at the water after you have 'steamed' a cauliflower in a colander if you don't believe me. So when you are steaming your dim sum, pop them on a plate before putting them to steam, or you will sacrifice some or much of their goodness.

DUCK

The most rewarding whole birds to go for are the wild ones: mallards, which might serve two; or single-serving widgeons and teals. Whatever you do, persuade your supplier *not* to singe the down, for this can flavour the flesh very nastily. I always cut the tail from all ducks as close as possible to the body, thus removing the preen gland, for if this is damaged or you are cooking the flesh in a liquid it will appallingly contaminate the rest of the flesh.

There is now an entirely new type of duck on this earth, a series of crosses between the domestic and the wild. In Israel they plead the Mulard; in Britain the Gressingham is the most favoured. There is greater flesh and less fat proportionately, and the flavour is richer than domestic ducks. They are mainly sold directly to finer catering establishments, so it may be to a friendly restaurant that you must apply for supply. Very much worth the effort.

I recommend keeping a *magret* or *maigret* or two on hand, too. A *magret* is not, as you often see, merely a boneless breast of duck: breasts are properly only given this name if they have been removed from a duck which has been fattened for *foie gras*. Thus they will be French, and as these are generally vacuum-packed, can be frozen as they are with impunity. The choice of boneless duck breasts for your frozen storecupboard also includes breasts of Barbary duck, which are meatier and almost enough for two, if you are mean or have much else to offer; of course, a dab hand with the fanning of diagonally sliced breasts can make three servings from two breasts seem positively generous. It is quite as useful, maybe more so, to have one or two duck breasts or *magrets* ready cooked, so they may be defrosted and cut into *aiguillettes* (slivers) for adding to salads, pasta dishes or sandwiches; these will retain enough flavour to be worth eating on a

D

picnic. They quite transform a potato salad, hot or cold, particularly if the dressing is generous with garlic.

Whole ducks are rather bulky for freezer storage, and casseroles made with them tend to be rather fatty. For this reason the recipes that follow are based on portions of various kinds, which is the best way to approach freezing duck dishes. You can, of course, freeze carved roast duck meat, or a whole boned and stuffed duck.

DUCK WITH APPLE AND GREEN PEPPERCORN SAUCE

A vegetable purée − celeriac, potato, carrot or pumpkin − and a crisp green vegetable are the ideal accompaniments for this dish.

6−8 duck thighs weighing 2.5−3 kg (5½−7 lb)
175−250 g (6−8 oz) onion, sliced thinly
2 garlic cloves, chopped finely
5 large cooking apples weighing about 1 kg (2 lb), peeled, cored and sliced
a sliver of lemon rind
200 ml (7 fl oz) duck stock, plus extra if necessary
200 ml (7 fl oz) dry white wine or apple juice
juice of 1 lemon, plus extra if necessary
1 bay leaf
a sprig of thyme
4 cloves
1½ teaspoons green peppercorns
salt

Serves 6

Remove the fat and skin from the duck and gently sauté a piece of the skin in a heavy casserole until the fat runs. Remove the skin and sauté the onion and garlic until they are just golden. Transfer to an ovenproof casserole and top with the apple slices and lemon rind.

Sauté the duck portions until golden-brown and add them to the casserole with the stock, wine or apple juice and lemon juice. Wrap the bay leaf around the thyme and cloves and tie the bundle together. Add to the casserole with half the peppercorns. Add salt to taste, and cover and cook in a preheated oven at Gas Mark 4/180°C/350°F for 1 hour or until the duck is just tender. Cool and FREEZE, or continue to cook for about 30 minutes more until the duck is really tender. Remove the bay leaf bundle, transfer the duck portions to a serving dish and keep them warm.

Liquidise the vegetable and apple mixture, stir in the remaining peppercorns and simmer these together for 2−3 minutes. Check the seasoning, adding lemon juice or more stock if needed, and pour the sauce around the duck.

To serve from frozen: Thaw the duck casserole for at least 1 hour; then bake in a preheated oven at Gas Mark 4/180°C/350°F for 30 minutes or until piping hot. Continue as above.

CHINESE BAKED DUCK WITH PINEAPPLE

Serve with string beans and steamed or stir-fried rice.

**6 duck portions each weighing about
400 g (13 oz)
50 g (2 oz) butter
250 g (8 oz) onion, chopped
2 garlic cloves, chopped
1 tablespoon plain flour
2 sun-dried tomatoes, cut into strips
200 g (7 oz) shitake mushrooms,
halved
500 ml (18 fl oz) duck or chicken
stock
1–3 tablespoons dark soy sauce
1 pineapple, peeled and cut into
bite-size cubes
salt and freshly ground black pepper**

Serves 6

Cut each duck portion into two or three pieces. Heat the butter in a pan and brown the duck in the butter until the pieces are crisp and golden. Transfer the duck to a flameproof casserole dish.

Sauté the onion and garlic in the butter in the pan until soft. Stir in the flour and cook for 1–2 minutes, stirring well. Add the tomatoes, mushrooms and stock and bring slowly to the boil, stirring constantly. Pour the mixture over the duck, cover and simmer for 1 hour until the duck is almost cooked. Cool and FREEZE, or remove the lid of the casserole and leave the sauce to simmer until reduced to a rich gravy.

When the duck is tender, add seasoning and the soy sauce to taste. Stir in the pineapple and simmer for a further 15 minutes.

To serve from frozen: Reheat gently for 30–45 minutes and continue as above.

DUCKLING WITH COINTREAU

Accompany with small, crisp roasted potatoes and courgettes.

**6 large duckling breast fillets each
weighing about 300 g (10 oz)
3 leeks, sliced
1 celery stick, sliced
2 carrots, sliced
400 ml (14 fl oz) chicken or veal
stock
200 ml (7 fl oz) medium-dry white
wine
4 large oranges
75 g (3 oz) pecan nuts
1 tablespoon Cointreau
salt and freshly ground black pepper**

Serves 6

Score the fatty skin of the duckling breasts and lay them, skin side down, in a preheated heavy-based frying pan. Leave them until the skin is crisp and golden. Pour off the excess fat, turn the duckling and sauté the flesh side for 20 seconds. Lift out the breasts and set them aside.

Pour all but 2 tablespoons of fat from the frying pan. Add the vegetables and stir-fry them until they are soft and tender. Spread the vegetables in a layer in a shallow ovenproof casserole and lay the duckling, skin side up, on top. Pour on the stock and wine and season to taste. Cover and cook in a preheated oven at Gas Mark 3/160°C/325°F for 30 minutes or until the duckling is tender.

Meanwhile, cut the rind and pith from three of the oranges and cut out the segments. Peel the rind from the remaining orange and cut it into matchstick-thin strips; then squeeze the juice from the orange. Blanch the orange rind for 5 minutes in boiling water and then drain.

Slice the cooked duckling, top

D

it with the orange segments and pecans and scatter over the orange rind. Keep warm or cool for freezing.

Purée the vegetables, sieve them, add the juice from the orange and the Cointreau and check the seasoning. FREEZE with the duck in one container or reheat and serve with the duck.

To serve from frozen: Bake from frozen in a preheated oven at Gas Mark 4/180°C/350°F for about 45 minutes until it has thawed completely and is piping hot.

GLAZED DUCKLING WITH GINGER AND MANDARIN

Duckling breast fillets cooked in paper parcels not only look pretty, they also stay beautifully moist and tender. Serve them with watercress and crisp straw potatoes.

**8 mandarin or satsuma tangerines
2 tablespoons lemon juice
4 teaspoons soy sauce
2 tablespoons yellow bean sauce
a 2 cm (1-inch) piece of fresh root ginger, chopped finely
2 tablespoons dry sherry
1 tablespoon oil, plus extra for greasing
6 large duckling breast fillets each weighing about 300 g (10 oz) *or* 12 smaller ones
salt and freshly ground black pepper**

Serves 6

Pare and shred the rind from two of the mandarins or satsumas, and squeeze and strain their juice. Mix together the rind, strained juice, lemon juice, soy sauce, bean sauce, finely chopped ginger, sherry and oil. Season with salt and pepper. Remove the duckling skin, cover the breasts with the marinade and FREEZE, or leave for 1 hour.

To cook, cut six 30 cm (12-inch) squares of greaseproof paper or foil and trim them into heart shapes. Oil the insides and put a duckling breast on to each one. Spoon over the marinade. Cut the peel and pith from the remaining tangerines and cut out the segments. Scatter these over the duckling. Fold the heart shapes in half and seal the edges to form cornish pasty shapes. Place them on a baking tray and bake in a preheated oven at Gas Mark 4/180°C/350°F for about 30 minutes if parcelled in greaseproof paper or 35 minutes if parcelled in foil.

To serve, tear open the parcels and slip the contents on to six warmed plates.

To serve from frozen: Thaw the duckling in the marinade overnight in the refrigerator and continue as above.

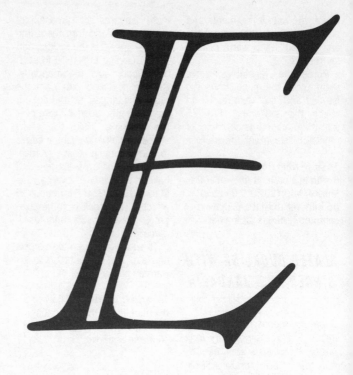

Elderflower

ELDERFLOWER

Wine-makers will know to keep a stock of elderberries for when they have the time to brew up. They are equally useful for strewing into apple pies as an alternative to blackberries. Elderflowers are a more useful and elegant thing to freeze. Defrost them in warm double cream which will then be perfumed with their muscat scent, or cook them from frozen. Equally impressive is their inclusion in cheesecakes, like my Fragrant Cheesecake (page 48). A bunch or so left in a bottle of Germanic wine overnight, later sweetened slightly with honey, gives you your own pudding wine at a fraction of the cost of a muscat from the South of France.

see also
GOOSEBERRIES (page 97)
Elderflower Sorbet (page 182)
Fragrant Cheesecake (page 48)

ELDERFLOWER FRITTERS

This is a dish for using your frozen stock of elderflowers rather than for freezing. Frozen elderflowers heads make a quick and delicate dish of fritters if taken straight from the freezer, dipped into batter and then deep-fried and served either as a starter with segments of lime or lemon or as a dessert with greenage sauce.

18 frozen elderflower heads
oil for deep-frying
Batter
125 g (4 oz) plain flour, sifted
a pinch of salt
2 tablespoons olive or sunflower oil
1 large egg, separated
150 ml (5 fl oz) dry white wine

Serves 6

To make the batter, sift the flour and salt into a large bowl. Make a hollow in the centre, add the oil and egg yolk and then gradually

stir in the wine, continuing until the mixture is the consistency of smooth cream. Whisk the egg white until stiff and fold lightly into the batter.

Heat the deep oil for frying until a small cube of bread dropped in cooks to a golden *croûton* in about 1 minute. Dip the frozen elderflower heads into the batter, one at a time. Shake off the excess and drop them into the hot oil without crowding them. Cook for 2–3 minutes; then lift out and drain well before serving.

ELDERFLOWER AND GOOSEBERRY CHEESE

Fresh fruit preserves set with gelatine are particularly good eaten with fromage frais or greek yogurt or with cold meat or poultry.

125 g (4 oz) sugar
400 ml (14 fl oz) water
1–2 elderflower heads
500 g (1 lb) ripe green gooseberries
250 g (8 oz) ripe red gooseberries
1 tablespoon gelatine
2 tablespoons lemon juice

Serves 6

Dissolve the sugar in the water. Add the elderflower heads and leave in a warm place to infuse for 20 minutes.

Top and tail the gooseberries, strain over the cool syrup and simmer for 20 minutes until the fruit is just beginning to break up.

Dissolve the gelatine in the lemon juice and stir into the fruit *compote*. Cool until just beginning to set and spoon into a damp, oblong mould. FREEZE or chill until firm. Turn out and serve, cut into slices.

To serve from frozen: Thaw the gooseberry cheese at room temperature for 1 hour before slicing.

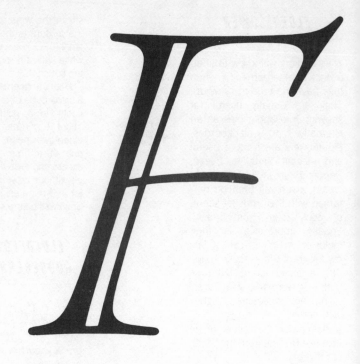

F

FENNEL

The most useful thing to do when you notice a glut of this perfumed, liquorice-flavoured vegetable is to braise it, which takes ages, and to freeze it in that state. Good enough to serve as a first course, cold or hot, and a wonderful substantial buffet dish, although I should cut it into more manageable slices on such occasions. Of course you can also freeze it blanched for use in other dishes, when it can be cooked from frozen.

see also
Rabbit and Fennel in Yogurt Sauce (page 166)

FIGS

These are always nicest ripened on the tree, but they freeze well before they are over-ripe. Store them whole. Or poach, purée or slice them into a lemon- or orange-flavoured syrup first for easier use, and cook from frozen.

I would enhance their flavour with the tiniest drop of Pernod, either in poaching or while defrosting.

FRESH FIG AND ORANGE GRATINÉE

2 large oranges
24 fresh ripe figs, cut into quarters
Topping
500 ml (18 fl oz) milk
4 egg yolks
125 g (4 oz) sugar
2 tablespoons plain flour
30 g (1¼ oz) unsalted butter
2 tablespoons brandy

Serves 6

Trim the peel and pith from the oranges and cut away the flesh in segments. Divide the figs and oranges between six individual flameproof *gratin* or soufflé dishes, adding any remaining juice from the oranges.

To make the topping, heat the milk until just boiling. Meanwhile, beat the egg yolks and sugar until light and fluffy. Stir in the flour and gradually whisk in the hot milk. Return this sauce to the saucepan and bring slowly to the boil, stirring constantly to make a thick custard. Take off the heat, beat in the butter and brandy and leave to cool.

Spoon over the fruit and FREEZE, or grill under a high heat until the top is brown. Serve at once.

To serve from frozen: Thaw at room temperature for 1½–2 hours; then grill as above, making sure the fruit has thawed by plunging a knife through the topping.

CHOCOLATE AMARETTI FIGS

Quick, simple and absolutely delicious! Serve with brandy-flavoured cream sweetened with sifted icing sugar.

18 fresh plump figs
200 g (7 oz) bar of plain chocolate, grated
4 tablespoons finely chopped almonds
1 tablespoon Amaretto liqueur

Serves 6

Cut a small lid from the top of each fig and lift out a coffee-spoonful of the flesh. Discard.

Mix the chocolate, almonds and liqueur and press them well together. Press spoonfuls into the hollows of the figs and FREEZE, or bake in a preheated oven at Gas Mark 2/150°C/300°F for 5 minutes.

To serve from frozen: Bake the frozen figs in a preheated oven at Gas Mark 2/150°C/300°F for 8–10 minutes until the figs are totally thawed and piping hot.

FISH

My freezer is usually stuffed with exotic fish, including smoked ones (page 174). The variety of fish now available has never been better and as supplies of some of the most useful and interesting are unreliable, freezing when you discover them is better than having none at all.

Filleted fish is clearly simpler to store and more useful, for it will defrost faster than whole fish; but there are other ways. A simple alternative, which gives you much choice as to eventual use, is to gut and bone whole smallish fish, which is far easier than you might imagine. There are two ways.

For very small and fiddly fish, up to the size of a medium trout, the way to start is by gutting from the stomach as usual and then snipping out the gills, a vital and often overlooked step for they can give great bitterness. Then you spread each fish on its recently degorged stomach sack and run a thumb firmly along the backbone a number of times. When you turn the fish back you will find you are able to lift out all of the spine together with most of the other small bones, and need only snip the spine top and bottom.

Rather more effort but amazingly more efficient for stuffing a fish is to gut it from the top. This means you not only get rid of most of the bones, but the stretchy stomach sack will become a perfect recipient for the stuffing, making it less likely that any ingredients will tumble out and more likely that such stuffings might actually flavour the flesh – impossible if you merely fill the pouch where digestion, egg production and so forth once went on. With a sharp knife – a serrated bread knife does it brilliantly – cut along the length of the back, as close to one side of the spine as possible. Then using the sharp point of the knife, cut through the flesh on the side of the upright bones until you get to the rib cage bones, which you will have to cut through, thus getting you into the gut; continue down to the tail without cutting through the skin. Now do the other side, which is a little trickier to start. Snip out the spine and the gills. Pick up the innards and snip them from the head and the vent, again being very careful not to pierce

F

the floor of the stomach. And there you are. It works for everything from trout and mackerel right up to something as big and grand as carp or salmon. Don't worry if you seem to mash the flesh as you go here and there – it always seems to be alright once it has cooked.

Another neat way to store fish is in rolled fillets, and this is a way of cooking for a large number as each takes up much less space in the pan. First the prepared fillets must be partially skinned. Using a knife that is not too sharp in this instance, cut between the skin and flesh at the tail end of the fillet and, once you have purchase, continue skinning (the secret of which is to move the skin from side to side rather than the knife). Stop once you get to where the fish is at its widest. Roll the fish from the tail end as far as you can go and then wrap the skin neatly around the fish; this keeps it in shape and will, when you eventually cook it, keep it moist. Some flavourings, such as a herb butter, might be rolled in, especially if you think you might eventually bake or steam the rolled fillets.

There are three distinct choices, other than smoked, of fish to have on standby, however you prepare it: small, individual or snack fish usually stored whole; unusual fillets or steaks; and whole exotic fish or chunks of major ones.

Of the small fish **anchovies** are really rather boring, particularly when compared with fresh sardines, from which they are distinguishable by a particularly large mouth which grimaces well back on each side of their head. They can be grilled and served as sardines, but a better way to serve them if you have time is to gut and bone them as above, and to lay them flat in a shallow dish with a little white wine, vinegar or lemon juice, parsley and garlic. Once the flesh has marinated, remove and dress again with more of the same just before serving.

Red mullet are the overall winner for flavour and appearance. Those bought frozen are many times cheaper than fresh ones. Traditionally cooked with at least the liver intact, they may also be grilled with all their innards intact. This is a fish which benefits from having its scales left on, especially if you are barbecuing, for they protect the skin from unsightly tearing or untasty burning. If they are to be baked, wok-smoked or rolled, the scales are best removed. An excellent, up-to-the-minute first course consists of neatly trimmed fillets of mullet cooked over a low heat and served in a puddle of warm olive oil; I make this even more interesting by allowing the oil to sit with fresh mint leaves, which are then strained out.

Sardines are available fresh or frozen with price differences. If I am grilling them I don't bother to remove the scales, which makes eating simpler for the whole skin peels away and, as with mullet, the scales protect the flesh better anyway. Although added oil might seem over the top, a shower of olive oil is excellent, as is the Corsican conceit of putting a mint leaf or two into their cavities. Yes, they will smell out the house if you grill them in an enclosed, centrally-heated flat during winter, but oh! the summer-pleasure memories of so doing.

Slipper soles are the most fulfilling of the flat fish to keep in store, for their smallness is a treat, visually as much as anything else, and there are many dishes you can make with them. Their main advantage is that there is space in a pan for other ingredients. They are the correct size of fish to use for the delicious Venetian combination of sole with baby artichokes, for instance.

The only **whitebait** worth eating are the Spanish *anguillas* or elvers. Transparent and thread-like they turn into a milky opaqueness when cooked, usually tossed in flour or an eggy batter, and have the most wonderful nutty flavour. There are no accusative eyes! And, yes, New Zealand exports them frozen and they are easier to find than the Spanish.

Of fillets and larger fish the most obvious are **salmon** and **trout**, and of the two I would rather give space to salmon; not because it is in any way superior necessarily, but because it allows much more flexibility. Small catering companies will be pleased to know that Scottish salmon farmers are now supplying fillets and individual portions both boneless and skinless, so salmon can be served in a much wider variety of outlets than ever before. But now you might also keep fillets of **parrotfish**, of **bourgeois** or **red snapper**, **sea bream** or **coral trout**. Two fish that can only be bought frozen and filleted are **orange roughy** and **hoki**, yes, both from New Zealand. Orange roughy is a recently discovered deep-water fish with extremely white flesh, which behaves as well as sole; that is, you can keep it warm, reheat it and generally do most things to which fish should not be subjected without violating its edibility.

For all that it is worth giving space to salmon in your freezer, the fact remains you can probably buy it fresh most, if not all, of the year. Thus I am more readily persuaded to freeze

chunks, slices and steaks of rarer fish when I see them for sale: fresh **tuna**, **shark**, **swordfish**, **sailfish** and other varieties.

The special advantage of all these large, rarer fish is that there is such an abundance of flesh upon each that it is easy to buy pieces without bones and to store these as chunks. I tend to keep chunks of shark, tuna and swordfish. Each chunk originally starts as a piece of fish of several pounds weight, approximately triangular to rectangular and 15–20 cm (6–8 inches) long. In other words, each is rather bigger and thicker than the thicker end of a beef fillet, and about half the dimensions of a small sirloin. Each one is then cut in half and one half frozen, the other cut further into six steaks for use. Thus the whole one, although it might be cut into six steaks eventually, also gives me the choice of cutting it into very thin slices while still slightly frozen (as you would for a beef carpaccio). These slices are good for serving raw with a marinade, or for cooking quickly in butter or oil, both serving up to twelve people as a first course or as an intermediate course with salads.

It is important when cooking all these fish, especially if fashionably grilling or barbecuing them, to do no more than cook them through or they will quickly dry out. The secret is always to let them come to room temperature before being cooked. A further advantage of these fish in today's confused world of diet and counter-diet is that sliced or cubed, each is a perfect substitute for white meats, especially veal and rabbit, and knowing this you can adapt every such recipe you like. The difference, of course, is that the sauces must be

F

made first and the fish merely cooked through in the sauce at the last minute.

In my experience the best results are obtained from frozen fish if they are allowed to defrost as slowly as possible. Planning ahead so you defrost them overnight or longer in a refrigerator seems by far the best plan. The bonus is that less liquid seems to drain away.

SEAFOOD TARTLETS WITH CHERVIL SAUCE

Smaller tartlets make a wonderful starter, but these larger cases are perfect for a main course dinner or luncheon dish.

Pastry Tartlets
225 g (7½ oz) unsalted butter
375 g (12 oz) plain flour, sifted
2 tablespoons iced water
Filling and Sauce
5–6 large soles, filleted
12–18 small scallops
150 ml (¼ pint) dry vermouth
250 ml (8 fl oz) fish stock
1 garlic clove, chopped finely
1 shallot, chopped finely
1 sprig of flat-leaf parsley
milk or fish stock
150 g (5 oz) unsalted butter
100 g (3½ oz) plain flour
1 tablespoon freshly chopped chervil
284 ml (10 fl oz) carton of double cream
salt and freshly ground black pepper

Serves 6

To make the pastry, use a fork to cream the butter with 125 g (4 oz) of the sifted flour and the iced water. Stir in the rest of the sifted flour and knead together to make a smooth dough. Chill for 30 minutes.

Roll out the dough and use to line six individual tartlet or quiche tins measuring about 12 cm (4¾ inches) in diameter. Chill well, line with foil and fill with baking beans and bake blind in a preheated oven at Gas Mark 6/200°C/400°F for 10–12 minutes. Remove the baking beans and foil and continue to bake for a further 10 minutes or until the cases are crisp. Cool and remove from the tins. FREEZE or set aside for filling.

Season the fillets of fish and roll each one up with the skin side inside. Place the fish and scallops in a single layer in a flameproof dish. Add the vermouth, stock, garlic, shallot and parsley and poach gently for 2–3 minutes if freezing or 7–8 minutes if serving at once. Keep the fish warm, strain off the cooking liquid and make it up to 1 litre (1¾ pints) with milk or fish stock.

For the sauce, melt the butter in a small saucepan. Stir in the flour and cook for 30 seconds without colouring before adding the fish cooking liquid. Bring to the boil, stirring constantly, to make a smooth sauce. Season well, add the chervil and simmer for 2–3 minutes. Add the cream.

Pour half the sauce over the fish, FREEZE and FREEZE the remaining sauce separately. Or, to serve, reheat the sauce, arrange the fish in the pastry cases and pour over the sauce to cover. Serve the remaining sauce separately.

To serve from frozen: Thaw the fish and sauce in the refrigerator overnight. Thaw the pastry cases in a preheated oven at Gas Mark 6/200°C/400°F for 5 minutes. Reheat the fish in its sauce and the remaining sauce over a gentle heat, and use to fill the pastry cases as above.

CRUSTED TROUT CREAMS

40 g (1½ oz) butter
2 tablespoons finely chopped shallot
40 g (1½ oz) plain flour
250 ml (8 fl oz) milk
4 tablespoons dry vermouth
1 teaspoon Dijon mustard
1 tablespoon freshly chopped parsley
2 teaspoons freshly chopped tarragon
142 ml (5 fl oz) carton of double cream
375 g (12 oz) filleted pink-fleshed or salmon trout, skinned, poached lightly and broken into bite-size pieces
50 g (2 oz) Gruyère cheese, grated
25 g (1 oz) almond flakes
salt and freshly ground black pepper

Serves 2

Melt the butter in a saucepan and lightly sauté the shallot in the butter until it is soft. Stir in the flour and cook for 1 minute before slowly adding the milk. Bring to the boil, stirring constantly to make a smooth sauce. Beat in the vermouth and mustard and season with salt and pepper. Simmer gently, stirring constantly, for 1 minute. Add the herbs, cream and trout and turn into individual *gratin* dishes. FREEZE or sprinkle with the grated cheese and almond flakes and grill until the cheese melts and the fish is piping hot.

To serve from frozen: Thaw the trout creams in the refrigerator for 1–2 hours. Sprinkle with the grated cheese and almond flakes and bake in a preheated oven at Gas Mark 4/180°C/350°F for about 30 minutes until piping hot.

SOLE AND VODKA TERRINE

250 ml (8 fl oz) dry white wine
1 tablespoon freshly chopped tarragon
2 teaspoons freshly chopped dill
400 g (13 oz) filleted sole, skinned
2–3 tablespoons olive oil
1 garlic clove, chopped finely
175 g (6 oz) smoked salmon, chopped roughly
175 g (6 oz) unsalted butter
2 tablespoons vodka
salt and freshly ground black pepper

Serves 6

Bring the wine, herbs and a little pepper to a gentle simmer for 1–2 minutes. Add the sole and poach for about 1 minute (depending on the thickness of the piece of fish). When cooked, remove the sole and leave it to cool. Reduce the poaching liquid to 2–3 tablespoons and set aside. Strain when cool.

Heat the olive oil and sauté the garlic in the oil for 30 seconds. Add the smoked salmon and sauté over a high heat for 30 seconds. Remove and pat dry with kitchen towel. Blend or process both the sole and the smoked salmon until smooth. Beat in the strained wine reduction, butter, vodka and seasoning and pack the mixture into a small oblong 400 ml (14 fl oz) mould or dish. FREEZE or cover and chill for 3–4 hours.

To serve, either unmould the terrine and cut it into thin slices and serve with Melba toast, or, using two tablespoons dipped in boiling water, shape ovals of pâté and arrange one or two on individual plates. Garnish with herbs or salad and serve with triangles of toast and fresh lemon or lime.

F

To serve from frozen: Thaw the terrine for 1–2 hours in the refrigerator, slice or shape and then thaw for about 1 hour at room temperature before serving as above.

GOUJONS OF SALMON WITH DILL

Serve with garlic- and herb-flavoured greek yogurt or wedges of fresh lemon.

500 g (1 lb) filleted salmon, skinned
2 large egg yolks (size 1 or 2)
2 tablespoons olive oil
2 tablespoons water
125 g (4 oz) dry breadcrumbs
4 tablespoons freshly chopped dill
oil for deep-frying

Serves 2

Cut the fish into diagonal strips about 2 cm (¾ inch) wide. Beat the egg yolks, olive oil and water together and dip the strips of fish into this mixture. Mix together the breadcrumbs and dill and coat the fish with this. Shake off the excess crumbs.

FREEZE the coated fish or heat the deep fat for frying until a cube of bread dropped into it sizzles immediately and turns golden-brown. Cook the *goujons* quickly, a few at a time, turning them once or twice until golden. Lift out, drain well and keep hot while frying the remainder.

To serve from frozen: Deep-fry the *goujons* from frozen until they are golden.

FRICASSEE OF SEAFOOD WITH CHERVIL CREAM

1 kg (2 lb) monkfish fillet, skinned and cut into 1 cm (½-inch) cubes
2 tablespoons lemon juice
300 ml (½ pint) dry vermouth or white wine
250 g (8 oz) scallops, cleaned and cut in half
1 kg (2 lb) fresh mussels, cleaned and steamed open
375 g (12 oz) fresh lobster, cooked
1 tablespoon oil
1 shallot, chopped finely
10 tomatoes, peeled, de-seeded and chopped
150 ml (¼ pint) fish stock
284 ml (10 fl oz) carton of double cream
1 tablespoon freshly chopped chervil
salt and freshly ground white pepper

Serves 6

Season the monkfish with the lemon juice and salt and pepper and poach in the vermouth or wine for 1–2 minutes. Lift out the fish and reserve the wine. Poach the scallops in the vermouth or wine for 1–2 minutes and leave them to cool in the liquid; then strain, reserving both the liquid and the fish. Shell the mussels and lobster and cut the lobster into bite-size pieces.

Heat the oil in a pan and gently sauté the shallot in the oil until soft. Add the tomatoes, stock and strained vermouth. Simmer for 10–12 minutes, check the seasoning and liquidise or sieve. Stir in the cream, chervil and fish and reheat gently. FREEZE or serve in shallow soup plates.

To serve from frozen: Thaw overnight in the refrigerator and reheat gently until piping hot.

PRAWN AND SOLE PASTRIES WITH WATERCRESS CREAM

3 large sheets of Filo Pastry (page 143)
75 g (3 oz) unsalted butter, melted, plus extra for greasing
375 g (12 oz) filleted lemon or Dover sole, skinned and cut into 1 cm (½-inch) cubes
175 g (6 oz) fresh peeled prawns
125 g (4 oz) garlic and herb cream cheese
1 egg, beaten lightly
freshly ground black pepper
Watercress Cream
1 shallot, chopped
1 garlic clove, chopped
2 bunches of watercress, stalks chopped
150 ml (¼ pint) dry white wine
200 ml (7 fl oz) vegetable stock
142 ml (5 fl oz) carton of double cream
a little lemon juice if necessary
salt and freshly ground black pepper

Makes 6

Separate the sheets of pastry. Use them one at a time, keeping the remainder rolled up and covered.

Brush the sheet to be used with some of the melted butter; then cut it in half with a knife to make two oblongs each about 15 × 50 cm (6 × 20 inches). Arrange one-sixth of the cubed sole slightly off-centre at one end of the strip. Top with four or five of the prawns, a spoonful of the cheese and a sprinkling of pepper. Fold a corner of the pastry over the filling to make a triangle and make sure that the filling is completely enclosed. Turn the triangle over and along the pastry, keeping the edges straight. Continue folding the triangle over and over to the end of the strip, keeping the edges matching and straight all the time. Repeat this procedure with the rest of the pastry, butter and filling.

FREEZE or brush each triangular pastry with a little of the lightly beaten egg and bake on a greased baking tray in a preheated oven at Gas Mark 5/190°C/375°F for 15–20 minutes.

For the sauce, add the shallot, garlic and chopped stalks from the watercress to the wine and stock. Bring to the boil, and boil hard to reduce the liquid by half. Strain. In a separate saucepan of boiling water, blanch the watercress leaves. Drain them and refresh them in cold water. Add them to the sauce and reheat gently. Liquidise the sauce, strain if liked, and FREEZE or chill. To serve, stir in the cream and seasoning and add lemon juice if needed.

To serve from frozen: Thaw the pastries and sauce at room temperature for 30 minutes. Brush the pastries with the beaten egg and bake in a preheated oven at Gas Mark 5/190°C/375°F for 30 minutes. Reheat the sauce gently, add the cream and chill.

FLOWERS

Petals come from the freezer in the same soggy state as herbs and thus must be disguised in some way before or afterwards and used from frozen. Fragrant rose petals, from which you have cut the bitter white bases, make super additions to a baked peach pie, to rice pudding you have flavoured with rose-water, to chocolate icings flavoured the same way, or as a frosted decoration for a rose sorbet; or they might simply be mixed with cream cheese in small moulds lined with rose geranium leaves to serve with raspberries.

see also
ELDERFLOWER (page 83)
ICE BOWLS AND JACKETS (page 107)
Fragrant Cheesecake (page 48)

F

Marigold petals are a delicious and slightly spicy old-fashioned way to add colour to stews, and should simply be frozen on the head in a plastic bag; ensure you use the English rather than the French marigold.

Flowers also make entrancing butters and can be used to flavour double cream when they are heated gently together. Both freeze very well. Use a good reference book to tell you which are edible and ensure they have not been sprayed. Imagine serving a pudding with cream you have imbued with red clover, day lily, jasmine, pansy or violet . . . especially if the occasion is in midwinter.

FOIE GRAS

There are two types: goose and duck. Goose *foie gras* is the more classic I suppose, but has the complication of being more likely to decompose or explode during cooking into the fat of which it is comprised. Duck *foie gras* in quantity is relatively new, and those who have had the opportunity to compare generally agree that it is somewhat firmer of texture, better behaved in cooking and has a more complex flavour. As it is often cheaper (comparatively) it thus has much to recommend it. If you do not trust your source you can tell the two from one another by looking. David Chambers, Michelin-star executive chef of London's Meridien Hotel, claims that you can invariably tell one from the other just by looking at them whilst they are whole: the smaller of the two lobes of goose *foie gras* looks fat and round and plump; that of duck is slimmer and longer looking.

Vacuum-packing now means the livers come fresh and safely firmed for freezing in that state. A friendly local restaurateur should be able to get some for you if you cannot get to Harrods, where a telephone call will have a supply put to one side for you. If you can buy it fresh, open freeze it as you would other livers before storing.

The current fashion is to use *foie gras* as it is, sliced thinly, pan-fried and served as a garnish, on a *salade tiède* for instance. Although it seems widely accepted, I do not recommend eating it pink, but cooking it through – just.

Whether you are going to serve it freshly cooked, bake it, or attempt a *pâté de foie gras*, it is usual to excavate the few veins, arteries and other channels which you will easily find. It is then common to marinate the liver in a little cognac or port, but not for too long or in more than is enough to moisten the surface or you will murder much of the flavour. In the south-west of France, *foie gras* is baked very simply, the lobes lightly seasoned and pressed or cut if necessary to neatly fill the baking container. In Alsace, where duck is something of a rarity, they usually knead the goose *foie gras* and mix in spices: an echo of the Middle Eastern tastes of the Jewish population, which continued the heritage of goose-raising introduced by the Romans – not for the liver but for the goose fat, one of the permitted cooking media in a kosher diet.

Do not confuse, in conversation or otehwise, baked *foie gras* with *pâté de foie gras*. The latter is *foie gras* baked in a farce of pork and in turn robed with pastry, the sort of thing to buy sliced from a shop rather than to make yourself.

GALETTES

see CRÊPES

GAME BIRDS

A splendid thing to freeze, if you take time to think first. By which I mean that here is where the axiom that you only get out what you put in is doubly proven. You really must let the poor dead things develop some flavour or some tenderness before you freeze them.

Grouse, for instance, can be eaten immediately it falls to the ground, for it is tender and sweet enough; but it is much improved if allowed to age a couple of days, which it will do without developing the 'gamy' flavour that some people do not like. But a **pheasant** really must be hung before it is eaten, as without time it has neither tenderness nor flavour: it is precisely this lack of hanging time that gives commercially frozen game birds such a bad name. Although birds are best hung in their feathers, even naked birds will improve a little if left for a few days in the refrigerator after defrosting.

All these game birds are what makes cooking whole unpeeled cloves of garlic most worthwhile. Add them to accompanying sauces, so you and your guests may mash the soft garlic into juices; or squash them through a sieve, thus painlessly removing the skins, and serve with the birds, perhaps dribbled with outstanding hot or cold olive oil.

Don't forget that game birds are also perfect for giving flavour to any pâté. Thus it is worth your while to store away those that may be unattractive or damaged in some way.

see also
APPLES (page 15)
BERRIES (page 32)
BUTTERS, FLAVOURED (page 40)
CITRUS FRUITS (page 62)
DUCK (page 78)
GUINEA-FOWL (page 99)
PIGEON (page 153)
QUAIL (page 163)
SMOKED MEATS AND POULTRY (page 179)
Chestnut Polenta (page 52)
Wild Rice Timbales (page 168)

FEUILLETÉS OF PHEASANT WITH RED WINE SAUCE

Follow these with a crisp mixed red-leaf and nut salad for a perfect balance of flavours.

6 pheasants
1 carrot, chopped roughly
500 g (1 lb) onion, chopped roughly
1 celery stick, chopped roughly
1 garlic clove, chopped finely
1 sprig of fresh thyme
2 tomatoes, chopped roughly
150 ml (¼ pint) red wine
2 ginger biscuits, crumbled
15 g (½ oz) butter
2 quantities (500 g/1 lb) of Puff Pastry (page 142)
1 egg, beaten
salt and freshly ground black pepper

Serves 6

Remove the breasts from the pheasants. Place the carcasses in a roasting tin with the carrot, onion, celery, garlic and thyme and roast in a preheated oven at Gas Mark 5/190°C/375°F for 10 minutes. Transfer the contents of the roasting tin to a large saucepan. Add the tomatoes, cover with cold water, bring to the boil and simmer, covered, for 3 hours. Strain the stock and leave it to cool.

Bring the stock, red wine and crumbled biscuits to the boil, whisk well and simmer until reduced to about 300 ml (½ pint). Check the seasoning. FREEZE or keep warm.

Meanwhile, trim the skin and any fat from the pheasant breasts and sauté them in the butter over a high heat for about 1 minute on each side. Lift them out of the sauté pan and leave to cool.

Roll out the pastry thinly into a rectangle and cut into six long strips. Brush the edges of the pastry with some of the beaten egg and wrap each pheasant breast completely in a strip of pastry, overlapping the edges of the pastry slightly and sealing the ends. FREEZE or brush with the rest of the beaten egg and bake in a preheated oven at Gas Mark 6/200°C/400°F for 25–30 minutes, until the pastry is crisp and golden. Reheat the sauce and serve with the *feuilletés*.

To serve from frozen: Thaw the pastry-wrapped pheasant breasts in the refrigerator for 1 hour. Brush with beaten egg and bake as above. Gently reheat the sauce before serving.

PHEASANT PÂTÉ

This is a firm but slightly crumbly pâté which is suitable for spreading or slicing very carefully. If you want a firmer mixture, add up to 25 g (1 oz) of dry breadcrumbs.

1 well-hung pheasant
375 g (12 oz) streaky bacon
600 ml (1 pint) strong red wine
125 g (4 oz) onion
2–3 garlic cloves
24 black peppercorns
8 juniper berries
2 blades of mace
4 bay leaves
4 teaspoons brandy, whisky or gin
375 g (12 oz) chicken livers
1 tablespoon flour
175 g (6 oz) belly of pork, cut into small pieces
1 teaspoon dried thyme *or* a mixture of thyme and rosemary

Makes about 1.25 kg (3 lb)

Remove any remaining feathers from the pheasant and chop it into quarters. Cut the bacon into strips or cubes. Put the pheasant quarters, bacon, wine, onion, garlic, peppercorns, juniper, mace and bay leaves in a saucepan. Simmer gently until the meat is tender and falling from the bones. Remove the pheasant pieces

and leave to cool slightly. Remove the breasts, pour over the brandy, whisky or gin and leave to marinate.

Take the rest of the flesh and the skin and fat off the pheasant bones and put into a food processor or liquidiser. Drain the stock from the pan and reserve; add the rest of the contents of the pan to the food processor or liquidiser, with the chicken livers. Process until the mixture is smooth; then add the flour and mix well. Turn the mixture into a bowl and add the pork.

Add the dried thyme or thyme and rosemary to the reserved stock and reduce it over a gentle heat to 200–250 ml (7–8 fl oz). Mix 150 ml (¼ pint) of it into the pâté mixture.

Put two-thirds of the pâté into a 1.75-litre (3-pint) bowl or loaf tin. Cut the marinated pheasant breast into long, thick strips and arrange them on top of the pâté in the tin, sprinkling over any extra alcohol. Spread on the remaining pâté and pour over the rest of the stock.

Stand the bowl or tin in a roasting tray and pour in boiling water to a depth of 5–7 cm (2–3 inches). Bake in a preheated oven at Gas Mark 4/180°C/350°F for 1¼ hours or until the cooking juices are no longer pink. Leave to cool; then cover and chill well for at least 24 hours. FREEZE or turn out and serve.

To serve from frozen: Thaw the pâté overnight in the refrigerator.

Variation:

GROUSE PÂTÉ

Replace the pheasant with 2 grouse, marinate the breasts in whisky and replace the thyme with rosemary.

© Glynn Christian

G

GNOCCHI

You might find making and storing unusual types of your own gnocchi more than a good idea. They're so easy to make and at least your guests won't be able to compare them with something the local all-night has on special offer. They go marvellously with any stewed meat.

LENTIL GNOCCHI

439 g (15½ oz) can of green or
brown lentils, drained
1 egg yolk
2–3 heaped tablespoons wholemeal
flour, plus extra for rolling
1 teaspoon hot paprika
1 teaspoon ground cumin
salt

Serves 4–6

Mash the lentils and egg yolk together with a fork. Mix in the flour and spices and a little salt. The mixture should leave the sides of the bowl but still be slightly sticky. Leave it to firm for 1 hour.

Knead the lentil mixture for a few minutes and then roll walnut-size pieces into balls with floured hands. Press each ball on to the back of the tines of a fork and roll off across the tines to give a ridged, slightly folded shape. Leave them to dry.

FREEZE the gnocchi or cook in boiling, salted water or stock until they float to the surface. Serve with meat or poultry – you shouldn't need any butter or oil if the meat has a good stock to spoon over.

To serve from frozen: Cook the lentil gnocchi as above from frozen.

© Glynn Christian

see also
PUMPKIN (page 160)

see also
ASPARAGUS (page 19)
FOIE GRAS (page 93)
Apple and Lime Rosti
(page 159)
Chestnut Polenta (page
52)

see also
PHYSALIS (page 153)
Elderflower and
Gooseberry Cheese
(page 83)

GOOSE

Because the goose is the only bird which cannot be induced to reproduce more than once a year it is a wickedly delicious thing to serve out of season. As more and more geese are being reared, and on grass at that, the chance of finding one to freeze is getting ever better: some of the better supermarkets seem to keep a small supply year round.

Don't forget to pull out the chunks of fat just inside the back vent to freeze as it is or to render beforehand: it keeps longer than most fats and is quite the best thing for frying, especially potatoes, and is the proper fat to use for large or small Swiss rosti. If you have goose fat it really is worth considering making small rosti with it (like the one on page 159) and freezing those. Very satisfying to serve unexpectedly.

GOOSEBERRIES

If you really want to freeze them, do so whole or as a purée with elderflower and use from frozen. Much better to go for what used to be called cape gooseberries, but which are becoming better known as physalis (page 153).

GRANITA

see SORBET

GROUSE

see GAME BIRDS

GUAVA

Juicy and very rich in vitamin C, these are easy freezers. Freeze them whole or, if the skin is tough, peeled, halved or sliced and poached beforehand. Otherwise store away a purée of the flesh for later use in fools, mousses, sorbets, pies and jellies.

see also
Basic Meringues (page 122)

LEMON CREAM TORTE WITH FRESH GUAVA AND GINGER

Genoese sponge
2 eggs
50 g (2 oz) caster sugar
½ teaspoon triple-strength rose-water
50 g (2 oz) plain flour
½ tablespoon cornflour
20 g (¾ oz) unsalted butter, melted, plus extra for greasing
Filling
125 g (4 oz) unsalted butter
150 g (5 oz) caster sugar
3 large eggs (size 1 or 2), separated
finely grated rind and juice of 2 lemons
200 g (7 oz) medium-fat soft cheese, e.g. Philadelphia Light
2 teaspoons gelatine
284 ml (10 fl oz) carton of double or whipping cream
Guava and Ginger Sauce
8 ripe guavas, peeled and halved
2 tablespoons ginger syrup from preserved ginger
lemon juice to taste

Serves 6

To make the sponge, place the eggs, sugar and rose-water in a mixing bowl standing over a saucepan of gently simmering water. Whisk until the mixture is thick and quite pale and leaves a trail when the whisk is lifted out of the bowl. Take the bowl off the heat and continue to whisk for about 5 more minutes until the mixture is cool. Sift the flour and cornflour together and gently fold half into the whisked eggs. Gently pour in the melted butter and sprinkle on the remaining flour. Fold the mixture together to make a smooth sponge.

Turn the sponge mixture into a 23 cm (9-inch) lined and buttered deep spring-release cake tin and bake in a preheated oven at Gas Mark 5/190°C/375°F for 30–35 minutes. Let it cool and then cut it in half horizontally. Wash the cake tin, dry it and line it with greaseproof paper. Put the bottom layer of sponge into the base.

To make the filling, cream the butter and sugar until light and fluffy. Beat in the egg yolks, finely grated lemon rind and cheese. Dissolve the gelatine in the lemon juice. Whip the cream until it forms soft peaks. Whisk the egg whites until stiff. Whisk the dissolved gelatine into the egg yolk mixture; then fold in the cream and egg whites.

Spoon the filling mixture on to the sponge base in the tin and cover with the remaining circle of sponge. FREEZE or chill for at least 2 hours before unmoulding the cake and slicing it.

To make the sauce, blend together the guavas, ginger syrup and lemon juice to taste in a liquidiser. Sieve the sauce and FREEZE it, or serve it with the sliced cake.

To serve from frozen: Thaw the cake for 2–3 hours in the refrigerator and the sauce for 3–4 hours at room temperature. Unmould the cake, slice it and serve it with the sauce.

G

GUINEA-FOWL

Sounds better than it usually is: a decent corn-fed, free-range or *poulet noir* chicken is invariably better. The corn-fed guinea-fowls from France are a definite cut above the rest, if you really want one. Even better if you can find them are very young guinea-fowl, which are now being marketed from the West Country. Remarkably, they seem more readily available in Australia. At Gay Bilson's gorgeous Berowa Waters Restaurant, just up a bit from Sydney, where guests arrive by seaplane or boat, mine had been baked in clay and stuffed with a jellied herbal glaze which melted through the flesh during the sealed cooking.

see also
APPLES (page 15)
CHICORY (page 58)

30 minutes until they are almost tender.

Meanwhile, soften the onion in a little oil until lightly golden. Stir in the olives, orange juice, sugar, lemon juice and water. Simmer together for 3–4 minutes.

Bone the cooked guinea-fowl and add to the sauce with the cinnamon stick and tomato purée. Simmer for 15 minutes. Check the seasoning, and add more lemon juice if necessary. Remove the cinnamon stick and FREEZE or serve.

To serve from frozen: Thaw overnight in the refrigerator and reheat gently, adding a little more water if the sauce dries up.

BRAISED GUINEA-FOWL WITH OLIVES

Serve with a pumpkin or celeriac purée and fresh green vegetables.

sunflower oil for frying
a brace of guinea-fowl, cut into neat joints
250 g (8 oz) onion, chopped finely
175 g (6 oz) black olives, halved
250 ml (8 fl oz) unsweetened orange juice
a pinch of sugar
juice of 1 lemon, plus extra if necessary
4 tablespoons water
½ cinnamon stick
1 tablespoon tomato purée
salt and freshly ground black pepper

Serves 6

Heat a little oil in a frying pan. Add the guinea-fowl joints and brown them thoroughly. Reduce the heat and cook them for about

Hare
Hazelnuts
Herbs

HARE

The saddle and hind legs are the usual pieces to keep for later use. I also like to freeze potted hare (below) or a hare pâté. Those wishing to make a jugged hare properly will freeze the blood for final thickening.

see also
SMOKED MEATS AND POULTRY (page 179)
Rabbit, Olive and Red Pepper Terrine (page 165)

POTTED HARE

Only the legs are needed for this dish, store the tender saddle for roasting or sautée-ing, perhaps to serve in slivers scattered on top of an interesting mixed salad as a modern first course.

50 g (2 oz) onion, chopped
1 garlic clove, crushed
1 tablespoon oil
50 g (2 oz) smoked bacon, cut into small pieces
75 g (3 oz) lean belly of pork, cut into small pieces
250 g (8 oz) hare on the bone
150 ml (¼ pint) red wine, plus extra if necessary
1 tablespoon pickling spice
4 juniper berries
2 bay leaves
5 cm (2-inch) piece of orange rind
125 g (4 oz) unsalted butter
1–2 tablespoons cognac
freshly ground black pepper

Makes about 375 g (12 oz)

Brown the onion and garlic lightly in the oil. Add the bacon and pork pieces and fry for about 3 minutes until the fat begins to run. Remove the meat and onion mixture from the pan, replace with the hare and brown it lightly.

Return the meat and onion mixture to the pan and add the wine, pickling spice, juniper berries, bay leaves and orange rind. Cover the pan and simmer for up to 1 hour until the meat is falling from the bones, adding more liquid if necessary.

Take out the hare and remove the flesh from the bones. Simmer the cooking liquid until it is reduced and syrupy. Put the hare flesh and the cooking liquid into a food processor or blender, add the butter and process, making the mixture as smooth or rough as you like. Alternatively, process half the hare flesh, the cooking liquid and the butter until smooth; then process the remaining hare roughly to give some texture. Leave the mixture to cool.

Season the hare mixture with pepper and stir in the cognac. Spoon the mixture into a suitable container, cover tightly and FREEZE, or leave for 24 hours before serving.

To serve from frozen: Thaw the mixture in the refrigerator overnight before serving.

© *Glynn Christian*

MÉDAILLONS OF HARE WITH CHERRIES

Serve with a cauliflower and potato gratin.

3 hares
3 leeks
175 g (6 oz) butter
25 g (1 oz) raisins
300 ml (½ pint) red wine
10 juniper berries
4 tablespoons double cream
4 tablespoons Armagnac
200 g (7 oz) wild cherries or morello cherries, poached in a little red wine and sugar and then drained
salt and freshly ground black pepper

Serves 6

Fillet the saddle from the hares and cut the meat into 2 cm (1-inch) *médaillons*. Roast the bones together with the leeks and 125 g (4 oz) of the butter in a preheated oven at Gas Mark 6/200°C/400°F for 30–40 minutes.

When brown, transfer the bones to a large saucepan, add the raisins, cover them with water and boil for 3–4 hours. Skim and strain off the stock and transfer it to a smaller saucepan. Add the red wine and juniper berries and boil again until the liquid is reduced to 500 ml (18 fl oz). Taste frequently, adding salt and pepper if necessary. Stir in the cream.

Heat the remaining butter in a heavy-based frying pan and sauté the *médaillons* of hare for a few seconds on both sides. Add the Armagnac and *flambé* the meat. Pour over the sauce and simmer together for 2–3 minutes. FREEZE or stir in the well-drained cherries before serving.

To serve from frozen: Thaw the *médaillons* in their sauce in the refrigerator for 4–5 hours. Reheat very gently until piping hot; then stir in the well-drained cherries.

HAZELNUTS

see also
BUTTERS, FLAVOURED
(page 40)
Praline Japonaise (page
123)

Like all nuts, the oil of which deteriorates with age, these are much better kept frozen, in any form except salted, if you are not able to buy reliable supplies easily; it's specially important for makers of continental-style cakes which rely on ground hazelnuts for their special texture and flavour. Like all nuts, they can be used straight from the freezer.

Otherwise, the only hazelnuts I would bother to freeze are the brand-new ones, the cob nuts of the hedgerows, also found in decent greengrocers. Their milky, creamy greenness is a special treat as a snack, with tomatoes, or in any salad mixture. Coarsely chopped, they make a wondrously fresh-tasting scatter for fish, especially poached salmon.

NUT BASKETS

These are delicate, crisp containers for ice cream, mousse or fresh berries.

**2 egg whites
125 g (4 oz) caster sugar
50 g (2 oz) plain flour
25 g (1 oz) flaked hazelnuts
50 g (2 oz) butter, melted, plus extra
for greasing**

Makes about 12

Beat together the egg whites and sugar until light and frothy. Sift in the flour. Add the nuts and melted butter and stir well.

Drop dessertspoons of the mixture on to greased baking trays, leaving space for the baskets to spread. Bake in a preheated oven at Gas Mark 4/180°C/350°F for about 5 minutes until golden at the edges but still pale in the centre.

Leave the biscuits on the trays for a minute; then, using a palette knife, lift one biscuit at a time and shape it over a lightly greased tumbler so that it hardens to a basket shape. Transfer to a wire rack to cool completely while baking and shaping the remaining mixture. FREEZE or fill and serve.

To serve from frozen: Thaw the baskets at room temperature for about 1 hour and, if necessary, re-crisp the baskets in a warm oven for 2–3 minutes and re-shape.

H

CHOCOLATE HAZELNUT TORTONI

125 g (4 oz) plain chocolate
150 g (5 oz) carton of hazelnut
yogurt
284 ml (10 fl oz) carton of whipping
cream, whipped lightly
3 tablespoons hazelnuts, toasted
and sliced
4 tablespoons brandy
2 tablespoons milk
12 large sponge biscuits *or* 18
boudoir biscuits
Decoration
284 ml (10 fl oz) carton of whipping
cream, whipped
chocolate curls

Serves 6

Melt the chocolate in a bowl set over a saucepan of hot water. Cool slightly and whisk in the yogurt. If the chocolate hardens on contact with the yogurt, warm the mixture over a pan of hot water, whisking all the time to make a smooth sauce. Cool slightly; then fold in the lightly whipped cream and nuts.

Line an 11 × 23 cm (4½- × 9-inch) loaf tin with clingfilm, letting it overhang the top edges. Mix the brandy and milk in a shallow dish and dip the sponge fingers one at a time into this mixture. Arrange half of them in the base of the tin. Spoon in the chocolate filling and top with the remaining biscuits. Wrap the overhanging clingfilm over the biscuits and FREEZE the *tortoni*, or turn out and decorate the top two long edges with whorls of whipped cream. Fill the centre with chocolate curls.

To serve from frozen: Thaw for 30 minutes in the refrigerator before decorating as above.

HERBS

Summer's green herbs, which are generally at their most potent just before flowering, are not successful frozen if you want to use them lavishly to strew as you would fresh ones, for they go mushy when defrosted. In that less than perfect state they are thus good for crumbling from frozen into soups, stews, sauces, purées and stuffings; I usually strain them out of soups and stews before serving. Pack them chopped or in sprigs in plastic bags and remember to make up generous quantities of *bouquet garni* when the herbs are available, for later use.

A common way to freeze herbs is in cubes with water, giving measured doses for such cooking; add only just enough water or you will unnecessarily dilute your dishes. Far more original is to make rather smaller ones of suitable flavours for use in long and short drinks, or to first have extracted the herb's goodness into the water with minimal heat, perhaps in a microwave, so the melting cubes will add a stronger and more useful flavour. Fresh ginger processed this way gives a very distinct lift to non-alcoholic drinks or the sensible weak spritzers of fashion. I always add a little sugar, strain out the ginger and then refresh the flavour by squeezing in fresh juice through a garlic press before freezing. Of course, ginger isn't a herb, but I thought this might give you some ideas.

A herb I always look out for is chervil: this is an absolute must to keep whenever you see it. It is quite the thing to use in egg dishes or beguilingly with tarragon, which has a similar but stronger flavour.

see also
BUTTERS, FLAVOURED
(page 40)
CREAM (page 69)
CREAM CHEESE (page
69)
FISH (page 86)
ICE BOWLS AND
JACKETS (page 107)
PASTA (page 134)
PASTRY (page 140)
RICE (page 167)
SMOKED FISH (page
174)
Herb Cream (page 178)
Herb Sauce (page 48)

PESTO

Frozen pesto has a far better flavour than bottled versions, and although it separates on thawing, it just needs a thorough stir to combine all the ingredients before spooning over pasta.

75–100 g (3–3½ oz) fresh basil
3 tablespoons pine kernels
125 ml (4 fl oz) olive oil, plus extra
if necessary
3 large garlic cloves
4 tablespoons freshly grated
parmesan cheese
salt and freshly ground black pepper

Serves 6

Wash the basil, remove the leaves and discard the stems. Sauté the pine kernels in 1 tablespoon of the oil until they are lightly golden. Drain them well.

Put the basil leaves, pine kernels, peeled garlic and seasoning into a food processor or pestle and blend or pound with a mortar until the mixture becomes a smooth paste. Add the remaining oil a little at a time, as if making mayonnaise.

Once all the oil is added, stir in the cheese. If the mixture seems too stiff, add a little more oil to make a sauce the consistency of double cream. FREEZE or serve with freshly cooked pasta.

To serve from frozen: Thaw for 30–60 minutes at room temperature and whisk well to reconstitute.

HERB ROULADE WITH MUSHROOMS

Light and fluffy, a herb roulade lends itself well to a variety of different fillings – from lightly cooked vegetables, fish or shellfish in a cream sauce, to slivers of chicken or ham with sliced avocado; from a ratatouille-type vegetable mixture, to this tasty mushroom filling.

Herb Roulade
50 g (2 oz) butter, plus extra for
greasing
50 g (2 oz) plain flour
500 ml (18 fl oz) milk
4 eggs, separated
3 tablespoons freshly chopped
tarragon, basil or dill *or* a mixture of
these herbs
salt and freshly ground black pepper
Filling
2 tablespoons oil
25 g (1 oz) butter
175 – 250 g (6–8 oz) onion,
chopped
500 g (1 lb) sliced mushrooms
a dash of lemon juice
142 ml (5 fl oz) carton of double
cream
salt and freshly ground black pepper
To serve
fresh soured cream

Serves 6

For the roulade, melt the butter in a saucepan, stir in the flour and cook for 30 seconds. Gradually add the milk and cook until the sauce is smooth and thick, stirring continuously. Season and take off the heat. Cool for a minute before beating in the egg yolks, one at a time. Whisk the egg whites until stiff and fold them into the soufflé, with the herbs.

Grease and line a 35 × 24 cm (14- × 9½-inch) swiss roll tin with non-stick baking paper and spread the soufflé mixture evenly over the tin. Bake in a preheated oven at Gas Mark 3/160°C/325°F for 45 minutes until golden and set. Turn on to a sheet of non-stick baking paper and peel off the lining paper.

To make the filling, heat the oil and butter in a frying pan and sauté the onion until soft. Add the sliced mushrooms and stir-fry until almost all the liquid has evaporated. Take off the heat, stir in a dash of lemon juice, the cream and seasoning. Spread the mixture over the roulade and roll up lengthways. FREEZE or serve hot, with fresh soured cream for spooning over each serving.

To serve from frozen: Reheat the roulade in a preheated oven at Gas Mark 4/180°C/350°F for 25–30 minutes until piping hot. Serve with soured cream for spooning over each serving.

CARROT AND CHERVIL CREAMS

These make a perfect accompaniment to grilled or roast meats.

750 g (1½ lb) carrots, sliced
1.5 litres (2½ pints) chicken stock
a pinch of grated nutmeg or ginger
4 large eggs (size 1 or 2), beaten lightly
200 g (7 oz) Emmental cheese, grated finely
butter for greasing
salt and freshly ground black pepper

Chervil Sauce
15 g (½ oz) butter
2 spring onions, chopped finely
1 tablespoon plain flour
250 ml (8 fl oz) dry white wine or stock
142 ml (5 fl oz) carton of double cream
2 tablespoons freshly chopped chervil
salt and freshly ground black pepper

Serves 6

Simmer the carrots in the stock with seasoning and the nutmeg or ginger until they are very tender. This will take about 20 minutes. Cool and purée them until smooth. Add the eggs and stir in the cheese.

Divide the carrot mixture between six buttered individual soufflé dishes and FREEZE, or bake in a preheated oven at Gas Mark 4/180°C/350°F for 30 minutes or until firm. When cooked, loosen the edges of the moulds with a knife and turn them out on to warmed plates.

To make the sauce, melt the butter in a saucepan and soften the spring onions. Stir in the flour and cook for a few minutes before slowly adding the wine or stock. Season and bring to the boil, stirring constantly. Liquidise the sauce to a purée and then sieve it. Reheat the sauce, add the cream and chervil and FREEZE, or serve it spooned over the carrot creams.

To serve from frozen: Thaw the carrot creams completely and bake as above until firm. This may take 40–45 minutes. Reheat the sauce, whisk it well and serve it spooned over the carrot creams.

HOKI

see FISH

Ice Bowls and Jackets
Ice Cream

Ice bowls make pretty and unusual containers for serving frozen food. The best way is to use two freezerproof bowls or cake tins – one slightly smaller than the other. Put about 5 mm (¼ inch) of iced water into the larger bowl and freeze until hard. Arrange sprays of flowers, herbs or greenery around the sides. Place the smaller inside, weight lightly with well-scrubbed pebbles, fill the gap between them with iced water and freeze until hard. Fill the small bowl with tepid water and stand the larger in warm water to remove both; freeze the resulting ice bowl.

Vodka parties just aren't the same if at least one of the bottles isn't presented with a jacket of ice. Simplest and nicest results come from putting a small bottle into an empty milk or fruit juice carton of suitably large size, filling the remaining space with water, flowers, leaves and the like, and freezing that. When you are ready the carton peels away. You can also line other favourite, suitable shapes with cling film or foil and use them as a mould. If you have small enough bottles and large enough vases, the currently fashionable rectangular and square vases would be worth a go.

It is increasingly less sensible to make your own ice cream. More and more manufacturers are offering dairy ice cream made the proper way and with natural and beguiling flavours. But they can't *always* make the flavour you fancy and thus there will always be a place for home-made, too. Especially such goodies as my favourites: Earl Grey, Rose Pouchong or Jasmine tea ice cream (page 108). These are surprisingly highly flavoured and satisfying, and they mix well with virtually any fruit or fruit pudding; you might even consider serving a tea ice cream with a tea sorbet (page 183) for a stunning dessert.

A home-made basic ice cream is a good standby for the freezer: it can be flavoured with fruit or whatever suits your menu. Of all the recipes I have made and you will have seen, nothing is simpler than ice cream made with condensed milk, for its texture and behaviour is almost identical with that of the egg custard with which you might otherwise have begun, and it is the perfect base for any ice cream flavoured with a fruit purée. Quick and easy too, is an ice cream made simply from cream and eggs. But wetter flavourings, such as fruit juice or tea, are best incorporated into a thicker base: those who do not use cornflour or arrowroot but thicken these only with egg will have runny ice cream.

The other kind worth their keep are savoury ice creams – these make deliciously different first courses.

see also
CHOCOLATE (page 60)
PERSIMMONS (page 152)
WAFFLES (page 201)
Brandy Basket Biscuits (page 36)
Chocolate Brandy Sauce (page 61)
Chocolate Nests (page 60)
Nut Baskets (page 102)

CUSTARD-BASED ICE CREAM

This version cheats a little by including flour, which avoids the horror of a curdled egg custard base.

125 g (4 oz) caster sugar
1 tablespoon plain flour or cornflour
2 egg yolks
a pinch of salt
300 ml (½ pint) milk
284 ml (10 fl oz) carton of double cream
½ teaspoon vanilla essence

Serves 4–6

Mix together the sugar, flour or cornflour, egg yolks and salt in a large bowl and beat until creamy. Scald the milk in a saucepan and pour it over the egg mixture, blending thoroughly. Return to the pan and bring gently to the boil over a low heat, stirring continuously. Once it has thickened, let it simmer for 3–4 minutes; then strain and cool, covering the surface with plastic film to prevent a skin forming.

Whip the cream and fold it in with the vanilla essence. Pour the mixture into a suitable container, cover and freeze for 2–3 hours until it has begun to solidify around the edges. Turn out into a bowl and beat until it is creamy; then return to the freezer and FREEZE.

To serve from frozen: Soften the ice cream for 30 minutes in the refrigerator or for 15–20 minutes at room temperature before serving.

Variations:

CHOCOLATE ICE CREAM

Use 150 ml (¼ pint) of milk and add 125 g (4 oz) of plain chocolate melted in 8 tablespoons of water. Replace the vanilla essence with 2 tablespoons of coffee essence.

TEA ICE CREAM

The best flavours to use are Rose Pouchong, Lapsang Souchong, Jasmine, Earl Grey or Green Gunpowder. Infuse 25 g (1 oz) of tea leaves or of tea bags in the hot milk. Leave it to stand for 5–9 minutes, turning from time to time. Strain well (you may need muslin) and make up to the original volume with cold milk. Add an extra 25 g (1 oz) of sugar to the egg mixture and omit the vanilla essence.

© *Glynn Christian*

CONDENSED MILK ICE CREAM

Flavour this simple, rich ice cream with any of the following variations, or a flavour of your choice.

175 ml (6 fl oz) sweetened condensed milk, chilled
142 ml (5 fl oz) carton of double cream, chilled

Serves 4–6

Put the condensed milk in a chilled bowl and beat it until it has thickened. Pour in the cream and continue to beat until the mixture has almost doubled. Flavour and FREEZE.

To serve from frozen: Soften the ice cream for 30 minutes in the refrigerator before serving.

APPLE AND CINNAMON ICE CREAM

Fold in 300 ml (½ pint) of slightly sweetened apple purée, about 4 teaspoons of lemon juice and at least ½ teaspoon of cinnamon.

Add raisins that have been soaked in rum or orange juice to make Apple Strudel Ice Cream.

APRICOT AND ORANGE ICE CREAM

Soak 250 g (8 oz) of dried apricots overnight in enough water, fruit juice or other flavoured liquid to cover; then strain and purée. Sieve the purée directly into the ice cream mixture and add 2½ tablespoons of lemon juice, 4 teaspoons of brandy and 2 teaspoons of grated orange rind.

BANANA ICE CREAM

Mash 3 very ripe bananas with 5 drops of vanilla or rum essence and a squeeze of lemon or lime juice; fold into the ice cream mixture.

You can substitute the pulp of 1 or 2 passion-fruit for 1 of the bananas if wished.

© *Glynn Christian*

BASIC ICE CREAM

The perfect ice cream: it goes straight into the freezer once mixed and just needs to be left until firm. Flavour it with chopped glacé fruit, chopped lightly toasted nuts, chopped chocolate truffles, crumbled meringues or chopped brandy-soaked fruit, remembering that the more alcohol used the harder it is to freeze the ice cream.

6 eggs, separated
150 g (5 oz) icing sugar, sifted
425 ml (15 fl oz) double cream

Serves 6

Whisk the egg whites until they form firm peaks. Gradually whisk in the icing sugar. Lightly beat the egg yolks and fold them into the meringue. Whip the cream until it forms soft peaks, fold into the ice cream and FREEZE.

To serve from frozen: Transfer to the refrigerator to soften for 30–40 minutes before serving.

Variations:

CHOCOLATE ICE CREAM

Fold in 175 g (6 oz) of melted plain chocolate with the cream.

MOCHA ICE CREAM

Fold in 175 g (6 oz) of melted plain chocolate and 3 tablespoons of really strong coffee with the cream.

FRUIT ICE CREAM

Stir in up to 200 ml (7 fl oz) of thick fruit purée just before freezing.

TOASTED COCONUT AND GINGER ICE CREAM

The nutty texture of coconut is particularly good when combined with the pungency of ginger. This ice cream is delicious served with a fruit salad made from lychees and passion-fruit or pineapple.

50 g (2 oz) desiccated coconut
125 g (4 oz) stem ginger in syrup
1 quantity of Basic Ice Cream
mixture (page 109)

Serves 6

Spread the coconut on a baking tray and toast under a medium-hot grill until lightly golden, watching carefully to prevent the coconut burning. Allow it to cool. Chop half the ginger and cut the remainder into strips to be used later for decoration.

Fold the cooled coconut into the basic ice cream mixture. Freeze until the ice cream is just beginning to go firm at the outer edges. Fold in the chopped ginger and continue to freeze until firm. Shape into 18 balls and FREEZE.

To serve from frozen: Transfer the ice cream from the freezer to the refrigerator for 4–5 minutes to soften slightly before sprinkling it with the remaining strips of stem ginger and serving.

CARAMELISED PECAN ICE CREAM

150 g (5 oz) granulated sugar
250 g (8 oz) pecan nuts
butter for greasing
1 quantity of Basic Ice Cream
mixture (page 109)
Decoration
double cream, whipped
pecan nuts, chopped

Serves 6

Heat the sugar in a saucepan without stirring until it turns to caramel liquid. Add the nuts and cook for a further 30 seconds. Turn out on to a sheet of lightly greased aluminium foil and leave to cool. Coarsely grind the caramelised nut mixture in a coffee grinder.

Fold the caramel into the ice cream mixture and divide between six base-lined tall dariole moulds or yogurt cartons. FREEZE.

To serve from frozen: Turn out the ice cream bombes and decorate the top of each one with whipped cream and chopped nuts.

AMARETTI ICE CREAM SAMBUCA

1 quantity of Basic Ice Cream
mixture (page 109)
125 g (4 oz) amaretti macaroons,
crumbled coarsely
75 g (3 oz) toasted almonds,
chopped coarsely
To serve
175 ml (6 fl oz) Sambuca Romana
liqueur
2 tablespoons powdered espresso
coffee

Serves 6

Freeze the basic ice cream mixture until it is just beginning to set. Fold in the crushed amaretti and chopped nuts and FREEZE.

To serve from frozen: Arrange scoops of ice cream in sundae dishes or goblets and pour over the Sambuca Romana. Dust the tops with the powdered espresso coffee and serve.

ICED MARRON AND GINGER CREAM

250 g (8 oz) can of sweetened chestnut purée
2 tablespoons brandy
1 tablespoon syrup from preserved stem ginger
142 ml (5 fl oz) carton of double cream
To serve
284 ml (10 fl oz) carton of single cream
2 pieces of stem ginger, cut into matchsticks

Serves 6

Mix together the chestnut purée, brandy and ginger syrup. Whip the cream until it forms soft peaks and fold it through the chestnut mixture. Freeze until hard.

Using a potato scoop, shape small balls of the ice cream on to a metal tray lined with non-stick baking paper and FREEZE.

To serve from frozen: Thaw the ice cream in the refrigerator for 5 minutes while swirling the cream on to six small dessert plates. Top with the scoops of marron ice cream and sprinkle with the sticks of ginger.

The heady flavour of this ice cream goes wonderfully well with lightly chilled fruits, particularly slices of orange sprinkled with cinnamon and orange-flower water. You will find that canned lychees work better than fresh ones.

567 g (1 lb 4 oz) can of lychees
3 egg yolks
4 teaspoons cornflour or arrow-root
250 ml (8 fl oz) milk
4 teaspoons rose-water
3 tablespoons ground almonds
284 ml (10 fl oz) carton of whipping cream, whipped

Serves 6

Drain the syrup from the can of lychees and put the syrup into a pan. Heat gently until the syrup is reduced to 4 tablespoons.

Purée the lychees in a liquidiser or food processor and force the purée through a sieve. Mix in the reduced syrup.

In a pan, mix the egg yolks with the cornflour or arrowroot and stir in the milk. Cook until thickened and then cook for 2 more minutes. Stir in the lychees, rosewater and almonds and leave to cool with clingfilm on the surface.

Fold the whipped cream lightly into the cooled custard. Pour into a suitable container and freeze until hard round the edges and mushy in the middle. Remove from the freezer and whisk again; then FREEZE.

To serve from frozen: Soften the ice cream in the refrigerator for 30 minutes before serving.

© *Glynn Christian*

AVOCADO AND LIME ICE CREAM

It is important to scrape out the bright green lining of the avocado skin to get a good colour. Serve it with almost any sub-tropical fruit, which helps to balance the rich flavour. Try it with mango, papaya, pineapple, banana or orange slices; or dribble the pulp of half a passion-fruit over each serving.

500 g (1 lb) ripe avocado flesh (about 2 large fruit)
4 teaspoons clear honey
2½ tablespoons lime juice, plus extra if necessary
2 teaspoons grated lime rind, plus extra if necessary
142 ml (5 fl oz) carton of double cream, whipped lightly

Serves 6

Put the avocado flesh, honey and lime juice into a liquidiser or food processor and blend to a fine purée. Stir in the grated lime rind, turn into a container and freeze until hard around the edges and mushy in the middle.

Remove the ice cream from the freezer and beat it thoroughly until the texture is even. Blend in the lightly whipped cream. Taste and add a little more lime juice or rind if necessary. FREEZE.

To serve from frozen: Soften the ice cream for 30 minutes in the refrigerator before serving.

© *Glynn Christian*

SMOKED SALMON AND DILL ICE CREAM WITH PRAWNS

100 g (3½ oz) white bread, crusts removed
125 g (4 oz) smoked salmon
2 tablespoons lemon juice
150 ml (5 fl oz) cold water
about 4 tablespoons olive oil
15 g (½ oz) gelatine
142 ml (5 fl oz) carton of double cream, whipped lightly
1 teaspoon freshly chopped dill
salt and freshly ground black pepper
To serve
150 g (5 oz) fresh watercress
250 g (8 oz) shelled prawns
a pinch of Cayenne pepper

Serves 6

Soak the bread in a little water for 5 minutes. Remove and gently squeeze out the excess liquid. Purée with the smoked salmon, seasoning, lemon juice and 2 tablespoons of the water. Add the oil, a teaspoon at a time, blending between each addition to make a smooth purée.

Dissolve the gelatine in the remaining water. Slowly whisk this mixture into the salmon purée. Stir in the cream and dill and FREEZE.

To serve from frozen: Soften the ice cream for 30–40 minutes in the refrigerator. Arrange nests of the watercress on six small plates and scoop one large or two smaller balls of ice cream on to the watercress. Sprinkle with the prawns and the Cayenne pepper. Serve with Melba toast.

CAMEMBERT AND ALMOND ICE CREAM

Serve with crusty bread or crisp Melba toast.

**3 eggs, separated, plus 3 extra egg
yolks
2 × 284 ml (10 fl oz) carton of
single cream
375 g (12 oz) Camembert cheese
1 tablespoon gelatine
4 tablespoons water
salt and freshly ground black pepper**
To serve
**150 g (5 oz) fresh watercress or
baby spinach leaves
50 g (2 oz) flaked almonds, toasted**

Serves 6

Whisk all the egg yolks and 150 ml (5 fl oz) of the cream in a double boiler to make a smooth sauce the thickness of double cream. Dice the cheese into small cubes and add to the sauce. Stir and leave for 5 minutes to soften; then take off the heat. Season well and sieve.

Dissolve the gelatine in the water. Whisk the egg whites until stiff. Whisk the gelatine and egg whites into the sauce with the remaining cream and FREEZE.

To serve from frozen: Soften the ice cream in the refrigerator for 30–40 minutes. Arrange nests of the watercress or spinach on six small plates and scoop balls of the ice cream on to the nests. Sprinkle with the toasted almond flakes.

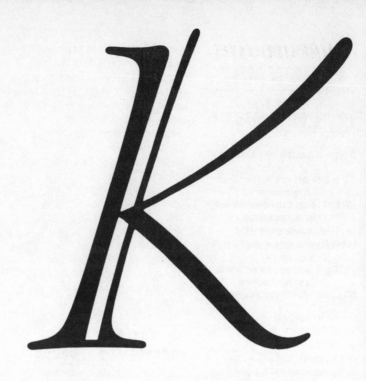

Kaffir Lime Leaves
Kid
Kohlrabi

KAFFIR LIME LEAVES

The kaffir lime looks rather specially unwell, with a lumpy wrinkled skin. The flavour is coarser than the lime we know as a friend of vodka. What I keep in my freezer is not the fruit but the leaf of the tree, which is increasingly available in oriental supermarkets. The clean clear flavour is a signature of Thai food, especially when combined with lemon grass.

Kaffir lime leaves freeze terribly well and thus can be used from frozen as though fresh; sliced very finely, for instance, to scatter on to steamed fish, or as an assertive note in a salad. In soups, stews and sauces where you use lemon, kaffir lime will add nuance and depth, or can be used solo. The thinner you slice the leaves the stronger the flavour. I also like to refresh its tang by adding extra for the last few minutes, though I strain them out if possible, to create added mystery.

If the kaffir lime leaf is not available, other citrus leaves may also be used, but not to the same intriguing effect.

KID

Called *chevron* if it is imported; the flavour is very much like milk-fed lamb. It freezes exceptionally well, but as you might buy it direct rather than from a butcher, do let it hang a few days before storing it to ensure tenderness.

KOHLRABI

This turnip-rooted cabbage was clearly designed by a committee with other things on its mind. Some sense prevailed though, compensating for the vegetable's weird appearance with a beguiling overall foam-green pallor. Rare enough to justify its inclusion in any gourmet book, it might be treated in the same way as any other root vegetable; or used for chilled or hot soups, served as a purée or a sauce, or baked with the richness of cream and other affinities, notably orange and almonds. And like other root vegetables it freezes well – either blanched whole when young and tender, or blanched in cubes; both to use from frozen.

KOHLRABI WITH ORANGE AND ALMONDS

50 g (2 oz) butter
1½ tablespoons olive oil
1 tablespoon finely chopped onion
500 g (1 lb) small kohlrabi, trimmed
300 ml (½ pint) orange juice
flaked almonds, browned lightly

Serves 4

Melt the butter and oil in a pan, add the onion and soften well. Cut the unpeeled kohlrabi into 4 or 8 pieces, depending on size, and add them to the pan. Cook until they start to absorb the butter and oil and then add the orange juice. Simmer gently for about 30 minutes until the kohlrabi is tender and the sauce is rich and syrupy. FREEZE or serve scattered with toasted almond flakes.

To serve from frozen: Thaw the kohlrabi over a gentle heat until piping hot and serve as above.

© *Glynn Christian*

KUMQUATS

see CITRUS FRUITS

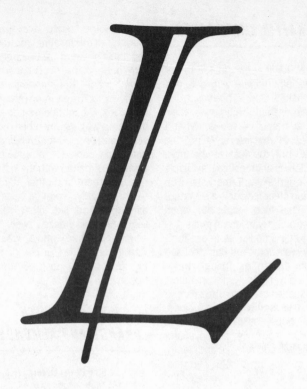

Lamb
Liver
Lobster
Lychee

LAMB

Lamb fillets, the darling of *à la minute* chefs, freeze well. They are not the same muscle as the beef fillet, but the eye of the chops and/or the neck muscles. They should be cooked pink by pan-frying or baking in pastry, and must be allowed to sit for five minutes or so to set and tenderise before slicing to serve.

see also
CELERIAC (page 44)
CITRUS FRUITS (page 62)
QUINCE (page 163)
Aubergine, Tomato and Olive Sauce (page 22)
Terrines of Hot Aubergine with Tomato and Sherry Sauce (page 21)

NOISETTES OF LAMB EN CROÛTE

6 thick *noisettes* of lamb each weighing about 125 g (4 oz)
oil for frying
6 large sheets of Filo Pastry (page 143)
75 g (3 oz) garlic and herb cream cheese
125 g (4 oz) butter, melted
salt and freshly ground black pepper
To serve
1 quantity of Tomato and Coriander Sauce (page 191), heated

Serves 6

Trim the *noisettes* of fat. Heat a lightly oiled frying pan until it is very hot and then seal the *noisettes* on both sides. Allow to cool.

Cut each sheet of pastry in half to make 12 squares and arrange the sheets one on top of the other. Place a *noisette* of lamb on the first sheet. Top with a spoonful of garlic and herb cream cheese, season and fold the pastry over the meat, tucking under the ends to make a neat parcel. Brush the second sheet with some of the melted butter. Place the parcel of lamb in the centre and bring the four corners up and over the parcel, pinching and twisting them at the neck to make a bundle. Gently flatten the pointed corners on top of the bundle, shaping them into a rosette-like decoration. Repeat with the remaining *noisettes*.

Brush the bundles with more of the melted butter and FREEZE, or bake in a preheated oven at Gas Mark 6/200°C/400°F for 20–25 minutes, covering the pastries with foil if they brown too quickly. Serve on a pool of the hot sauce.

To serve from frozen: Thaw the pastries in the refrigerator for at least 1 hour. Brush them with a little more melted butter, bake as above for 30–35 minutes and serve with the sauce.

AVGOLEMONO LAMB

2–3 tablespoons oil
2 kg (4½ lb) leg of lamb, boned and cubed
175 g (6 oz) onion, chopped finely
2 garlic cloves, chopped finely
2 leeks, sliced finely
1 litre (1¾ pints) chicken stock
1 cinnamon stick
500 g (1 lb) spinach, shredded
400 g (13 oz) can of artichoke hearts, drained and quartered
2 egg yolks
2 tablespoons plain flour
juice of 2 lemons
salt and freshly ground black pepper
Garnish
3 tablespoons freshly chopped dill

Serves 6

Heat the oil in a heavy-based saucepan and brown the meat in batches. Lift out the meat and set aside. Add the onion to the pan and soften it gently in the remaining oil. Add the garlic and leeks and stir well. Return the meat to the pan with the stock and cinnamon stick. Heat gently until boiling; then cover and simmer for about 45 minutes until the meat is just becoming tender.

Remove the cinnamon stick. Add the shredded spinach and artichokes, check the seasoning and simmer hard for 10–15 minutes. FREEZE or continue to cook for about 45 minutes until the meat is really tender and the liquid has been reduced by one-third.

Beat the egg yolks and flour together; then slowly add the lemon juice and a little of the hot stock. Stir well and whisk into the lamb casserole, whisking continuously until the sauce has thickened slightly. Check the seasoning again, sprinkle with the dill and serve.

To serve from frozen: Reheat the casserole over a gentle heat until piping hot. Simmer for about 45 minutes until the meat is really tender; then thicken and season the sauce as above, sprinkle with the dill and serve.

LEMONS

see CITRUS FRUITS

LIMES

see CITRUS FRUITS

LIVER

Best undoubtedly is calves' liver, unless you like to keep pig's liver for pâtés, stuffings and the like. As it usually comes vacuum-packed it is safe and ready for freezing as it is, otherwise open freeze it fresh beforehand. Slice it while still half frozen to use eventually fried, grilled or braised. The only cooked dish you are likely to freeze it in is a terrine.

see also
Fricassee of Seafood with Chervil Cream (page 91)

see also
CHICKEN (page 53)
FOIE GRAS (page 93)

LOBSTER

This is best kept frozen raw, if the supplier has done this. If you want to freeze your own lobster it must be exceptionally fresh, that is, frozen the same day that it is caught; otherwise you must have a very reliable supplier. But whether you freeze it raw or cooked, it will keep for four to six weeks.

Many people find that the bigger lobsters are not necessarily the best – often the flavour is less sweet and intense. Some claim that the hen lobster has the best flavour and perhaps this is the case, but certainly it seems to yield more flesh per shell.

Lobster is always enhanced by a dash of alcohol, notably sherry.

LOBSTER AND SCALLOP MOUSSE

850 ml (1 pint 8 fl oz) water
25 g (1 oz) flavoured aspic crystals
4 teaspoons gelatine
juice of ½ small lemon, plus 1 tablespoon
oil for greasing
250 g (8 oz) scallops out of their shells
4 tablespoons dry vermouth
2 lobsters each weighing 375 g (12 oz), cooked
125 g (4 oz) cream cheese
4 tablespoons Armagnac
284 ml (10 fl oz) carton of double cream, whipped lightly
salt and freshly ground white pepper
Garnish
sprigs of fennel

Serves 6

Bring 650 ml (22 fl oz) of the water to the boil, take off the heat and sprinkle over the aspic crystals and 2 heaped teaspoons of the gelatine. Stir until they have dissolved; then stir in the tablespoon of lemon juice. Spoon a thin layer of the aspic into a lightly oiled 750 ml (1¼-pint) seamless loaf tin or mould. Chill until set.

Slice the scallops thinly and cook in the vermouth for 20 seconds. Set aside to cool.

Carefully remove the lobster flesh and coral from the shells and set aside. Simmer the shells with the rest of the water for 10–15 minutes. Strain and cool the resulting stock.

Arrange the meat from two of the lobster claws and a little of the coral on the aspic in the base of the mould. Spoon over another thin layer of the aspic and chill until set. Pour the rest of the aspic into a tray and FREEZE, or chill until set and cut into cubes.

Put the remaining lobster meat, the cream cheese, Armagnac and lobster stock into a food processor and blend lightly. Dissolve the rest of the gelatine in the remaining lemon juice with a spoonful of the scallop cooking liquid if needed. Add to the lobster mousse. Fold in the whipped cream, the remaining coral, the sliced scallop and seasoning. Spread the mousse over the lobster and coral in the mould and chill until it is firm to the touch. FREEZE or turn out the mousse and surround it with the cubes of aspic to serve.

To serve from frozen: Thaw both the mousse and the extra aspic in the refrigerator overnight. Turn out and serve as above.

LOGANBERRIES

see BERRIES

Fresh lychees can be frozen in syrup once peeled and pipped. Much more worthwhile is to purée the fruit from a large can, straining a couple of times, add a few drops of rose-water and then freeze. Blend in the very reduced syrup from the can and a couple of lightly whipped egg whites at some stage too. Quite the most fragrant and prettiest sorbet you can possibly imagine.

see also
Lychee Ice Cream (page 111)

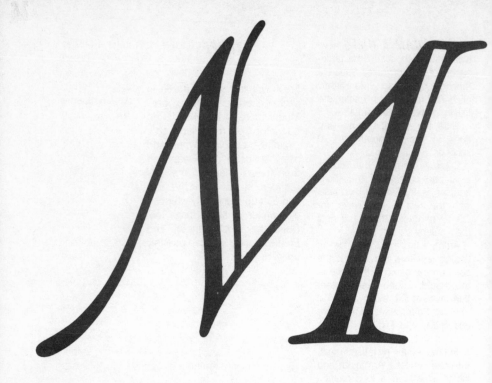

Macadamia Nuts
Mangetout
Mangoes
Melons
Meringue
Muffins
Mussels

MACADAMIA NUTS

If you can get any which have not been roasted or salted, I heartily recommend you freeze them, for their very high oil content puts them very much at risk from oxidation through bad storage. Most of them are lightly flavoured with extra coconut oil (the American ones are anyway) and that makes them even more fragile. Use them straight from the freezer as you would other nuts.

MACKEREL

see FISH

MANDARINS

see CITRUS FRUITS

MANGETOUT

Well of course, you might say. But rather than the thin ones, I would blanch and keep the fatter 'sugar-snap' peas. Those with time on their hands, or the disposal of the hands of others, might make the neatest of all cocktail snacks. Blanched peas are split down their curved longest sides and stuffed with something like a prawn or smoked salmon pâté (page 174) and then frozen. It does take time, but can be done over several days or weeks for a big day or night (but freeze them as you stuff them!)

see also
SMOKED FISH (page 174)

MANGOES

You can make and freeze a mango purée to use as a coulis, although I am convinced that

see also
Skewered Pork with Mango (page 157)

the flavour of mango changes dramatically when it is puréed and have stopped doing it for ice creams and most other things – the exceptions being such things as Sue's mousse (below).

I use cans of Alphonso mangoes to make a sorbet, simply by puréeing the drained contents of the can. The Alphonso is the most widely available of the fragrant varieties of mango. The combination of its silken texture, the canning process, and the sugar retained in the drained flesh makes one of the simplest and best of sorbets: once it is almost frozen and you are giving it a whisk to even out the crystals, it is good to fold through one or two beaten egg whites, as it prevents the sorbet melting too quickly and gives a better, lighter texture.

Fresh ripe mango is worth freezing in slices in a lime- or lemon-flavoured syrup – the former giving a better flavour.

MANGO MOUSSE WITH COINTREAU SAUCE

3 ripe mangoes or 3 × 425 g
(15 oz) can of mangoes in syrup
sifted icing sugar to taste
2 teaspoons gelatine
2 tablespoons water
200 ml (7 fl oz) double cream
1 large egg white (size 1 or 2)
2 tablespoons Cointreau
1–2 tablespoons brandy
Garnish
fresh mint sprigs

Serves 6

Peel and slice the fresh mango flesh or drain the canned mango slices. Blend the flesh and measure 375 ml (13 fl oz) of the resulting purée into a bowl. Sweeten with icing sugar if liked. FREEZE the rest of the purée, or set it aside the make the sauce.

Dissolve the gelatine in the water and whisk this into the measured quantity of mango purée. Lightly whip the cream until it thickens and fold this gently into the mango mixture. Whisk the egg white until stiff and fold into the mousse. Pour into a 500 g (1 lb) loaf tin or mould. FREEZE or chill until set.

To serve, flavour the remaining mango with the Cointreau, brandy and icing sugar to taste. Turn out the mango mousse and slice. Serve each portion on a pool of the mango sauce and garnish with sprigs of mint.

To serve from frozen: Allow both the mousse and the mango purée to thaw at room temperature or in the refrigerator. Slice the mousse and flavour the purée as above. Serve as above.

see also
Basic Ice Cream (page 109)

MELONS

see also
SMOKED FISH (page 174)

A store of melon purée is useful to have at hand for a fruit coulis or to mix into mayonnaise. It also makes cooling and refreshing chilled soups. One of the simplest of these is made by mixing 1.2 litres (2 pints) of melon purée with 300 ml (½ pint) of cucumber purée and 8 to 12 sprigs of crushed peppermint; this is then chilled overnight and the mint removed before serving. Or you could try combining two types of melon purée – perhaps cantaloupe flavoured with lemon juice and honeydew flavoured with lime juice – to flavour and chill the same way.

If you put by cubes or balls of melon tossed in caster sugar, syrup or lemon juice, use them while they are still a little chilled in case they collapse. But don't freeze water melon, it doesn't give good results.

MERINGUE

A good thing to have in the freezer for creating an impressive dessert quickly and easily. Cream, fruit, liqueur, nuts – all these things are happy to be associated with meringue. Of course the latter, in the form of ground almonds, is the basis for *japonaise*.

Bear in mind that meringues are fragile things and pack them carefully for freezing.

BASIC MERINGUES

Puffs of crisp meringue sandwiched with Chantilly or whipped cream and served on a pool of fresh fruit purée make a quick and very delicious dessert. Try serving on a swirl of purées: fresh or frozen kiwi fruit with strawberry; peach with raspberry; guava sprinkled with strips of preserved ginger.

**5 egg whites
300 g (10 oz) caster sugar**

Makes 12

Whisk the egg whites until stiff. Gradually whisk in the sugar and continue whisking until the mixture is very stiff and shiny.

Line a baking sheet with non-stick paper and spoon or pipe on 12 large meringues. Bake in a preheated oven at Gas Mark ¼/100°C/200°F for 1½–2 hours until they are crisp. Peel the meringues from the paper and FREEZE or fill them.

To serve from frozen: Thaw the meringues for 30 minutes to 1 hour before filling them.

M

MARRON MERINGUES WITH BLACK CHERRY SAUCE

1 quantity of basic Meringue mixture
(opposite)
Filling
250 g (8 oz) chestnut purée
3 tablespoons brandy
sugar to taste (optional)
284 ml (10 fl oz) carton of double
cream, whipped lightly
Black Cherry Sauce
425 g (14 oz) can of pitted black
cherries
brandy to taste

Serves 6

Line a baking sheet with non-stick paper and spoon or pipe on to it 12 large meringues. Bake in a preheated oven at Gas Mark ¼ 100°C/200°F for 1½–2 hours until they are crisp. Peel the meringues from the lining paper and FREEZE, or set aside to fill.

To make the filling, beat the chestnut purée with the brandy and sweeten with sugar if liked. Fold this mixture into the lightly whipped cream. FREEZE or use to fill the meringues, sandwiching two meringues together with the filling.

To make the sauce, drain all but 1 tablespoon of juice from the cherries and liquidise the fruit. Stir in the brandy and a little more juice if the sauce seems too thick. Sieve the sauce and FREEZE, or serve each meringue on a pool of sauce.

To serve from frozen: Thaw the filling and sauce in the refrigerator overnight. Thaw the meringues at room temperature for 30 minutes to 1 hour before assembling and serving as above.

BERRY JAPONAISE

2 large egg whites (size 1 or 2)
50 g (2 oz) ground almonds
125 g (4 oz) caster sugar
750 g (1½ lb) raspberries,
redcurrants, mulberries, blueberries
or strawberries *or* a mixture
icing sugar to taste
284 ml (10 fl oz) carton of double
cream, whipped lightly

Serves 6

Whisk the egg whites until stiff; then fold in the almonds and sugar. Spoon or pipe 6 circles of meringue mixture on to a baking tray lined with non-stick baking paper, allowing space between for them to spread. Bake in a preheated oven at Gas Mark 1/140°C/275°F for 45–60 minutes until firm and almost dried out in the centre. Cool, lift off the paper and FREEZE, or arrange with the slightly hollow underside facing upwards on individual dessert plates.

Purée one third of the berries, sieve if liked and sweeten to taste with icing sugar. FREEZE or set aside to serve.

Just before serving, top the *japonaise* with the whipped cream, spoon over the whole berries and serve with the berry sauce.

To serve from frozen: Thaw the fruit purée for 2–3 hours and the meringue for about 1 hour at room temperature. Assemble and serve as above.

PRALINE JAPONAISE

This masterpiece of French pâtisserie is fairly difficult and time consuming to make, and so it is worth making ahead; it will taste as though you have slaved for days. The addition of cornflour to the crème is not strictly traditional, but it helps to prevent it curdling and will stop it separating during freezing.

Meringue
375 g (12 oz) white sugar
6 egg whites
Praline
175 g (6 oz) caster sugar
175 g (6 oz) hazelnuts or unblanched almonds
oil for greasing
Crème au beurre
300 ml (½ pint) milk
125 g (4 oz) white sugar
6 egg yolks, beaten well
4 teaspoons cornflour
425 g (14 oz) unsalted butter, softened
1 tablespoon coffee powder, dissolved in 1 tablespoon water

Serves 12

To make the meringue, beat the sugar and egg whites together until standing in firm peaks. Divide the meringue between three 23 cm (9-inch) circles of foil or non-stick baking paper. Bake in a preheated oven at Gas Mark ¼/100°C/200°F for at least 4–5 hours, perhaps overnight. Invert the meringues, remove the foil or paper and leave to cool.

To make the praline, heat the caster sugar and nuts together over a low heat without stirring. When the sugar starts to colour, stir until the nuts are toasted and the sugar is a rich, golden-brown. Pour on to a cold, oiled metal baking sheet and leave to cool. When cool, roughly break or grind into a coarse powder.

To make the *crème au beurre*, bring the milk and sugar almost to the boil and pour on to the well-beaten egg yolks, stirring all the time. Mix the cornflour to a paste with a little of the mixture and stir back into the custard. Cook the mixture in a double boiler until it is thick, but do not let it curdle. Leave to cool to lukewarm with clingfilm on the surface.

Cream the butter with an electric beater and *slowly* add it to the custard mixture. If it curdles, beat in a couple of tablespoons of tepid melted butter. Flavour the mixture with most of the praline and the coffee.

Divide the *crème* into four. Cement the three meringue layers together with two of the portions of *crème*. Spread the third portion of *crème* evenly over the top. Trim the cake evenly with a sharp knife and mix the trimmings into the remaining portion of *crème*; use this to cover the sides of the *japonais*, using a knife heated slightly in warm water. Sprinkle the rest of the praline over the top and sides and FREEZE or serve.

To serve from frozen: Thaw the *japonaise* for 2–3 hours at room temperature or for 6 hours in the refrigerator.

© *Glynn Christian*

MONKFISH

see FISH

MUFFINS

Muffins are a lovely treat to have in the freezer, especially if you make a big batch to flavour both sweet and savoury. Savoury muffins are good with soups, salads, soufflés and snacks, in fact anything with which you would normally serve some form of bread. Sweet muffins make a delicious tea-time treat, especially if eaten the traditional way in the depths of winter beside a roaring fire. Or serve your muffins warm, as the Americans would, for breakfast.

MUFFINS

This basic muffin recipe is easily adapted to make a variety of different flavours (below).

250 g (8 oz) self-raising flour
1 tablespoon caster sugar
½ teaspoon baking powder
½ teaspoon salt
1 large egg (size 1 or 2)
200 ml (7 fl oz) milk
50 g (2 oz) butter, melted, plus extra
for greasing

Makes 12

Sift together the flour, sugar, baking powder and salt. Lightly whisk the egg and milk with the cooled, melted butter and stir lightly into the dry ingredients until the flour is moistened. The batter should still be very lumpy.

Spoon the batter into 12 well-buttered muffin tins and bake in a preheated oven at Gas Mark 6/200°C/400°F for about 20 minutes or until the mixture springs back into shape when pressed lightly. Cool and FREEZE or serve.

To serve from frozen: Reheat the muffins in a preheated oven at Gas Mark 4/180°C/350°F for 10–15 minutes until piping hot.

Variations:

PARMESAN MUFFINS

Add 50 g (2 oz) of grated parmesan cheese to the dry ingredients, with a pinch of paprika.

CHEESY MUFFINS

Add 4 tablespoons of grated mature Cheddar cheese and a teaspoon of mustard powder to the dry ingredients.

BACON MUFFINS

Add 4 tablespoons of crisply fried chopped bacon to the dry ingredients.

BERRY MUFFINS

Add 125 g (4 oz) of blueberries or cranberries to the dry ingredients.

FRUIT MUFFINS

Add 2 tablespoons of sultanas or raisins to the dry ingredients.

BANANA MUFFINS

Add a large, roughly mashed banana and reduce the quantity of milk by 1–2 tablespoons.

BANANA AND CHOCOLATE MUFFINS

Add banana as for Banana Muffins (above), with 75 g (3 oz) of roughly chopped plain chocolate.

MULBERRIES

see BERRIES

MUSSELS

It is dangerous to freeze uncooked mussels as it will kill them, and then you will never know which are safe to eat, and which are not, by observing their behaviour – if they are safe they'll be closed before cooking

see also
Fricassee of Seafood with Chervil Cream (page 91)

and open afterwards. Like all shellfish, cooked ones run the risk of being dried and ruined if you want to use them in a dish after defrosting: best to freeze sauces and the shellfish separately and put the fish into the hot sauce just long enough to heat through.

If you see them, I recommend you try green-lipped mussels from New Zealand; these have many advantages, their only disadvantage being that they are big, very big compared to the sweeties we expect from Wales or France. Green-lipped mussels, a description which applies to the irridescent outline of their shells rather than the creatures, are 5–7 cm (2–3) inches long, and fat with it, which seems off putting to those of the northern hemisphere. Yet they are available on the half-shell or without shells, and, as they have been farmed and processed within a few yards of harvesting, they are absolutely reliable.

GRILLED GARLIC MUSSELS

750 g (1½ lb) mussels (about 32)
200 ml (7 fl oz) dry white wine
Topping
125 g (4 oz) butter
1–2 garlic cloves, crushed
1 tablespoon freshly chopped parsley
2 tablespoons fresh white breadcrumbs
salt and freshly ground black pepper

Serves 2

Clean the mussels thoroughly, discarding any that are broken or open. Remove the beards. Steam the mussels in the white wine for 1–2 minutes until they open. Discard any that do not open. Cool and loosen the mussels from their shells and place two mussels in each half shell.

Beat the butter and garlic together until soft and fluffy. Stir in the parsley and seasoning and spread the mixture over the mussels. Sprinkle with the breadcrumbs and FREEZE, or grill under a high heat for 5–10 minutes until crisp and golden on top.

To serve from frozen: Thaw the mussels at room temperature for 30 minutes; then grill until piping hot and crisp and golden.

MUSSEL AND SAFFRON SOUP

1.25 kg (3 lb) mussels
175–250 g (6–8 oz) onion, sliced
3 celery sticks, sliced
a *bouquet garni*
2 teaspoons white peppercorns
3 garlic cloves
300 ml (½ pint) dry white wine
1.2 litres (2 pints) fish or vegetable stock
a scant teaspoon of saffron, soaked in 1 tablespoon warm water
284 ml (10 fl oz) carton of double cream
2 egg yolks
salt
Garnish
2 tablespoons freshly chopped parsley

Serves 6

Clean the mussel shells thoroughly, discarding any that are broken or open. Remove the beards.

Put the sliced onion and celery into a large saucepan with the *bouquet garni*, peppercorns and garlic. Add the mussels and wine with enough stock to three-quarters cover the mussels. Cover and bring to the boil. Cook, shaking the pan from time to time, until the mussels open. This will take about 5 minutes. Discard any mussels that do not open. Remove the mussels from their shells and FREEZE, or set aside. Strain off the liquid, add the saffron and return it to the clean pan. Boil hard until the soup is reduced by a quarter.

Whisk the cream and egg yolks together; then slowly whisk them into the soup. Adjust the seasoning, and add a little more stock if the soup seems too thick. FREEZE the soup, or stir the mussels into the soup and heat gently for 1 minute. Sprinkle with the parsley.

To serve from frozen: Reheat the soup from frozen and whisk it until smooth. Add the mussels and heat through before serving sprinkled with the parsley.

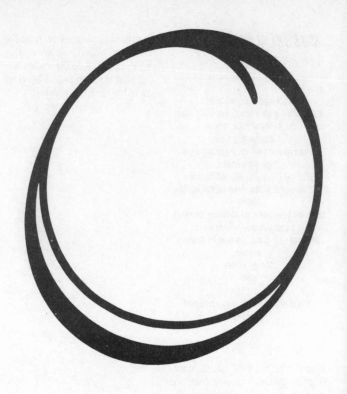

Olives
Oxtail
Oysters

OLIVES

Olives freeze well but they will also keep in the refrigerator for up to six months. I would rather keep a store of Olivade (below) or similar.

see also
BUTTERS, FLAVOURED
(page 40)
Aubergine, Tomato and
Olive Sauce (page 22)
Carpaccio with Olivade
and Pine Kernels (page
32)

OLIVADE

Serve in little pots as a savoury with crisp celery sticks or as an hors-d'oeuvre with hard-boiled eggs or freshly grilled tuna.

**24 stoned black olives
8 anchovy fillets
1 tablespoon capers
5 tablespoons olive oil
lemon juice to taste
brandy to taste**

Serves 6

Pound the olives, anchovies and capers together to form a thick purée. Add the olive oil a little at a time, as you would for mayonnaise. Flavour the mixture with lemon juice and brandy and pack into little pots. FREEZE or serve.

To serve from frozen: Thaw overnight in the refrigerator or use from frozen to flavour sauces and casseroles.

ORANGE ROUGHY

see FISH

ORANGES

see CITRUS FRUITS

OXTAIL

see also
CITRUS FRUITS (page
62)

It is gourmet! Gary Rhodes of the Castle Hotel in Taunton, who boasts a Michelin star for his relentless championing of British food, makes oxtail sing, and once he had sung its praises at a chefs' conference it suddenly became the most fashionable dish imaginable. For today's tastes it is important to take the trouble to remove as much of the fat as possible. Gary actually renders it and uses it for browning the oxtail, but this is a technique for the master chef rather than the home. My recipe (below) has always had enormous success, but it relies very much on the celery. If you want to freeze the made-up dish, leave out the celery and stir quite a lot of celery leaves into the oxtail a few minutes before serving. That should do you nicely. Otherwise, store oxtail raw to make into dishes as you wish.

OXTAIL CASSEROLE

**2 oxtails
seasoned flour for coating
125 ml (4 fl oz) olive oil
4 celery sticks *or* a bunch of celery
leaves
a bottle of strong beer
875 g (1¾ lb) tomatoes *or*
2 × 397 g (14 oz) can of tomatoes
2 bay leaves
6 unpeeled garlic cloves**

Serves 2–6

Chop the oxtails into 5 cm (2-inch) lengths and trim them of all the excess fat. Coat them in seasoned flour.

Heat half the olive oil in a heavy-based frying pan and fry the oxtail pieces until they are golden in colour. Remove them and discard any excess oil or flour.

If serving the dish straight away, chop the celery sticks into 2.5 cm (1-inch) lengths. Add the rest of the oil to the pan and cook the celery until it starts to soften. Add the beer and leave to bubble through, scraping the bottom of the pan at the same time. If freezing the dish, omit the celery.

Layer the oxtail, celery (if used) and beer, tomatoes, bay leaves and garlic in a large casserole, so that the liquid just covers the meat. Simmer gently for 1½–2 hours until the meat is falling from the bones. FREEZE or serve.

To serve from frozen: Thaw the casserole gently over a low heat until it is piping hot. Just before serving, chop the celery leaves and add to the casserole.

© *Glynn Christian*

OYSTERS

I wouldn't freeze flat-shelled native oysters, for these are only to be eaten still a-shiver from sea and ice. Most oysters are not of that aristocratic breed these days, but are the frill-shelled interlopers which are easier to farm and more resistant to pests; their flavour is stronger, bolder and coarser, thus advantageously making them more suited to cooking. It is generally cheaper to look for oysters which have been frozen abroad than to do your own. If you should find yourself with a supply in excess of immediate demand, freeze them raw and with as much of their saline juices as possible.

A new ploy is to buy Pacific oysters which have been frozen as nature intended – in their double shells. The process ensures extraordinary freshness, although of course it kills the oysters. The very special advantage is that as the oysters defrost, the shells magically open – and there you are,

see also
BEEF (page 28)
Steak and Oyster Pies (page 30)

oysters on the half shell without a single fracturing of a knife or bloody splitting of a finger. Serving these lightly warmed on the shell is a neat trick. Heat the oven as high as it will go, wedge the open oysters in something like sea salt, and then slam them into the oven just long enough for the edges to curl and the liquid to warm through. I top them with a little soured cream, and maybe a spoonful of caviare.

Extra flavourings for oysters are things of personal preference, but please remember that, as with caviare, lots of lemon juice, raw onions and shallots, vinegars and chillies mask the flavour and expense. They are the refuge of the tired or non-existent palate, or of people who do not actually like oysters: things like bacon are the refuge of tired chefs. Yet there are plenty of flavours which enhance the oyster's natural gifts. The most popular way I've served oysters recently was this: I reduced a decent quantity of California Chardonnay by half with lots of butter and then turned down the heat so that the liquid barely moved. Into that went a few Pacific oysters at a time, from Washington State as it happens, with their juices. As soon as they had plumped they were popped atop leaves of fresh basil in a small hot brioche. The pepperiness of the basil and the explosion of its oils when ignited by the heat of the brioche, the flavour of the oyster itself, and a generous slurp of the butter-wine liquid meant there was no need for pepper, and the natural salts of everything else did the rest.

O

CRUSTED OYSTERS ON THE SHELL

12–18 oysters on the shell
125 g (4 oz) butter
1–2 garlic cloves, crushed
2 tablespoons freshly chopped
parsley
2 tablespoons grated parmesan
cheese
2 tablespoons fine white
breadcrumbs
salt and freshly ground black pepper

Serves 2

Open the oysters and pour off the excess liquid. Arrange the oysters in their deeper shells, propped-up with balls of crumpled foil.

Beat the butter until soft. Add the garlic and seasoning and beat well. Stir in the chopped parsley and spread the mixture over the oysters. Mix together the cheese and breadcrumbs and sprinkle them over the oysters. FREEZE or grill until the tops are crisp and golden.

To serve from frozen: Grill from frozen until bubbling and golden.

GRILLED OYSTERS TRICOLORE

12 oysters
75 g (3 oz) butter
1 tablespoon finely chopped shallot
1 garlic clove, chopped finely
25 g (1 oz) spinach leaves
2 tablespoons freshly chopped
parsley
2 sun-dried tomatoes, cut into thin
strips
2 tablespoons fresh breadcrumbs
2 tablespoons grated Gruyère
cheese
salt

Serves 2

Open the oysters and arrange them in their deeper shells on a shallow baking tray, propping them up with crumpled balls of foil.

Melt 25 g (1 oz) of the butter and stir-fry the shallot until soft. Add the garlic, spinach and parsley and continue to sauté for 30 seconds. Take off the heat and stir in the tomatoes, bread-crumbs, cheese, a little salt and the remaining butter. Spoon over the oysters and FREEZE, or grill under a high heat for 2–3 minutes until golden.

To serve from frozen: Grill from frozen as above.

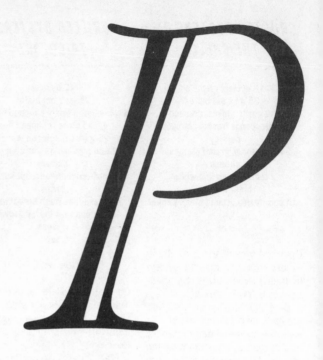

P

PALM SUGAR

This granular, syrupy extraction from certain palm trees has a unique toffee flavour that is addictive once tasted. A simple sprinkling on tropical fruit, even something as banal as bananas, makes a real treat. Buy it frozen from oriental supermarkets and use it in cooking from frozen.

PANCAKES

see CRÊPES

PARROTFISH

see FISH

PASSION-FRUIT

Passion-fruit freezes whole but is probably more worthwhile stored as a purée to use in sorbets, mousses and fools, or as a simple sauce (opposite). Passion-fruit pulp (*with* the seeds) also makes my favourite filled pancake to be stored and subsequently cooked in more of the same (page 71); or it is delicious mixed simply with cream, sugar and a sprinkling of sherry. It can be cooked from frozen.

see also
CRÊPES (page 71)
Physalis Fritters with Fresh Passion-fruit (page 153)

PASSION-FRUIT TERRINE WITH STRAWBERRY SAUCE

1 quantity of Genoese Sponge (page 98), sliced thinly
1 tablespoon brandy
2 large eggs (size 1 or 2), separated
50 g (2 oz) caster sugar
1 tablespoon gelatine
200 ml (7 fl oz) freshly squeezed or concentrated orange juice
50 g (2 oz) passion-fruit pulp (about 4 fruits)
200 ml (7 fl oz) whipping or double cream, whipped
sifted icing sugar for sprinkling
Strawberry Sauce
250 g (8 oz) ripe strawberries
sifted icing sugar to taste
To Serve
75 g (3 oz) passion-fruit pulp

Serves 6

Line a 1-litre (1¾-pint) loaf tin or basin with plastic wrap and then with the slices of sponge cake. Trim any of the sponge extending above the rim and sprinkle the cake with the brandy.

Beat the egg yolks and sugar until pale. Dissolve the gelatine in the orange juice and add with the passion-fruit pulp to the egg yolk mixture. Whisk well. Whisk the egg whites until stiff and fold in with the whipped cream. Pour this filling into the sponge-lined mould. FREEZE or chill until set.

To make the strawberry sauce, sieve the strawberries and sweeten to taste with sifted icing sugar. FREEZE or set aside.

Unmould the terrine, sprinkle with a layer of sifted icing sugar and slice. Spoon a little of the strawberry sauce over one corner of each slice and a little of the passion-fruit pulp over the other.

To serve from frozen: Thaw both the mould and the sauce overnight in the refrigerator before serving as above.

PASTA

A properly made dish of lasagne, or appropriate pasta sauces, all of which take forever to cook properly, deserve to be frozen after being made with care, rather than hurried at some other inconvenient time. Otherwise the only pasta related things I would give space to are fresh *ripieni* (stuffed pasta) of any kind, bought or home-made, and gnocchi (page 97) of all kinds, all of which can be used from frozen. Let me explain, for there are those who bother to buy and keep 'fresh' noodles and other pasta shapes in a freezer.

The fresh pasta revolution which has so transformed our eating habits is based on exceptionally shifty theory. You would think, wouldn't you, that most of Italy found itself chained to a drudge of daily kneading, rolling and shaping pastas, for fear of otherwise starving. Not so. Fresh pasta is a special and unusual thing these days, harder to buy in Italy than in Basingstoke or Stirling. By far the vast majority of pasta eaten is bought dried. The reasons are simple and inarguable. First the variety is infinitely better, although only half what is was said to be a century ago. And, more important, it is or can be of far better quality. The ordinary person in the *strada* cannot get the fine grades of semolina from durum wheat which makes the best pasta, and so does not bother. Incidentally, you can always tell if dried pasta has been made from inferior wheat or by a faster inferior process by its very shiny and smooth surface. Factory produced pasta made from top quality durum and dried slowly has a dull surface and grittiness to the surface; these cook and taste better than most freshly made pastas, believe me (and millions of Italians).

Now, this is not to say that much of the fresh pasta being sold in Britain these days is not up to scratch, for most of it is very good and the convenience is incontrovertible. Of these, the stuffed ravioli, cappelletti, tortellini and so on, make the best buys for the freezer if you are not going to make it yourself. But buy the best quality unstuffed pasta as dried pasta and store it elsewhere.

However, you might find freezing cooked noodles a good idea. Crisped in hot oil they make a quick accompaniment to vegetarian meals and, when pressed and deep-fried in a small metal sieve, they become crisply golden baskets that are ideal for containing fish or vegetable mixtures. You may also find it useful to make and store your own pasta, particularly as it can be filled and shaped as and when appropriate.

As well as proper lasagne, macaroni cheese and stuffed pasta, I would also freeze good sauces to serve with pasta. Simplest of these is tomato: a can of plum tomatoes cooked with olive oil and garlic until reduced and then sieved gives excellent results. Flavour it with onion instead of the garlic; fresh herbs (oregano, bay leaf, tarragon, parsley or mint); canned baby clams; mushrooms; ham . . . and so on. Your store of double cream is also an excellent basis for pasta sauces: allow 150 ml (¼ pint) per person simmered to reduce by half and flavour as appropriate. Suitable flavourings include: artichoke bottoms, canned or frozen red peppers and garlic; Danish blue cheese

PASTA DOUGH

and broccoli; mushrooms and potted shrimps; saffron, garlic and parsley; smoked salmon and dill or mint; canned baby clams or mussels, tomato purée, garlic and vermouth; wild mushrooms, ham or tongue and vermouth . . . the possibilities are endless.

I would also include in my freezer a good bolognese *ragù*: once you have browned the mince and added a little onion, a couple of bay leaves and some canned tomatoes (two 397 g/14 oz cans for every 500 g/1 lb of mince) in the usual way, be sure to cook the mixture for at least an hour until the liquid has practically disappeared, and then for another fifteen minutes after you have salted it lightly. This ensures that each morsel of mince is succulent and juicy. Add a few chopped celery leaves on defrosting. Vary it by adding some garlic and replacing one of the cans of tomatoes with 150 ml (¼ pint) of red wine and a little tomato purée. Use it to stuff pasta (if cooked until dry) or serve it poured over pasta. Otherwise I would use this quantity to make a proper lasagne for four, for which you will also need 600 ml (1 pint) of béchamel sauce and 250–325 g (8–11 oz) of lasagne that has been cooked in plenty of boiling water. Swirl a bit of each sauce in the base of a square dish to create a marbled effect and cover with a layer of pasta; continue in this way, strewing each layer of mixed sauces with a generous amount of grated parmesan or pecorino cheese. Finish with a decent layer of sauce strewn with cheese and bake in the usual way (page 138), or store away generous amounts for use at some later stage.

250 g (8 oz) plain flour or strong plain white flour
1 teaspoon salt
2 eggs, beaten lightly
3 tablespoons warm water, plus extra if necessary

see also
BUCKWHEAT (page 38)

Serves 2

Sift the flour and salt into a bowl. Lightly beat the eggs with the water and pour into the centre of the flour. Stir well, adding a little more water if the mixture seems dry. Knead to make a stiff dough. Wrap in a plastic bag and chill for 30 minutes.

Divide the dough into three or four pieces and keep each piece well wrapped in a plastic bag. Roll out one piece very thinly; then roll it up like a swiss roll, cut into ribbons and shape into loose neat circles. Alternatively, use a pasta machine to shape the dough. Place on tea towels while rolling and shaping the remaining dough. FREEZE or use.

To serve from frozen: Plunge the pasta into plenty of boiling, salted water and cook for 3–4 minutes until tender. Drain well and toss in melted butter or oil before serving.

RAVIOLI WITH CRAB AND ARMAGNAC

1 quantity of Pasta Dough
(page 135)
1 egg, beaten lightly
salt
Filling
2 cooked crabs each weighing about
500 g (1 lb)
a few drops of Tabasco sauce
125 g (4 oz) ricotta cheese
2 tablespoons grated parmesan
cheese
1 tablespoon melted butter
2 tablespoons Armagnac
salt and freshly ground black pepper
To serve
½ quantity of Vegetable Cream
Sauce (page 192), heated
freshly grated parmesan cheese

Serves 2

Begin by preparing the filling. Shell the crabs and mash the meat and coral with a drop or two of Tabasco sauce, the cheeses, butter, Armagnac and seasoning.

Roll out the pasta dough to a large rectangle about 3 mm (⅛ inch) thick. Cut into strips 5–7 cm (2–3 inches) wide. Place teaspoonfuls of the filling at 5 cm (2-inch) intervals on one side of each strip. Brush the cut edges of the pasta and between the piles of filling with the beaten egg. Fold the unfilled side of the pasta strips over the filling and press well to seal the edges and expel any air. Cut the strips into individual ravioli and FREEZE, or poach in plenty of boiling, salted water for 5–6 minutes.

To serve, drain the pasta and pour the hot sauce around it. Serve sprinkled with freshly grated parmesan cheese.

To serve from frozen: Cook the frozen squares of pasta in gently simmering, salted water for 10–15 minutes until the filling is piping hot. Serve as above, with the hot sauce and freshly grated parmesan cheese.

CAPPELLETTI WITH GOAT'S CHEESE AND PINE KERNELS

1 quantity of Pasta Dough
(page 135)
1 egg, beaten lightly
salt
Filling
150 g (5 oz) goat's cheese
75 g (3 oz) pine kernels, chopped
roughly
3 garlic cloves, chopped finely
1 tablespoon Pesto Sauce (page
104)
freshly ground black pepper
To serve
½ quantity of Tomato and Coriander
Sauce (page 191), heated
freshly grated parmesan cheese

Serves 2

Roll out the pasta dough to a large rectangle 3 mm (⅛ inch) thick. Cut into 5 cm (2-inch) diameter circles.

For the filling, trim the rind from the cheese and mix with the pine kernels, garlic, pesto and pepper.

Place a quarter to half a teaspoonful of the filling on to the centre of each circle. Brush one half of each circle with the beaten egg. Fold each circle in half over the filling and press to seal the edges. Pick up each semi-circle and bend the folded side around one index finger; then press the two points together forming a little circular pouch of pasta.

FREEZE the pasta or poach in plenty of boiling, salted water for about 5 minutes until *al dente.* Serve with the hot sauce and grated parmesan cheese.

To serve from frozen: Cook the frozen cappelletti in plenty of boiling, salted water for 6–7 minutes until the filling is piping hot. Serve as above, with the hot sauce and grated parmesan cheese.

P

CAPPELLETTI, WILD MUSHROOM AND ARTICHOKE PIE

Use a mixture of dried mush-rooms to perfume this pie — porcini, girolles, cèpes or morilles. It can be as lightly or heavily perfumed with them as you wish. The earthy flavour of the artichokes bridges the gap between the wildness of the mushrooms and the smooth-ness of the pasta. Follow it with a crisp salad.

about 15 g (½ oz) dried mushrooms
300 ml (½ pint) dry white wine
284 ml (10 fl oz) carton of double cream
40 g (1½ oz) butter
125 g (4 oz) onion, chopped finely
40 g (1½ oz) plain flour
450 ml (¾ pint) milk
1–2 large garlic cloves, crushed
2 bay leaves
750 g (1½ lb) Rough Puff Pastry (page 142)
175 g (6 oz) cooked artichoke bottoms, sliced thickly
500 g (1 lb) cooked Cappelletti (opposite)
about ½ teaspoon ground allspice
salt and freshly ground black pepper

Serves 4–6

Put the mushrooms into a pan with the wine and simmer, uncov-ered, until the mushrooms are tender and the wine has reduced to about half its original volume. Add the cream and keep warm.

Melt the butter in a pan and soften the onion. Stir in the flour and cook for 2 minutes. Pour in the mushroom and cream mix-ture and whisk until the sauce has thickened. Slowly add the milk, garlic and bay leaves. Cook gently for 10 minutes; then sea-son. Remove from the heat, cool slightly and then leave to cool but not set with clingfilm covering the surface.

Line a 23 cm (9-inch) round dish at least 5 cm (2 inches) deep with two-thirds of the pastry. Stir the artichoke slices into the mushroom sauce and remove the bay leaves. Mix the sauce into the pasta, pour the filling into the pie and sprinkle with the allspice. Cover the pie with the rest of the pastry, seal well and prick the top with a fork. FREEZE or bake the pie in a preheated oven at Gas Mark 8/230°C/450°F for 15 minutes. Reduce the heat to Gas Mark 6/200°C/400°F and cook for another 30 minutes until the pastry is golden-brown.

To serve from frozen: Thaw the pie at room temperature for 1 hour and then bake as above for 30 minutes.

© *Glynn Christian*

LENTIL AND SPINACH LASAGNE

This is perfect for a vegetarian meal; the cinnamon gives it a warm, exotic flavour and adds a touch of mystery.

250 g (8 oz) green or brown lentils
3–4 tablespoons oil
2 × 397 g (14 oz) can of plum tomatoes
1 teaspoon ground cinnamon
50 g (2 oz) butter, plus extra for greasing
50 g (2 oz) plain flour
600 ml (1 pint) milk
250 g (8 oz) frozen leaf spinach
½ teaspoon grated nutmeg
50 g (2 oz) percorino or parmesan cheese, grated
175 g (6 oz) dried wholemeal or spinach lasagne sheets
salt and freshly ground black pepper

Serves 6

Cover the lentils with boiling water and leave to soak for 2 hours. Drain the lentils, cover with fresh water, add 2 tablespoons of the oil and cook for about 45 minutes. Drain and reserve the liquid.

Purée the lentils with about 5 tablespoons of the juice from the can of tomatoes. Add some of the lentil cooking liquid if necessary until the texture is like that of a thick béchamel sauce. Add the cinnamon and seasoning.

Melt the butter in a pan, add the flour and cook without browning. Add the milk and whisk over the heat until is is thick. Put the frozen spinach into the sauce and allow it to defrost. Add the nutmeg and seasoning and three-quarters of the cheese.

Cook the lasagne sheets in plenty of boiling, salted water with the rest of the oil until just tender. Drain and rinse under running cold water.

Grease a large ovenproof dish and pour a little of the spinach sauce around the edges; then add a layer of pasta. Spoon in some of the spinach sauce and some of the lentil sauce and swirl together until even but not completely mixed. Squash the tomatoes gently and add a layer of them to the dish; sprinkle with a little seasoning. Continue layering, finishing with a layer of spinach sauce. Sprinkle this with the remaining cheese. FREEZE or bake in a preheated oven at Gas Mark 6/200°C/400°F for 25 minutes.

To serve from frozen: Thaw the lasagne at room temperature for 1 hour and bake as above for 45–50 minutes.

© *Glynn Christian*

P

COD, LEEK AND PRAWN LASAGNE

see also
BREAD (page 36)

Serve this pretty dish as a main course, or halve the quantities and serve individual portions in ramekins as a first course.

**500 g (1 lb) cod fillet
300 ml (½ pint) dry white wine
1 bay leaf
600 ml (1 pint) milk
175 g (6 oz) butter, plus extra for greasing
50 g (2 oz) plain flour
750 g (1½ lb) leeks, sliced thinly
2 teaspoons seed mustard
175–250 g (6–8 oz) dried lasagne sheets
1–2 tablespoons oil
250 g (8 oz) peeled prawns
salt and freshly ground black pepper
chopped fresh parsley to garnish**

Serves 6

Poach the cod in the wine with the bay leaf until it is tender, adding a little water if necessary. Remove the cod and flake it into generous pieces, removing any skin or bone. Make up the cooking liquid to 600 ml (1 pint) with some of the milk.

Melt 50 g (2 oz) of the butter in a pan, add the flour and cook without browning for 30 seconds. Mix in the fish cooking liquid, whisking until thickened. Season and add the cod flakes.

Put the leeks and the remaining milk (ensure that this is no more than 300 ml/½ pint) in a pan and cook until the leeks begin to soften. Reserve a quarter of the leeks and purée the rest with the mustard and the rest of the butter. Stir in the reserved leeks.

Cook the lasagne sheets in plenty of boiling, salted water with the oil until just tender. Drain and rinse under running cold water.

Grease a large ovenproof dish and cover the base with a thin layer of lasagne. Spoon on some of the cod sauce and some of the leek sauce and swirl together until even but not completely mixed. Sprinkle with some of the prawns. Continue layering, finishing with a layer of fish sauce. FREEZE or bake in a preheated oven at Gas Mark 5/190°C/375°F for about 25 minutes. Serve sprinkled with chopped parsley.

To serve from frozen: Thaw the lasagne for 1 hour at room temperature and bake as above for 45–50 minutes. Serve sprinkled with parsley.

© *Glynn Christian*

MACARONI CHEESE

It really is worth making and storing a proper macaroni cheese. The finished dish is colourful and tasty, and nothing like the usual inedible offering.

250 g (8 oz) dried macaroni
65 g (2½ oz) butter, plus extra for melting
50 g (2 oz) plain flour
900 ml (1½ pints) milk
½ teaspoon grated nutmeg
125 g (4 oz) bacon, cut into strips
1 small red or green pepper, sliced
175 g (6 oz) strong Cheddar cheese, grated
125 g (4 oz) fresh breadcrumbs
salt and freshly ground black pepper
Garnish
8 slices of tomato
grated strong Cheddar cheese

Serves 4

Cook the macaroni in plenty of boiling, salted water until it is almost tender; then drain. Melt a little butter and toss the macaroni in this; then cover and reserve.

Melt the butter in a pan and cook the flour without browning for 30 seconds. Stir in the milk and whisk until thickened. Add the nutmeg and seasoning and simmer gently over a low heat.

Fry the bacon gently in a pan until the fat runs. Add the pepper slices and cook them until they are soft and bright in colour. Stir the bacon and pepper into the warm sauce and then stir in the cheese.

Fold the sauce into the macaroni and spoon into a 1.75-litre (3-pint) ovenproof dish. Cover with the breadcrumbs. FREEZE or arrange the tomato slices on top and bake in a preheated oven at Gas Mark 4/180°C/350°F for 20–25 minutes until the top is crisp and golden. Sprinkle with grated strong Cheddar cheese before serving.

To serve from frozen: Thaw the macaroni cheese for 1 hour at room temperature; then top with the tomato slices and bake as above for 45–50 minutes. Sprinkle with grated strong Cheddar cheese before serving.

© *Glynn Christian*

COCONUT PASTA WITH ORANGE-ALMOND SYRUP

This dish is stunning by itself, but magical when combined with other puddings. Try it with chocolate ice cream, with mango purée, mixed into a fruit salad, or topped with toasted coconut and almonds.

175–250 g (6–8 oz) Pasta Dough
(page 135)
1–2 drops of almond essence
Filling
75 g (3 oz) desiccated coconut
2 tablespoons sugar
1 egg
4 tablespoons brandy or black rum
Syrup
450 ml (¾ pint) orange juice
250 g (8 oz) sugar
1–2 teaspoons almond essence

Serves 4–6

Flavour the pasta dough with a drop or two of almond essence, roll it out and cover with a barely damp cloth.

To make the filling, mix together the coconut, sugar, egg and brandy or rum. Shape and fill the dough into ravioli or cappelletti (page 136). Cook in plenty of boiling water until they float to the top.

To make the syrup, heat the orange juice, add the sugar and heat until the sugar dissolves. Add the almond essence so that the flavour blends with the orange juice rather than dominates it.

Arrange the cooked pasta evenly in a shallow serving dish. Pour in the hot syrup and toss the pasta in it until they are covered, ensuring that none sticks to another. Cool; then refrigerate for at least 4 hours to allow the syrup to penetrate the pasta and the flavours to blend. FREEZE or serve.

To serve from frozen: Thaw the pasta overnight in the refrigerator.

© *Glynn Christian*

PASTRY

see also
Ginger Bow Ties (page 185)
Hot-water Pastry (page 156)
Pastry Tartlets (page 89)
Rich Pastry Tartlets (page 14)

All pastry freezes well either cooked or uncooked. Ideally, it pays to roll or pipe and, in the case of filo, fill the pastries before freezing. Given five to ten minutes standing time out of the freezer, they can be baked for immediate use.

If you want to make pastry which puffs up, I should only bother to make rough puff unless you have lots of time and energy. The timing of the chore is such that whilst one recipe is resting the short time it needs, you can be making another for the freezer. If you leave it to defrost you can continue to express yourself by flavouring the pastry before use. Whilst giving the pastry a couple more turns to make it even lighter, sprinkle in something suitable. Fresh or dried thyme, oregano, black pepper or paprika, for instance, for savoury pies. Lemon, lime or orange rind, crushed cardamom, cinnamon or mixed spice for fruit pies. The technique works very well for real puff pastry and for bought puff pastry if you take the care first to unfold it somewhat. Then, as well as adding herbs, zest or spice, add in knobs of cool butter, making it thus taste like the real thing.

P

RICH SHORTCRUST PASTRY

A delicate pastry that is easier to press into a tin than roll out. It can be frozen either as a ball of dough for shaping later, an uncooked pastry case or a cooked pastry case ready for filling.

**175 g (6 oz) plain flour
a pinch of salt
1 tablespoon icing sugar
125 g (4 oz) butter, cut into small pieces
1 tablespoon iced water**

Makes 300 g (10 oz) pastry or a 25 cm (10-inch) pastry case

Sift the flour, salt and sugar into a mixing bowl. Rub in the butter until the mixture resembles coarse breadcrumbs. Stir in the water and gather the dough into a ball. FREEZE or use.

Alternatively, press the dough into a 25 cm (10-inch) loose-based quiche or tart tin (there is no need to grease this beforehand) and FREEZE, or chill until firm. Line the pastry with foil, fill with baking beans and bake in a preheated oven at Gas Mark 4/180°C/350°F for 15 minutes. Remove the beans and foil and continue to bake for a further 5 minutes until the pastry is firm. FREEZE or fill.

To serve from frozen: Thaw the ball of pastry dough for 1–2 hours at room temperature before using. For the frozen pastry case, bake from frozen in a preheated oven at Gas Mark 6/200°C/400°F for 10 minutes if already cooked or 25–30 minutes if uncooked.

CHOUX PASTRY

A hand-held electric mixer makes beating the eggs in a lot easier and more thorough.

see also
Chocolate Brandy Sauce
(page 61)

**50 g (2 oz) butter
150 ml (¼ pint) water
75 g (3 oz) plain flour, sifted with a pinch of salt
2 large eggs (size 1 or 2), beaten**

Makes 200 g (7 oz) pastry

Put the butter and water into a small saucepan and heat together gently until the butter has melted. Bring the mixture to the boil and add the sifted flour. Beat well for 1–2 minutes without burning, until the mixture leaves the sides of the saucepan to make a smooth ball. Allow to cool for 10 minutes.

Beat in the egg, and pipe or spoon the pastry on to a dampened baking sheet, leaving space between the pastries for them to swell. Bake in a pre-heated oven at Gas Mark 6/200°C/400°F for 15–16 minutes for small pastries and about 25 minutes for larger ones or until they are crisp. Cool and FREEZE or use.

To serve from frozen: Reheat the pastries in a preheated oven at Gas Mark 6/200°C/400°F for 5–7 minutes until crisp and golden.

Variation:

SAVOURY CHOUX PASTRY

Beat 2 tablespoons of grated Cheddar cheese into the mixture before piping. Just before baking brush the tops of the puffs or éclairs with a little beaten egg and dust with grated parmesan cheese.

ROUGH PUFF PASTRY

This requires little effort to make and yet it will look and taste professional. It is also easy to flavour (page 140).

250 g (8 oz) strong plain white flour,
plus extra for dredging
a pinch of salt
175 g (6 oz) butter or a mixture of
butter and lard or shortening
a generous squeeze of lemon juice
150 ml (¼ pint) water

Makes 500 g (1 lb) pastry

Sift the flour into a bowl with the salt. Cut the fat into small, cherry-size pieces and add to the flour. Stir well and make a well in the centre. Add the lemon juice to the water and pour it into the well in the flour. Mix it with a knife and then with one hand until it forms a ball, but do not knead it. Turn it on to a floured board and pat it into a rectangle; it should be sticky and have lumps of fat sticking through it.

Roll out the dough with short, sharp strokes until it is about 39 × 13 cm (15 × 5 inches). Fold the bottom third up and then the top third down over it, keeping the edges neatly on top of each other. Turn the pastry round, with the folded edge on the left hand side. Let it rest for a few minutes and then seal both ends and the side seam with a rolling pin to trap the air. Roll, fold, seal and rest twice more, dredging the top and bottom with flour before rolling and brushing off the excess before folding. Cover the pastry and chill for 10–15 minutes.

Roll and fold the pastry again, starting with the folded edge on the left hand side. Dredge with more flour if the pieces of fat are still showing through. Fold, roll and turn at least once more. Wrap and FREEZE or chill for at least 30 minutes before rolling out and using.

To serve from frozen: Thaw the pastry overnight in the refrigerator or for 2–3 hours at room temperature before using.

© Glynn Christian

PUFF PASTRY

Puff pastry must be one of the most rewarding pastries to make for the freezer, even though it is rather time-consuming to prepare and does need a cool work surface on which to do the rolling and folding.

250 g (8 oz) strong plain white flour,
plus extra for rolling
a pinch of cream of tartar
a pinch of salt
25 g (1 oz) white cooking fat, cut
into pieces
125 ml (4 fl oz) cold water
200 g (7 oz) butter

Makes 250 g (8 oz) pastry

Sift the flour, cream of tartar and salt into a mixing bowl. Rub in the white cooking fat. Add the water and stir with the prongs of a fork to make a rough ball of dough that leaves the sides of the bowl clean. Turn the dough on to a floured work surface and knead it lightly to remove the cracks. Wrap and rest the pastry in a cool place for 30 minutes.

Roll the butter between two sheets of greaseproof paper to an oblong about 1 cm (½ inch) thick. Roll out the pastry dough to an oblong a little wider than the butter shape and long enough for the two ends of the dough to fold over the butter and slightly over-lap. Place the butter in the centre and fold over the pastry to enclose it completely. Seal the edges by pressing with the rolling pin.

Give the dough a half-turn, bringing the sealed ends to top and bottom. Roll the pastry out to a rectangle about three times as long as it is wide. With the rolling pin, mark the pastry into thirds with firm lines across the pastry, without breaking through the layers, to trap air. Fold the pastry along these lines, and press down the edges to seal them. The pastry has now had one roll and fold. Repeat this rolling and folding once more; then wrap and chill the pastry for about 30 minutes. Repeat the rolling and folding twice more, allow the pastry to rest; then repeat twice more again, making a total of six rolls and folds. Wrap and FREEZE or chill before using.

To use from frozen: Thaw overnight in the refrigerator or for 1–2 hours at room temperature.

until it is about 1–2 cm (½ inch) thick; then leave the rolling pin and start stretching the pastry, keeping one hand under the pastry and one on top. If you have no assistance, weight the opposite end of the pastry to keep it in position. When the pastry starts to stretch and stay stretched, stroke out any thicker parts with your fingertips to the same thickness and stretch the borders. Don't worry if any holes appear.

Once the pastry is stretched as much as possible, trim off the thicker edge pieces and make the pastry into an oblong or oval shape. Roll in layers or fold up and FREEZE, or use.

To serve from frozen: Thaw the pastry overnight in the refrigerator or for 2–3 hours at room temperature before using.

© *Glynn Christian*

STRUDEL PASTRY

Strudel pastry is fairly hard to find and so it is worth making some to keep in the freezer if you have the time, and particularly if you have someone to help you. It is also very satisfying to make.

250 g (8 oz) strong plain white flour, plus extra for dredging
1 egg
1 tablespoon oil
a pinch of salt
4 tablespoons water

Makes 250 g (8 oz) pastry

Put the flour into a large bowl, make a well in the middle and add the egg, oil and salt. Slowly mix in the water until you have a smooth dough, and then knead until the surface is covered with tiny blisters. Cover with a barely dampened cloth and leave for 1 hour.

Cover a table top with a clean cloth or sheet, cover this with flour and put the pastry in the centre. Start rolling the pastry

FILO PASTRY

Filo pastry is fortunately increasingly available in Britain, although you might want to make your own for storing if you have the time and patience. This is the best recipe that I have come across. Because you layer it with butter and roll it thinly, every sheet is actually three much thinner sheets, each thinner than you could roll independently. You may find it easier to use something as thin as a broom handle for rolling, or, to get really excellent results, wrap the dough around the rolling pin and continue rolling, ensuring that both sides are well floured.

**500 g (1 lb) strong plain white flour,
plus extra for dredging
1 teaspoon salt
4 tablespoons olive oil
1 egg
1 teaspoon vinegar
175 ml (6 fl oz) water
125–175 g (4–6 oz) butter,
softened**

*Makes about 750 g (1½ lb) pastry
(8–10 sheets)*

Put the flour in a bowl, make a well in the centre and add the salt, oil, egg and vinegar. Mush them into some of the flour and then start kneading in the water until you have a smooth, unsticky dough. Cover with a barely dampened cloth and leave in a cool place for 1 hour.

Divide the dough into 18 even-size pieces and flatten them slightly. Smear 12 of the pieces evenly with the softened butter. Put 2 of the buttered pieces on top of each other, buttered side up, and top with one of the unbuttered pieces. Do this with the rest of the pieces to make 6 piles, each consisting of 3 layers of dough separated by 2 layers of butter.

Roll out one of the piles of dough, sealing the edges if the butter starts to spurt out and dredging with flour. When the pastry sheet becomes unwieldy, cut it in half and roll out both sheets separately. Continue with the other piles of dough. Once the sheets have been rolled out as thinly as possible, roll them in layers or fold up and FREEZE, or use.

To serve from frozen: Thaw overnight in the refrigerator or for 2–3 hours at room temperature before using.

© *Glynn Christian*

PÂTÉS

If they do not contain too much garlic, really good pâtés are a tremendously encouraging thing to have in store, and this is how I would treat game birds if they were not attractive (nasty skins, broken bodies, etc.) or were getting past any sense of decent edibility. Keep the fat content of the pâté high, as should be the case anyway, but don't bother with clever fat-sealing and decoration, which can crack or discolour. Freeze the pâté as it is, and decorate once it is edible again. If you have plenty, it is a good idea to put up puréed pâtés, such as chicken liver, or potted things, in small pots or ramekins, so they are a possibility for individual treats or dinners for two.

A quickly made pâté, more a potting really, is also an excellent way to preserve any leftovers of smoked salmon, prawns, smoked eel or decent kippers, which you might have after a party. By so doing you are much more likely actually to use them. I have a single infallible recipe for all cooked seafood and other goodies of bland or delicate flavour, including sweetbreads or vegetables (page 147). To preserve the lightness of the recipe and save space you might want to freeze at the halfway stage. All you do is purée the prawns or smoked salmon, say, with an equal weight of melted, barely warm butter, and flavour that with the tiniest amount of lemon and some very dry white vermouth or cognac. Freeze at this stage, or, when the mixture is cool but not set, fold in lightly whipped cream – if you started with 125 g (4 oz) each of fish and butter you might use up to

see also
CHICKEN (page 53)
CROISSANTS (page 73)
FOIE GRAS (page 93)
PHYSALIS (page 153)
SMOKED FISH (page 174)
VINE LEAVES (page 198)
Pheasant Pâté (page 96)
Potted Hare (page 101)
Venison Pâté (page 197)

P

300 ml (½ pint), but at least 150 ml (¼ pint) is needed. Be very light-handed. Scoop it into small containers or a large one. If you pack it gently you will be rewarded; the heavy-handed who push and shove will not be as happy with its look, although the flavour will be the same. It might later be covered with butter and sprinkled with herbs. To ensure lightness after freezing a basic purée/butter mixture, you must first return it to room temperature, and perhaps even microwave it for a few seconds, to ensure it is malleable enough to combine with the cream. Both poached sweetbreads, and smoked eel are exceptionally good treated in this way, and both are further improved by the use of Pernod rather than vermouth – strange, I know, but true.

When you do eventually serve your pâté it is much more interesting to do so with a couple of special relishes or sauces, a leaf or two of unusual lettuce and a few tiny cubes of raw vegetable, than with toast. Pâté eaten with a knife and fork is also much easier to serve. Allow about 50 g (2 oz) per person if serving it as part of a buffet, or 75–125 g (3–4 oz) as a first course, depending on the richness of the pâté.

WILD DUCK AND BRANDIED CURRANT PÂTÉ

125 g (4 oz) currants
150 ml (¼ pint) brandy
500 g (1 lb) dressed wild duck
175 g (6 oz) belly of pork, boned and skinned
125 g (4 oz) duck or chicken livers
1 garlic clove
1 egg, beaten
1 teaspoon ground allspice
500 g (1 lb) pork fat, cut into neat strips
25 g (1 oz) shelled pistachio nuts, blanched
salt and freshly ground black pepper

Serves 6–8

Soak the currants in the brandy overnight.

Put the duck into one roasting pan and the belly of pork into another. Roast both in a preheated oven at Gas Mark 5/190°C/375°F for 45 minutes. Take out and cool.

Remove the breast fillets from the duck and remove and discard the skin. Marinate the breasts in the brandy with the currants for 30 minutes to 1 hour. Strip the remaining flesh from the duck, dice the pork and mince the two meats with the livers and garlic.

Mix the egg, spice, seasoning, and the currants and brandy from the marinade into the minced meat mixture. Line a 1-litre (1¾-pint) pâté dish with three-quarters of the pork fat strips. Half-fill the dish with the minced meat mixture. Lay the duck breasts on top in a single layer and sprinkle with the nuts. Cover with the remaining minced meats and pork fat. Cover the dish with foil and a lid and stand the dish in a roasting tin of hot water. Bake in a preheated oven at Gas Mark 3/160°C/325°F for 2–2½ hours.

When cooked, allow the pâté to cool, remove the lid and weigh the pâté down overnight in the refrigerator. FREEZE or turn out and serve.

To serve from frozen: Thaw the pâté at room temperature for 5–6 hours or overnight in the refrigerator.

DUCK LIVER PÂTÉ WITH MARSALA ASPIC

The thin layer of Marsala aspic gives a wonderful richness to this simple pâté. Serve it with hot toasted Brioche (page 37).

butter for greasing
175 g (6 oz) duck livers
175 g (6 oz) chicken livers
3 large eggs (size 1 or 2)
275 ml (9 fl oz) Marsala wine
salt and freshly ground black pepper
Aspic
175 ml (6 fl oz) Marsala wine
2 teaspoons gelatine
4 tablespoons cold water
1 tablespoon pickled green or pink peppercorns

Serves 6

Butter six 7 cm (3-inch) soufflé dishes. Trim the livers of any fat or sinew and cut each one in half. Blend the livers with the eggs, Marsala and seasoning until smooth and divide between the dishes, spreading the tops flat. Stand the dishes in a roasting tin of hot water and bake in a preheated oven at Gas Mark 2/150°C/300°F for about 1½ hours until firm. Leave to cool.

For the aspic layer, heat the Marsala in a pan and boil it to reduce it by half. Dissolve the gelatine in the cold water, add the Marsala and peppercorns and spoon over the pâtés. FREEZE or chill and serve.

To serve from frozen: Thaw overnight in the refrigerator.

CHICKEN AND WATERCRESS TERRINE

This contains neither liver nor pork and so is a delicious alternative to the more usual pâtés. Serve it with a well-reduced tomato sauce flavoured and coloured with chopped watercress and a dash of Tabasco or chilli sauce.

50 g (2 oz) bulghur wheat
4 large boned and skinned chicken breasts weighing 875 g – 1 kg (1¾–2 lb)
125 g (4 oz) trimmed watercress (about 2 bunches)
125 g (4 oz) onion
1 teaspoon ground mace
1 teaspoon ground coriander
2 eggs
125 g (4 oz) ground almonds
284 ml (10 fl oz) carton of double or soured cream
fresh or preserved vine leaves for wrapping
oil for greasing
4 tablespoons brandy
salt and freshly ground black pepper

Makes 1.25 kg (3 lb)

Cover the bulghur wheat with water and leave to soak for 20 minutes.

Remove the long supreme underneath one of the chicken breasts, keeping it in one piece. Divide the rest of the breast into 3 long strips about the same size as the supreme and reserve.

Reserve a palmful of the watercress and put the rest in a food processor with the onion. Add the mace, coriander, 1 teaspoon of salt and 1 teaspoon of pepper and chop finely. Blend in the eggs.

Drain the bulghur wheat and gently squeeze out the excess water. Add the bulghur wheat and the almonds to the food processor. While the food processor is running, slowly add the 3 whole chicken breasts and continue blending until smooth. Add the cream and blend until evenly textured.

Wilt or soak some fresh or preserved vine leaves in hot water for 5 minutes. Line an oiled 1.25 kg (3 lb) loaf tin with some of the vine leaves, keeping the shiny sides outwards.

Generously season the reserved strips of chicken. Coarsely chop the reserved watercress. Roll the strips of chicken in the watercress.

Spoon just over half the chicken mixture into the loaf tin and arrange the chicken strips in two lines along the top. Spoon on the brandy and add the rest of the chicken mixture. Smooth well, ensuring that the corners are tightly filled. Cover with more vine leaves and weave in those from the sides.

Seal the tin with a dome of aluminium foil and stand it in a roasting tin. Pour in boiling water to come half-way up the sides of the terrine. Bake in a preheated oven at Gas Mark 4/180°C/350°F for 1¼–1½ hours.

Let the terrine cool in the pan. FREEZE or chill well, turn out and serve cut into slices.

To serve from frozen: Thaw the terrine overnight in the refrigerator.

© *Glynn Christian*

PÂTÉ OF LAMB'S SWEETBREADS AND PERNOD

On a hot summer's day this makes the most tantalising and stimulating start to any meal, as well as a perfect first course for any sophisticated dinner party. Serve it in scoops on a plate which has been covered with lightly dressed, crisp, raw spinach leaves. Scatter over slices of crisp endive or very thin circles of raw leek and dribble tiny cubes of raw or cooked beetroot on to the pâté. Top with a couple of perfect prawns.

500 g (1 lb) lamb's sweetbreads
1 teaspoon chopped onion
½ teaspoon chopped garlic
2 teaspoons lemon juice
1 egg plus 2 extra egg whites
1½ teaspoons Pernod
175 g (6 oz) butter, melted
142 ml (5 fl oz) carton of double cream, chilled
salt

Serves 6–8

Soak the sweetbreads in 3 changes of water over 4 hours to draw out any blood.

Plunge the sweetbreads into boiling water and simmer for 2 minutes until firmed. Drain and cool under running cold water. Remove any excess fat, membrane and gristle; then place in a liquidiser or food processor with the onion, garlic, lemon juice, egg and egg whites and salt. Process until smooth and then sieve.

Put the purée into an ovenproof dish and cover it with foil. Stand it in a tray of boiling water and bake in a preheated oven at Gas Mark 4/180°C/350°F for about 30 minutes until it is just set; do not let it brown. Leave to cool.

Beat the Pernod and slightly warm, melted butter into the

purée until it is smooth. Whip the chilled cream and fold it into the purée. Turn the mixture into a dish to set and make a decorative pattern on top with a fork or knife tip. FREEZE or serve.

To serve from frozen: Thaw the pâté overnight in the refrigerator.

Variation:

SEAFOOD AND SWEETBREAD PÂTÉ

Seafood goes extremely well with both sweetbreads and Pernod and makes the dish more substantial. Drain a can of Danish mussels and dress with enough lemon juice and olive oil to moisten them. Mix some mayonnaise with some powdered saffron and fold in the mussels. Add a lot of chopped parsley so the mixture is quite firm. Put into the base of a lightly oiled ring mould or tin and pile the pâté mixture on top. Unmould to serve.

You could also serve the pâté with any canned seafood. Or make up any of the Norwegian brands of dried seafood soups into a sauce, adding brandy and cream. Let it cool, add extra pieces of fish and serve the sweetbread pâté in a pool of it.

© *Glynn Christian*

PEACHES AND NECTARINES

My fancy is for the white peach and nectarine. Both have a delicate, rather more refined fragrance and flavour than their yellow relatives. I would peel and segment them before freezing with minimal sugar. Save them for winter parties and serve them instead of ice cubes in white wine spritzers. Or dribble a tiny amount of orange liqueur on to three or four segments in a nice glass, top up with champagne and leave in the refrigerator whilst you dine. Serve with an attractive fork so you and your guests may stick it into the peach from time to time whilst you slowly sip the champagne, exchanging flavours one for the other.

If you want to save either kind for making into sorbets (page 182, 183), mousses or soups, freeze them packed in syrup, poached or puréed.

see also
FLOWERS (page 92)
SORBET (page 181)
Basic Meringues (page 122)
Nectarine Sorbet (page 182)
Peach Sorbet with Champagne (page 183)

PEANUTS

The only thing to do with peanuts and peanut butter that does not involve bread is to make satay sauce and keep that ready to use from frozen for any sort of grill. Don't freeze any thing containing salted peanuts for more than a month: it will tend towards rancidity.

PEARS

I should do with pears what I suggest you do with peaches and nectarines, but only if you can find ripe and juicy specimens of superior varieties – *Williams Bon Crétien* for instance.

see also
PHYSALIS (page 153)
QUINCE (page 163)
SORBET (page 181)

P

Remember too that pears might be used wherever you would normally choose apples in pies, pastries, sponge puddings, steamed puddings or sauces . . . or use the two in combination. For future fools, sorbets, soufflés and soups, store away a pear purée. Pears poached in wine or cider before freezing will have extra flavour.

PECANS

Fresh pecans are so expensive that should you find some good ones it really is worth protecting them by freezing. More than most nuts, they are improved by a light toasting, however they are to be used. They can be stored whole, chopped or toasted, but not salted, to use straight from the freezer.

It sounds a seductively cheaper solution, but do resist the suggestion that walnuts are a substitute for pecans in recipes. At best, which probably means Californian these days, walnuts are an alternative, but must not be considered to have anything like the same flavour.

see also
Caramelised Pecan Ice Cream (page 110)
White and Dark Truffles (page 61)

PRUNE, PECAN AND ARMAGNAC TERRINE

15 g (½ oz) gelatine
250 ml (8 fl oz) fresh orange juice
625 g (1¼ lb) pre-soaked pitted prunes
125 g (4 oz) pre-soaked dried apricots
100 ml (3½ fl oz) Armagnac
25 g (1 oz) pecans, chopped

Serves 6

Soften the gelatine in 3 tablespoons of the orange juice. Simmer the prunes and apricots in the remaining orange juice for about 5 minutes or until tender.

Add the gelatine mixture to the fruit and bring back to simmering point. Take off the heat. Add the Armagnac and pecans and pour into a 750 ml (1¼-pint) loaf dish. Press down firmly so that the fruit is covered by the liquid. Cool completely and FREEZE or refrigerate overnight.

To serve, dip the dish into warm water and invert it on to a plate. Slice the terrine and serve it with *crème anglaise* or cream flavoured with Armagnac and icing sugar.

To serve from frozen: Thaw the terrine overnight in the refrigerator. Serve as above.

PEPPERCORNS, FRESH

see also
Duck with Apple and Green Peppercorn Sauce (page 79)

Peppercorns – green in their natural state – are usually only available canned or bottled in vinegar or brine, so if you do see them fresh it really is worth your while to freeze them. Open freeze them before you pack them so you can take out just the quantity you need each time. They will add a freshly hot and spicy flavour to any food that you would normally season with pepper. In particular they are essential for a proper Steak au Poivre, a dish that is otherwise often palate-searing. Their aroma also seems to enhance that of gorgeously ripe tomatoes, and they make the perfect final touch for mulled wine or lightly warmed vodka. They are also ideal as a last-minute addition to sauces, especially any you plan to serve with fish. Add them frozen – just a minute of heating through will defrost them sufficiently.

PEPPERS

You can buy peppers all year round, but they are very much cheaper at certain times of the year and so you might like to take the opportunity to save some. What I like to do is to cut the peppers into even and straight strips – not rings, please – and to blanch them just enough to soften them, which also reduces the burp factor. A combination of these strips in red, green and yellow, perhaps with some orange and white too, make a fabulous vegetable when reheated in olive oil, with or without garlic. They also make an excellent chilled salad, and a wonderful garnish on something as simple as plainly cooked chicken or fish.

Those of you who like to do things properly will want first to char and then peel away the skins of red or green peppers, which enhances the flavour considerably but is rather a bore. I shouldn't bother with the other colours, particularly the gorgeous purple ones, which will turn green when charred and skinned or blanched.

You could also store away peppers as a purée, or as partially cooked stuffed peppers to be baked from frozen. But whichever way you choose to freeze them, peppers can be added to hot dishes in their frozen state.

see also
BUTTERS, FLAVOURED
(page 40)
CHICKEN (page 53)
COURGETTES (page 64)
PASTA (page 134)
RICE (page 167)
SANDWICHES (page 171)
SWEETBREADS (page 187)
Red Pepper Marmalade (page 65)

RED PEPPER VICHYSSOISE

6 red peppers, de-seeded and chopped coarsely
3 leeks, chopped coarsely
2 medium-size potatoes, peeled and sliced
1.75 litres (3 pints) chicken stock, plus extra if necessary
142 ml (5 fl oz) carton of double cream
salt and freshly ground black pepper
Garnish
garlic *croûtons*

Serves 6

Put the peppers, leeks, potatoes and chicken stock in a saucepan and simmer, covered, over a medium heat for about 20 minutes, until the vegetables are tender.

Liquidise and sieve the vegetables and place in a clean saucepan. Check the seasoning, add a little more chicken stock if the soup is too thick, stir in the cream and reheat gently. FREEZE or serve scattered with garlic *croûtons*.

To serve from frozen: Thaw the soup for 1–2 hours at room temperature; then reheat gently until piping hot. Garnish with *croûtons* and serve.

YELLOW PEPPER POTS WITH FRESH GREEN SALAD

Endive or frisé, lamb's lettuce or watercress and chicory all work well with these delicate moulds.

500 g (1 lb) yellow peppers
3 tablespoons oil
125 g (4 oz) onion, chopped
1 tablespoon plain flour
4 teaspons gelatine
600 ml (1 pint) chicken stock
1 tablespoon sherry vinegar
salt and freshly ground black pepper
Garnish
fresh green salad
500 g (1 lb) peeled prawns *or*
3 × 105 g (3½ oz) can of smoked
mussels, drained

Serves 6

Roast the peppers under a hot grill, turning them until the skins are completely blackened. Cool them and peel off the skins. Cut them in half, remove the stalks and seeds and chop them roughly.

Heat the oil in a pan and soften the onion in the oil. Stir in the chopped pepper and stir-cook for 30 seconds. Sprinkle over the flour and cook for a further 30 seconds. Dissolve the gelatine in 4 tablespoons of the stock and add the remaining stock slowly to the pepper mixture, stirring constantly. Bring to the boil; then cool slightly.

Liquidise the pepper mixture until smooth. Sieve and stir in the dissolved gelatine, sherry vinegar and seasoning to taste. Divide between six small 125 ml (4 fl oz) dampened moulds and FREEZE or chill until set.

To serve the moulds, ease the edge of the pepper jelly away from the mould, invert and shake well or dip each one briefly into hot water and turn on to individual starter plates. Garnish with fresh green salad and the prawns or smoked mussels.

To serve from frozen: Thaw the moulds in the refrigerator for 2 hours. Turn out and serve as above.

PARMESAN AND RED PEPPER FRITTATA

500 g (1 lb) onion, sliced finely
150 ml (¼ pint) olive oil
3 cooked, cold potatoes, sliced
2 red peppers, de-seeded and sliced thinly
125 g (4 oz) mild chorizo sausage, sliced
6–8 large eggs (size 1 or 2), beaten
4 tablespoons freshly grated parmesan cheese
salt and freshly ground black pepper

Serves 2

Gently sauté the onion in 3 tablespoons of the oil until soft. Lift out and set aside.

In a 15–18 cm (6–7-inch) heavy-based frying pan, stir-fry half the potato slices in 3 more tablespoons of the oil until they are lightly golden. Add half the softened onion, half the sliced red pepper and half the sausage slices and stir-fry for a further 1 minute. Pour over half the beaten egg, season well and sprinkle with half the grated cheese. Leave the omelette mixture to set, reducing the heat if the bottom of the mixture begins to burn.

When the omelette is just set but still moist in the centre, slide the frying pan under a hot grill and leave until the top is lightly golden and the omelette firm. Cool slightly, loosen from the pan and slide on to a serving platter.

Use the remaining ingredients to make a second *frittata*. FREEZE the *frittatas* or serve them.

To serve from frozen: Reheat the *frittatas* in a preheated oven at Gas Mark 4/180°C/350°F for 15–20 minutes until piping hot.

BAKED YELLOW PEPPERS WITH BOURSIN SAUCE

4 medium-size yellow peppers
Filling
500 g (1 lb) minced turkey
125 g (4 oz) dried apricots, chopped
grated rind and juice of ½ large
orange
1 teaspoon dried mint
1 tablespon finely chopped onion
½ teaspoon finely chopped garlic
salt and freshly ground black pepper
Boursin Sauce
300 ml (½ pint) dry white wine
1 medium-size onion, sliced finely
3–4 parsley stalks
1 bay leaf
a large packet of garlic and herb
Boursin cheese

Serves 4

Slice the tops off the peppers and remove the seeds from inside the peppers.

To make the stuffing, lightly mix together the minced turkey, apricots, orange rind and juice, mint, onion, garlic and seasoning. Stuff the mixture into the peppers. Replace the lids if wished.

For the sauce, put the wine, onion and herbs into a baking dish. Stand the peppers in the sauce.

Bake the peppers in a pre-heated oven at Gas Mark 4/180°C/350°F for 45 minutes until the peppers are tender and the stuffing is cooked through. Cool and FREEZE or remove the peppers from the dish and slowly mash and whisk the cheese into the hot cooking liquid. Strain the sauce and pour it around the peppers on hot plates.

To serve from frozen: Thaw the peppers in the sauce for 1–2 hours at room temperature. Bake as above for 15–20 minutes until piping hot. Continue as above.

RED PEPPER SAUCE

A sauce to serve with fish, roasted or grilled meat or a hot vegetable terrine.

3 tablespoons olive oil
3 red peppers, de-seeded and cut
into strips
2 garlic cloves, chopped finely
1–2 tiny red chillies, chopped
roughly
300 g (10 oz) tomatoes, chopped
roughly
a sprig of thyme
90 ml (3 fl oz) chicken stock or
water
a pinch of sugar
salt

Serves 6

Heat the oil in a saucepan and soften the pepper strips in the oil. Add the garlic and chilli and stir well. Add the tomatoes, thyme, stock or water, sugar and salt. Cover and simmer gently until the vegetables have made a thick purée. Sieve and reheat gently. FREEZE or serve.

To serve from frozen: Thaw the sauce over a gentle heat until piping hot.

PERSIMMONS

The colour of this fruit can vary from yellow to orange to red, giving it an appearance not unlike that of the tomato. Thus it is perfect, if skinned and stored as a purée, for giving a gorgeous colour and flavour to ice cream, or to serve as a coulis with other desserts. A dash of a liqueur like Kirsch will enhance the flavour on defrosting. Otherwise skin it and freeze whole in syrup to add to fruit salads or similar.

© Glynn Christian

P

PHEASANT

see GAME BIRDS

PHYSALIS

Once known as cape gooseberries, these are amongst the most intensely flavoured fruits of all, and make wondrous bursts of flavour and colour if you include them as accents in pâtés or pies of any kind. They keep their flavour in hot fruit pies and thus make a tremendous difference to an otherwise ordinary apple, pear or plum pie.

The acidity of the fruit is so wonderful that physalis teams excellently with savoury foods too. I make a purée of it to serve as an instant sauce for pâté and cold meats – and what a terrific colour.

PHYSALIS FRITTERS WITH FRESH PASSION-FRUIT

Wonton wrappers, on sale at oriental grocers, freeze perfectly unfilled and make the most delicious crisp fritter coating for fresh or frozen physalis, pineapple pieces or chopped guava.

24 wonton wrappers about 8 cm (3 inches) square
500 g (1 lb) physalis
1 egg yolk, beaten with 1 teaspoon water
oil for deep-frying
a little icing sugar, sifted
pulp of 6 passion-fruit

Serves 6

Spread the wonton wrappers on a dry work surface and place 2–3 physalis in the centre of each one. Brush the edges of the wrappers with the egg yolk. Fold them over and seal them, making neat triangles. FREEZE or fry about 8 at a time in deep, hot oil until lightly golden. This will take about 1 minute. Lift out with a slotted spoon and drain while frying the remaining fritters.

Pile the fritters on to a warmed serving platter or individual plates and dust with sifted icing sugar. Spoon over the passion-fruit pulp and serve.

To serve from frozen: Deep-fry the fritters from frozen until golden-brown and serve as above.

PIGEON

An excellent standby, especially as an extender of dishes based on expensive and more elegant white-fleshed game birds. But pigeons themselves stew up wonderfully, and make good potted courses too. Even so, it is possibly best not to bother with wild ones if you have access to the corn-fed farmed squabs now being produced in this country. They are another world altogether and should be kept, once plucked and drawn, in the freezer, so you can enjoy them simply roasted. They will also give a truer approximation of the Middle East's succulent pigeons for such masterpieces as the pigeon, egg, cinnamon, sugar, parsley and filo pie called B'stilla. If you prefer eating just the breasts (the legs and back often have a bitter taste) as you might for a *salade tiède*, don't be tempted to cut the birds to size before storing or cooking; if you do, the breasts will shrink alarmingly when heat is applied.

see also
CHESTNUTS (page 51)
Rabbit, Olive and Red Pepper Terrine (page 165)

PIGEON AND WALNUT CASEROLE

Serve with a barley and raisin pilaff and braised red cabbage for a glorious winter feast.

75 g (3 oz) streaky bacon, diced finely
3 tablespoons olive oil
150 g (5 oz) brown breadcrumbs
50 g (2 oz) shredded suet
3 tablespoons freshly chopped parsley
75 g (3 oz) walnuts, chopped finely
finely grated rind of ½ orange
1 egg, beaten
6 pigeons
1 tablespoon plain flour
150 ml (¼ pint) port
550 ml (19 fl oz) jellied chicken or turkey stock
a *bouquet garni*
250 g (8 oz) pickling onions
142 ml (5 fl oz) carton of double cream
salt and freshly ground black pepper

Serves 6

Sauté the finely diced bacon in a little of the oil and mix with the breadcrumbs, suet, parsley, walnuts, orange rind, beaten egg and seasoning. Shape into 2 cm (1-inch) balls and brown them in a little more of the oil. Drain and set aside.

Tie the pigeons neatly and brown them slowly in the remaining oil in a flameproof casserole. Remove the pigeons and stir in the flour. Cook for 1 minute; then slowly add the port, stock, *bouquet garni* and seasoning. Bring to the boil stirring continuously, reduce the heat and add the pigeons. Cover and cook in a preheated oven at Gas Mark 4/180°C/350°F for 1 hour.

Blanch the peeled onions in boiling water for 5–6 minutes. Drain and add them with the forcemeat balls to the casserole. FREEZE or simmer for a further 15–20 minutes.

To serve at once, remove the pigeons and forcemeat and boil the gravy over a high heat to reduce the liquid by one-third. Remove the *bouquet garni* and stir in the cream. Check the seasoning and serve with the pigeons.

To serve from frozen: Thaw the casserole overnight in the refrigerator. Gently reheat until piping hot and continue as above.

PISTACHIOS

These rich and decorative nuts are worth freezing to preserve their freshness. Like other nuts, freeze them shelled in any form except salted and use from frozen. I would blanch them quickly before using to enhance their green colour and make them easier to skin. Chopped finely they are invaluable for decorating sweet or savoury, hot or cold food. Use them to make a proper Middle Eastern pilaff, which might also include saffron and pine kernels. Mix them into a thick smoked salmon and double cream purée and flavour this with grated lime rind and seasoning and you have a wonderful stuffing for chicken breasts. Their distinctive flavour is also perfect in ice creams and cakes. Or use them to make crisp, bite-size triangles of Pistachio Bread (page 176) to serve with a fish pâté, guacamole or hummus, a hearty vegetable soup, or any egg dish.

see also
Pistachio Bread (page 176)

PITTA

The smaller versions, and the more unusual types which

see also
Pistachio Bread (page 176)

P

come with sachets of unidentifiable spices, are tremendously
satisfying to have at hand in the
freezer, for they can be hot from
the grill or toaster and in service
in minutes, either as an aid to
dipping or to split along one
side (not in half please) and to
stuff with salad and those ingredients which otherwise would
not stretch far enough. Filled
pittas are excellent 'fist food':
the smart way to approach buffet food. Pitta flavoured with
pistachios (page 176) is good
as an accompaniment to food
which you would normally serve
with bread.

POLENTA

It is becoming increasingly difficult to dine in Italian and Californian restaurants without
polenta appearing on your
plate. This speciality of the Ven-
etians begins as a thick porridge of yellow cornmeal, made
from a relative of sweetcorn.
Once thickened and cooked it is
turned out. When cold and hor-
rid and solid it is cut into pieces,
which are revived by frying or by
being baked with a small bird or
something else which will drip
juices into its blandness. It
wouldn't be a bad wheeze to
make up some of the porridge
on a boring day so you could
withdraw nicely shaped pieces
of polenta from the freezer upon
which to bake a partridge or
some quail, or more simply to
fry until golden in olive oil and
garlic; they will defrost sufficiently in the oven or frying pan. If
you make small cubes these will
be the best hot *croûtons*
imaginable for soups and for
salads, as the insides will be
soft and thus mercifully more
silent to eat.

see also
*Chestnut Polenta (page
52)*

POLENTA WITH BLUE CHEESE AND TOMATO CREAM

900 ml (1½ pints) water
250 g (8 oz) polenta
125 g (4 oz) freshly grated
parmesan cheese
2 eggs, beaten lightly
oil for greasing
125 g (4 oz) butter, melted
150 g (5 oz) blue cheese, crumbled
salt and freshly grated nutmeg
Tomato Cream
500 g (1 lb) tomatoes, peeled, de-
seeded and chopped
1 tablespoon freshly chopped basil
1 tablespoon dry sherry or cognac
284 ml (10 fl oz) carton of whipping
cream
salt and freshly ground black pepper
To serve
75 g (3 oz) bresaola or Parma ham,
chopped roughly

Serves 6

Bring the water to the boil, adding
a pinch of salt and freshly grated
nutmeg. Reduce the heat. Stir in
the polenta and continue to cook,
stirring constantly, until the mixture is thick enough for a spoon to
stand unsupported. Take the
polenta off the heat and stir in the
grated parmesan and the beaten
eggs. Spread the polenta on to a
well-oiled baking tray and smooth
to a 5 mm (¼-inch) thickness.
Chill for 1 hour until firm.

Cut the polenta into 5 cm
(2-inch) squares and then cut
each square into two triangles.
Arrange the triangles in overlapping circles in six greased,
shallow ovenproof dishes.
FREEZE or spoon over the melted
butter and crumbled blue cheese
and bake in a preheated oven at
Gas Mark 4/180°C/350°F for
15–20 minutes.

For the sauce, simmer the
tomatoes, basil and sherry or cognac together in a saucepan for
10–15 minutes. Sieve and reheat
with seasoning to taste and the

cream. FREEZE or spoon the sauce over the hot polenta and sprinkle with the bresaola or Parma ham.

To serve from frozen: Bake the polenta as above until crisp, golden and piping hot. Reheat the sauce and serve.

POMEGRANATE

Freeze the seeds and the juice, but with care as the juice stains without mercy. Use the seeds straight from the freezer to sprinkle on poached fish, pastry pies, salads, curries, rice dishes, fruit dishes or fruit salads. The colour and effect is fabulous, but do warn your fellow diners about the juices.

PORK

see also
APPLES (page 15)
CHESTNUTS (page 51)
CITRUS FRUITS (page 62)
Caramel-crusted Baked Smoked Pork Loin (page 179)
Champagne and Truffle Patties with Champagne Sauce (page 193)
Spicy Cherry Sauce (page 50)

I would freeze the tenderloin or fillet only for true gourmet food. Spicy Cherry Sauce (page 50) is one of the best accompaniments, so make sure you have plenty in stock.

Raised pork pies, like the one following, make good freezer fare for later cold meals and buffets.

PORK, GAMMON AND CRANBERRY PIE

Filling
750 g (1½ lb) neck of pork
2 teaspoons coarsely ground coriander seeds
1 teaspoon coarsely ground cumin
2 teaspoons finely grated lemon rind
1 teaspoon allspice
250 g (8 oz) gammon steak
oil for frying
125 g (4 oz) cranberries
125 ml (4 fl oz) gelatinous stock (made from pork bones), reduced to 3 tablespoons
salt and freshly ground black pepper
Hot-water pastry
500 g (1 lb) plain flour
1 teaspoon salt
200 g (7 oz) lard, plus extra for greasing
375 ml (13 fl oz) milk and water mixed
1 egg, beaten

Serves 6

Finely chop or coarsely mince the pork. Add the coriander, cumin, lemon rind, allspice and salt and pepper. Set aside for 30 minutes for the flavours to develop.

Trim the gammon of any fat and sauté the steak in a lightly oiled frying pan until golden on both sides. Set aside to cool.

To make the pastry, warm a mixing bowl and sift in the flour with the salt. Make a well in the centre of the flour. Heat the lard and milk and water until just boiling and stir them quickly into the flour until all the ingredients are combined. When the dough has cooled slightly, knead it until smooth.

Set aside one-quarter of the pastry for the lid and keep it covered. Use the rest of the pastry to line a 14–15 cm (5½–6-inch) loose-based, greased, deep cake tin. Spoon half the pork mixture into the tin. Cover with the gammon steak. Add the rest of the pork and top with the cranberries.

P

Roll out the remaining pastry for the lid and use to cover the pie. Seal the edges, make a hole in the centre, decorate the top with any trimmings and brush with the beaten egg. Bake in a preheated oven at Gas Mark 6/200°C/400°F for 15 minutes; then reduce the heat to Gas Mark 4/180°C/350°F and continue to bake for 1 hour more. Leave to stand at room temperature for 10–15 minutes; then carefully unmould and leave until cold.

Using a funnel, fill the pie with the stock and FREEZE, or leave to set for 10–15 minutes.

To serve from frozen: Thaw the pie overnight in the refrigerator.

FREEZE or sauté them gently in butter until browned on both sides. Lift out and keep warm.

To make the sauce, melt the butter in a clean frying pan and gently sauté the garlic and mushrooms in the butter for 30 seconds. Add the wine and simmer for 3–4 minutes. Liquidise for a very smooth sauce or leave chunky. FREEZE or add the cream, sherry and salt and pepper and cook gently for 4–5 minutes.

To serve from frozen: Sauté the patties in butter until they are golden. Reheat the sauce and add the cream, sherry and seasoning as above.

PORK SCALOPPINI WITH WILD MUSHROOMS

1.25 kg (3 lb) minced pork
3 shallots, chopped finely
2 garlic cloves, chopped finely
3 tablespoons freshly chopped parsley
1 teaspoon dried oregano
4 eggs
plain flour for coating
butter for frying
salt and freshly ground black pepper
Wild Mushroom Sauce
50 g (2 oz) butter
2 garlic cloves, chopped finely
200 g (7 oz) wild mushrooms or shitake mushrooms, chopped
200 ml (7 fl oz) dry white wine
284 ml (10 fl oz) carton of double cream
2 tablespoons dry sherry
salt and freshly ground black pepper

Serves 6

Mix the pork, shallot, garlic, parsley and oregano with the eggs and seasoning. Shape into 12 round, flat rissoles and chill for 1–2 hours.

Roll each rissole out flat into the shape of an escalope between two sheets of non-stick baking paper. Flour them on both sides.

SKEWERED PORK WITH MANGO

3 pork fillets weighing 1 kg (2 lb)
150 ml (½ pint) hoisin sauce
3 tablespoons tomato ketchup
3 tablespoons soy sauce
3 tablespoons sherry vinegar
4 tablespoons olive oil
1 tablespoon freshly grated root ginger
To serve
2 mangoes, cut into 2 cm (¾-inch) cubes

Serves 6

Trim the pork of any fat and sinew and cut the meat into 2 cm (¾-inch) cubes. Mix all the remaining ingredients, except the mangoes, together and add the pork. Stir well and FREEZE, or leave to marinate for 2–3 hours.

To serve, thread the pork and mango on to wooden skewers. Brush with any leftover marinade and grill under a high heat or barbecue until golden-brown.

To serve from frozen: Thaw the meat in the marinade in the refrigerator overnight. Thread on to skewers with the mango cubes and grill or barbecue as above.

SPICED PORK WITH CORIANDER

2–3 tablespoons oil
1.75 kg (4 lb) lean pork, cut into
bite-size cubes
250–300 g (8–10 oz) onion,
chopped finely
2 garlic cloves, chopped finely
1 tablespoon curry powder
1 cinnamon stick
1 teaspoon coarsely ground
coriander seeds
1 teaspoon coarsely ground cumin
seeds
4 ripe tomatoes, peeled, de-seeded
and chopped
500 ml (18 fl oz) chicken stock
4 teaspoons mango chutney
lemon juice to taste
142 ml (5 fl oz) carton of single
cream
salt and freshly ground black pepper
Garnish
fresh coriander leaves, chopped

Serves 6

Heat the oil in a saucepan and brown the cubed meat in batches in the hot oil. Lift out and set aside while gently softening the onion and garlic in the remaining oil in the pan. Add the spices and stir well for 30 seconds. Add the pork, tomatoes and stock and bring slowly to the boil. Reduce the heat, cover and simmer gently for 40 minutes or until just tender.

FREEZE or uncover the pan, add the chutney, lemon juice and seasoning to taste. Simmer hard for 5–10 minutes, without burning, to reduce the sauce a little. Stir in the cream, check the seasoning, sprinkle with fresh coriander and serve.

To serve from frozen: Reheat gently until piping hot and continue as above.

POTATOES

I can't think it worth giving much space to whole potatoes, not even such arcane and delicious salad varieties as the Red Fir or Kipferl. Instead you might find it an advantage to cook, grate and fry potatoes in goose fat, to make in advance some big or small rounds of rosti (opposite). Or keep a store of small cooked potatoes that have been fried in oil, cumin seeds, ground coriander and ground chilli to re-fry from frozen. I like to make up and keep a batch of bolognese sauce to serve over hot potatoes. The secret of this lies in the addition of celery and the length of cooking: use lean mince, cubed carrot, cans of plum tomatoes and bay, and cook it for at least forty-five minutes before salting it lightly and cooking for another ten minutes or so; stir in plenty of chopped celery leaves once it has defrosted.

Of course cooked potatoes freeze well as a purée or in croquette, duchesse or gnocchi mixtures. Combine with any other root vegetable, spinach or pumpkin for any of these. Partially cooked *pommes frites* can be stored to deep-fry or oven-bake from frozen.

see also
CELERIAC (page 44)
DUCK (page 78)
GOOSE (page 97)
PUMPKIN (page 160)
SWEET POTATO (page 189)
Jerusalem Artichoke and Chervil Pie (page 18)
Potato and Celeriac Choux (page 45)

P

APPLE AND LIME ROSTI

1.1 kg (2½ lb) waxy potatoes
375 g (12 oz) Bramley or Granny
Smith apples, cored
grated rind and juice of 2 limes
1 garlic clove, crushed
melted goose fat for frying
salt

Serves 6–8

Cook the potatoes in their skins until just starting to soften; then cool.

Peel the potatoes and grate coarsely into a bowl. Coarsely grate the apples and add to the potatoes with the lime juice. Add half the grated lime rind, the garlic and salt. Blend together with your hands.

Pour melted goose fat into a large frying pan to a depth of 5 mm (¼ inch). Heat the fat over a high heat; then remove from the heat and add the potato mixture. Press down evenly and cook the base over a medium heat until it is crisp and golden-brown. Slide the rosti on to a plate and flip it back into the pan to cook the other side, or dribble over more goose fat and brown the top under the grill. FREEZE or serve in wedges, sprinkled with the rest of the grated lime rind.

To serve from frozen: Thaw and re-crisp the rosti over a medium heat in a frying pan lightly oiled with goose fat, until piping hot. Serve sprinkled with the rest of the lime rind.

© Glynn Christian

POTATO AND PARSLEY GALETTES

Eat these golden, grated potato cakes hot or cold as an accompaniment to a main dish or as the base of a snack topped with creamy scrambled egg and smoked salmon slices, with tomato or aubergine sauce or creamed mushrooms.

750 g (1½ lb) potatoes, peeled and
grated coarsely
3 tablespoons freshly chopped
parsley
2 teaspoons grated lime rind
3 garlic cloves, chopped finely
3 eggs, beaten lightly
40 g (1½ oz) plain flour
4–5 tablespoons milk
oil for frying
salt and freshly ground black pepper

Makes 12–15

Mix the potatoes with the parsley, lime rind, garlic, beaten eggs, flour, milk and seasoning, making a mixture the consistency of double cream.

Heat 1 tablespoon of oil in a frying pan and add a heaped tablespoon of potato mixture, spreading it with the back of the spoon to form a cake about 5 mm (¼ inch) thick. Fry briskly for 2–3 minutes until golden; then turn and sauté the second side. Lift out and keep the cake warm while frying the remaining mixture, adding more oil each time. FREEZE or serve.

To serve from frozen: Wrap three galettes at a time in a foil parcel and reheat in a preheated oven at Gas Mark 4/180°C/350°F for 20 minutes until piping hot, or toss each one into a hot, lightly oiled frying pan and re-crisp and thaw over a brisk heat.

PRAWNS

Only freeze really fresh raw or cooked prawns. They are best bought frozen raw from the supplier. The prawns I look for are the big striped tiger prawns or the even bigger giant Pacific prawns usually found in oriental stores – but look hard for the wickedness of ice crusts for which you pay the same price as the flesh. For extra succulence, let them defrost in the refrigerator.

As an alternative to the usual prawn cocktail, I layer small spinach leaves and radicchio on a large white or green plate and then arrange segments of kiwifruit that have been marinated in Pernod on top; on to this goes a pile of cooked prawns and a helping of mayonnaise that has been flavoured with grated lime rind and juice.

PRAWN, DILL AND LIME POTS

500 g (1 lb) cooked, peeled prawns
125 g (4 oz) butter, melted and kept warm
2 teaspoons freshly chopped dill
1–2 tablespoons lime juice
a pinch of Cayenne pepper
142 ml (5 fl oz) carton of double cream, whipped lightly
freshly grated nutmeg and salt
Garnish
sprigs of dill

Serves 6

Mash or liquidise 250 g (8 oz) of the prawns with 75 g (3 oz) of the butter. Beat in the dill and lime juice to taste, with plenty of grated nutmeg, a pinch of Cayenne pepper and salt if necessary. Fold in the cream.

Divide the remaining whole prawns between six base-lined

individual dariole moulds or ramekins. Spoon the pâté on top and smooth firmly. FREEZE or chill.

To serve, dip the moulds briefly into hot water and turn them out on to individual starter plates. Garnish with a sprig of dill and serve with hot toast or high-baked water biscuits.

To serve from frozen: Dip the moulds briefly into hot water and turn out; then thaw in the refrigerator for 2–3 hours. Leave at room temperature for 30 minutes before serving.

PUMPKIN

This under-appreciated vegetable appears only for a few months, or in some places just for a few weeks around Guy Fawkes Night and Hallowe'en, and so it is well worth keeping. Contrary to popular opinion, squash is exactly the same thing. The difference lies between summer and winter squash or pumpkins. The former are the soft ones – marrow, courgettes and so on – which will not last long; winter varieties are the firmer-fleshed ones, which do. It has become convenient to call soft summer varieties the squash and firm winter ones the pumpkins, but until everyone does, confusion will unnecessarily continue. For freezing, I should forget the summer varieties and go for the very firmest fleshed varieties – Queensland Blue is a real goodie – but you will have to do with what you can find unless you are growing them.

Care is needed when preparing. It is safer to cut tough-skinned pumpkins into relatively small pieces or slices before attempting to peel, although strictly speaking peeling is not necessary when cooking it, which may be in any of the ways you would employ for potatoes. Other ways I use include pouring orange juice over slices of pumpkin to half their depth and then scattering over dried apricots, almond flakes, coriander, seasoning and butter and baking in a moderate oven for up to forty-five minutes. This method can be varied to create a Provençal-style dish by sprinkling the slices with olive oil, covering with slightly squashed canned tomatoes and their juices and then scattering with chopped or finely sliced garlic cloves, fresh thyme, rosemary and bay and extra olive oil before baking.

Pumpkin kept as lightly blanched or cooked chunks and cubes in the freezer also means you always have something to add colour to soups or to make a golden soup of its own (like the one following). Or something with which to make gnocchi, to grate into scone and bread mixtures or to purée for a pumpkin pie. I prefer to mix the purée with semolina, sugar, butter and currants and then sprinkle it with cinnamon, allspice and flaked almonds as an alternative to the usual pie filling. Or the purée can be mixed with butter and allspice, cooked gently with chopped dried apricots and served as it is, with a sprinkling of fried pine kernels. The purée is useful in other ways too. The most popular vegetable dishes at recent occasions I have catered for have been mixed mounds of mashed pumpkin and potatoes and marbled swirls of puréed parsnip and pumpkin.

Just coming on to the market are baby pumpkin and squash. The size of a baby's fist or so, they can be cooked whole or cut into two or three pieces. They may be eaten skin and all, and their frilled edges (the so-called patty pan squash) and bright greens, yellows and pale greens of their skins open up new worlds of vegetable possibility. As they are very happy with robust Mediterranean cooking, cook them and store them in a rich tomato, herb and olive oil sauce, or simply dressed with hot olive oil with chunks of soft-poached garlic and fresh basil leaves.

CREAM OF PUMPKIN AND ORANGE SOUP

125 g (4 oz) butter
300–350 g (10–12 oz) onion, chopped finely
1.5 kg (3½ lb) pumpkin, diced
1½ teaspoons curry powder
5 tablespoons plain flour
1.5 litres (2½ pints) chicken stock
3 tablespoons finely grated orange rind
a pinch of grated nutmeg
600 ml (1 pint) milk
salt and freshly ground black pepper

Serves 6

Melt the butter in a heavy-based saucepan and cook the onion over a gentle heat until soft. Add the pumpkin cubes and cook for 10–15 minutes, stirring occasionally, until they start to soften. Sprinkle over the curry powder and flour and cook for 1 minute without browning. Gradually stir in the stock and orange rind, nutmeg and seasoning and bring to the boil. Reduce the heat and simmer for 20–25 minutes until the vegetables are really tender.

Purée and sieve the mixture. Add the milk to make a rich soup, check the seasoning and heat until piping hot. FREEZE or serve topped with a swirl of cream.

To serve from frozen: Reheat the soup over a gentle heat until piping hot.

Quail
Quince

Good freezers, once they have been plucked and singed and the neck and crop removed. They make good first courses and good main courses. I have seen individual breasts offered for sale, sometimes smoked, and these would make for a very gourmet freezer indeed.

see also
ASPARAGUS (page 19)
POLENTA (page 155)
SMOKED MEATS AND
POULTRY (page 179)

QUINCE

Slices of the best varieties of quince, which have an unmissable honey-like perfume of much intensity, are such a superb addition to so many dishes that it is worth travelling to ensure you have a stock. Some of the most useful are very firm and feel unripe when bought. Used in the Middle Eastern way, they complete voluptuously spiced stews of poultry and lamb, which you invariably feel like making in winter well out of the fresh quince season, or may be baked with additional honey and spice to be served cold with thick cream. Even a trove of one or two, frozen in slices, is worthwhile, for just one or two segments will transform an apple pie or the stuffing for baked apples or pears. Poach them for a couple of minutes before freezing, or peel, quarter and core and freeze chunks or slices in syrup or as a dry pack.

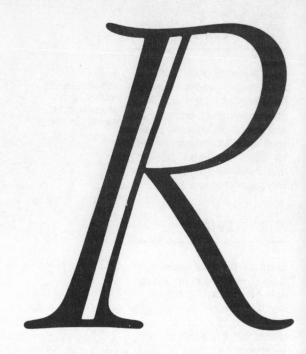

Rabbit
Rice

R

RABBIT

Frozen boneless rabbit, usually from China, is quite a useful thing to have in store, for you can use it any way you might use chicken but make it sound different. Indeed, you can actually use it to extend casseroles, *blanquettes* or pies of chicken or turkey. It is specially good combined with ham in sauces or pies where you might first think of using chicken.

RABBIT, OLIVE AND RED PEPPER TERRINE

Strong flavoured meats like hare and wood pigeon make an equally good mixture for this terrine. Although the terrine keeps well in the refrigerator for up to a week, it is fairly time-consuming to prepare, so make double the quantity and keep at least half in the freezer for a second or third meal.

1 kg (2 lb) rabbit, including saddle
250 g (8 oz) sliced streaky bacon
75 g (3 oz) cooked ham, diced
75 g (3 oz) pork fat, diced
2 tablespoons brandy
2 tablespoons Madeira
a pinch each of ground allspice,
cloves and nutmeg
200 g (7 oz) belly of pork
1 small red pepper, peeled, de-
seeded and diced
75 g (3 oz) stuffed green olives,
sliced thickly
salt and freshly ground black pepper

Serves 6

Cut the meat from the rabbit, keeping the saddle meat from the backbone and the fillets from under the ribs in whole pieces. Finely chop one of the rashers of bacon and fry it until the fat runs. Remove and reserve the fried bacon, slice the saddle meat and fillets into thick strips and cook them gently in the bacon fat for about 3 minutes until the meat is firm.

Turn the cooked meat into an earthenware or plastic bowl with the ham, pork fat, brandy, Madeira and spices and mix well. Cover and leave for about 1 hour.

Mince the remaining rabbit meat with the fried rasher of bacon and the pork. Stir in the marinated ham and pork fat, the diced red pepper, olives, seasoning and any marinade that is left. Fry a small piece and taste it to check that it is highly seasoned.

Line a 1-litre (1¾-pint) terrine with the remaining bacon rashers, reserving two or three for the top. Spread one-third of the minced mixture inside. Arrange half the strips of rabbit down the centre. Cover with another third of the mince, lay on the rest of the sliced meat and then cover with the remaining minced meat. Cover with the reserved bacon rashers. Stand the uncovered dish in a bain-marie and cook in a preheated oven at Gas Mark 4/180°C/350°F for 1½ hours or until firm and the juices run clear when a skewer is pushed into the centre. Cool; then cover with foil and press the top with a 1 kg (2 lb) weight. Leave in the refrigerator for 2 days to a week. Unmould, wrap and FREEZE or serve.

To serve from frozen: Thaw the terrine overnight in the refrigerator.

RABBIT AND FENNEL IN YOGURT SAUCE

250 g (8 oz) fennel
50 g (2 oz) butter
1 garlic clove, crushed
500 g (1 lb) rabbit meat, diced
150 ml (¼ pint) dry white wine
4 tablespoons dry white vermouth
strained greek yogurt
salt and freshly ground black pepper

Serves 4

Reserve the green fronds from the fennel and slice the rest thinly. Melt the butter in a pan and add the fennel slices and garlic. Add the rabbit and stir until the pieces are well coated with butter, but do not brown. Pour in the wine and vermouth, season and simmer for about 45 minutes until the rabbit is tender.

FREEZE or remove the pan from the heat and stir in as much yogurt as is necessary to make a thick white sauce. Chop the reserved fennel fronds finely and scatter them over the top. Serve with jacket potatoes.

To serve from frozen: Thaw the rabbit over a gentle heat and continue as above.

© *Glynn Christian*

RABBIT IN SOURED CREAM AND MUSTARD

The combination of soured cream and mustard counteracts the sweetness of the rabbit and the mustard prevents the cream separating.

750 g (1½ lb) boneless rabbit, diced
flour for coating
oil and butter for frying
450 ml (¾ pint) chicken stock or white wine *or* a mixture
a few sprigs of fresh thyme
4 tablespoons seed mustard, plus extra if necessary
142 ml (5 fl oz) carton of soured cream
salt and freshly ground black pepper

Serves 4

Toss the rabbit dice in flour and then season. Heat equal quantities of oil and butter in a pan or casserole and brown the rabbit. Add the stock and/or wine and the thyme, cover and simmer for about 45 minutes until the rabbit is tender.

Remove the thyme sprigs and stir in the mustard. Bring to the boil and cook, uncovered, until less than half the original amount of liquid remains. Stir in the soured cream and simmer over a very low heat to reduce a little more if necessary. FREEZE or check the flavour and add a little more mustard if necessary. Serve with baked potatoes.

To serve from frozen: Thaw the rabbit overnight in the refrigerator and reheat gently until piping hot.

© *Glynn Christian*

RABBIT IN CIDER

The cider does not need to be drastically reduced because of the sweetness of the rabbit.

1 large rabbit, cut into portions
oil for frying
175 g (6 oz) onion, sliced
3 shallots, sliced
1 garlic clove, chopped
1 teaspoon plain flour
1.2 litres (2 pints) dry cider,
reduced to 750 ml (1¼ pints)
1 clove
1 kg (2 lb) turnips, diced
salt and freshly ground black pepper

Serves 4

Brown the rabbit portions in hot oil in a large pan. Add the onion, shallots and garlic and cook until the rabbit is brown all over. Sprinkle over the flour and cook for 2–3 minutes more; then add the cider, clove and seasoning. Bring to the boil, cover and simmer gently for 45 minutes until the rabbit is tender.

Cook the turnip in boiling water for 10 minutes; then drain. Add the turnip to the rabbit and continue to simmer for 15 minutes. FREEZE or arrange the rabbit and turnips on a hot serving dish and serve.

To serve from frozen: Thaw the rabbit overnight in the refrigerator and reheat gently until hot.

© Glynn Christian

RASPBERRIES

see BERRIES

RED AND BOURGEOIS SNAPPER

see FISH

RED MULLET

see FISH

RICE

Rice is best frozen in made-up dishes. If you do want to freeze plain, cooked rice, open freeze it first and then stir-fry in hot oil from frozen. I would add to this crunchy and colourful goodies like shrimps, bits of bacon, cubes of ham, flakes of fish, strips of omelette, slices of pepper, pre-cooked onion, chives, herbs, garlic, leftover vegetables, pineapple, sticks of cucumber, or whatever takes your fancy. Serve your fried rice with soy sauce and Worcestershire sauce.

see also
CHESTNUTS (page 51)
COURGETTES (page 64)
DATES (page 77)
FLOWERS (page 92)
PISTACHIOS (page 154)
POMEGRANATE (page 156)
Tomato and Coriander Sauce (page 191)

ROSE AND RICE CREAMS

The lovely scented flavour and texture of these delicate moulds is delicious with a bowl of red summer fruits.

175 g (6 oz) pudding rice
750 ml (1¼ pints) full cream milk
2–3 tablespoons caster sugar
2 tablespoons triple-strength rose-water
1 tablespoon Muscat de Beaumes de Venise (optional)
142 ml (5 fl oz) carton of whipping cream, whipped lightly
75g (3 oz) almond flakes, toasted
Decoration
142 ml (5 fl oz) carton of whipping or double cream, whipped
10 g (¼ oz) crystallised or frosted rose petals

Serves 6

Put the rice and milk into the top of a double boiler. Cover and simmer for about 1¼ hours, stirring from time to time and adding more water to the bottom of the boiler if necessary. Once the rice is tender and creamy, stir in the sugar, rose-water and wine, if used, and leave to cool.

Fold in the whipped cream and almonds and chill before spooning into base-lined individual dariole moulds or yogurt cartons. FREEZE or chill until firm.

Turn out the creams and serve each one topped with a swirl of the cream and a frozen or crystallised rose petal.

To serve from frozen: Turn out the moulds and leave to thaw for about 1 hour before decorating and serving as above.

MOCHA RICE CREAMS

Serve each mould on a pool of double cream flavoured with brandy.

75 g (3 oz) freshly ground coffee
750 ml (1¼ pints) full cream milk
175 g (6 oz) pudding rice
sugar to taste
2–3 tablespoons brandy
4 tablespoons desiccated coconut, toasted
142 ml (5 fl oz) carton of double cream, whipped
Decoration
chocolate curls

Serves 6

Simmer the ground coffee in the milk for 1–2 minutes. Set it aside to infuse for 5–10 minutes.

Put the rice into a double boiler and strain the milk over it. Cook for about 1¼ hours or until the rice is tender, stirring from time to time and adding more water to the double boiler if necessary.

Sweeten the rice to taste and cool. Stir in the brandy, coconut and cream. Turn into six base-lined dariole moulds or ramekins and FREEZE, or chill until firm. Turn out and serve topped with curls of chocolate.

To serve from frozen: Turn out the moulds and thaw for about 1 hour in the refrigerator before decorating and serving.

WILD RICE TIMBALES

Individual packets of wild rice mixture wrapped in lettuce make a perfect accompaniment to roast meat or game.

175 g (6 oz) wild rice
50 g (2 oz) butter, plus extra for greasing
125–175 g (4–6 oz) onion, chopped finely
625 g (1¼ lb) *petits pois*
2 tablespoons flaked almonds, toasted lightly
1 tablespoon freshly chopped mint
12–18 large lettuce leaves
salt and freshly ground black pepper

Serves 6

Cover the rice with water and cook for 40 minutes or more or until the grains have butterflied open and the water is all absorbed. Cover and leave to steam for 10 minutes.

Meanwhile, melt the butter in a pan and slowly soften the onion until lightly golden. Add the peas and almonds and stir-fry together until all the vegetables are cooked. Stir in the mint and rice and check the seasoning.

Blanch the lettuce leaves in boiling, salted water, refresh in iced water, drain and pat dry. Use the leaves to line six well-greased timbales or ramekins, leaving some overhanging the edges. Pack with the rice mixture and fold the overhanging lettuce leaves on top. Cover with foil and bake in a preheated oven at Gas Mark 4/180°C/350°F for 10–15 minutes. FREEZE or unmould and serve.

To serve from frozen: Thaw the timbales at room temperature for 1 hour; then bake as above for 35–45 minutes until piping hot.

SUPPLI WITH RED PEPPER SAUCE

50 g (2 oz) butter
175–250 g (6–8 oz) onion, chopped finely
375 g (12 oz) risotto rice
150 ml (¼ pint) dry white wine
300 ml (½ pint) chicken stock
a pinch of saffron
275 ml (9 fl oz) water
3 tablespoons grated parmesan cheese
3 large eggs (size 1 or 2), beaten lightly
200 g (7 oz) mozzarella cheese, cubed
breadcrumbs for coating
oil for deep-frying
salt and freshly ground black pepper
To serve
1 quantity of Red Pepper Sauce (page 152), heated

Serves 6

Heat the butter in a pan and sauté the onion until soft. Add the rice, stir well and gradually add the wine, stock and saffron. Bring slowly to the boil, season and simmer until nearly all the liquid has evaporated.

Add the water, reduce the heat and continue cooking, uncovered, for 15–20 minutes or until all the liquid has been absorbed and the rice is just tender. Stir in the parmesan cheese and leave to cool.

Carefully stir the lightly beaten eggs into the rice mixture. Put a small tablespoonful of rice mixture into one hand. Add a cube of mozzarella and cover with a little more rice. Shape into a ball, completely enclosing the cheese, and roll the ball in breadcrumbs. Repeat until all the rice and cheese is made into balls.

FREEZE or chill for 30 minutes.

Deep-fry the rice balls in hot oil, three or four at a time, until they are crisp and golden. Drain them well and serve with the hot Red Pepper Sauce.

To serve from frozen: Thaw the rice balls for at least 30 minutes; then deep-fry them, allowing enough time for the mixture to be cooked right through. Test this by breaking one open. Serve with the hot sauce.

ROWANBERRIES

see BERRIES

SAILFISH

see FISH

SALMON

see FISH

SALSIFY

This wonderful winter vegetable is good to have at hand all year round. Scrub, blanch and peel it and store whole, in chunks or as a purée to treat as you would do kohlrabi or any other root vegetable. Cook it from frozen and dress with butter, cream, french dressing or hollandaise sauce, all of which go marvellously with its distinctive flavour. The purée is good whisked into soups and sauces. The tender young shoots and leaves only available in spring make wonderful additions to salads.

SANDWICHES

For gourmets with simple tastes it is worth keeping sandwiches in the freezer. But not to serve as they are. I defrost them in the microwave and then toast or fry them, although they can be toasted from frozen. The great trick is to butter the outside of toasted sandwiches just before serving, and that is where your flavoured butters (page 40–1) will make a huge difference.

Flamboyant and flavoursome versions of French-style cheese sandwiches can all be filled and frozen as they are, to be toasted later straight from the freezer. Try any of the following fillings.

see also
BUTTERS, FLAVOURED
(page 40)
DUCK (page 78)

Beef and Mustard Spread slices of rare roast fillet with French seed mustard and layer with slices of Emmental cheese.

Chicken, Tuna and Anchovy Layer slices of cooked chicken breast with flaked tuna, anchovy fillets and slices of mozzarella or Boursin cheese.

Ham, Aubergine and Tomato Sauté aubergine slices and layer with slices of mozzarella cheese and parma ham and slivers of sun-dried tomato.

Mushroom and Marjoram Cook slices of mushroom and mix with cubes of feta cheese and freshly chopped marjoram.

Pepper and Anchovy Roast and skin red peppers and cut them into strips. Layer them with slices of mozzarella cheese and drained anchovy fillets.

Salami and Olive Layer slices of salami and stuffed olives with grated Gruyère cheese.

Spinach Mix cooked, well-drained spinach with Boursin cheese and cubes of feta cheese. Add crumbled cooked bacon or toasted almond flakes if wished.

SARDINES

see FISH

SAUSAGES

see also
BRIOCHE (page 37)
Chilli Steak, Chorizo and
Bean Casserole (page
29)

Provided that they do not contain much onion, garlic or celery, the new varieties of meaty sausage and the re-created traditional ones are excellent freezer goodies. The long Cumberland sausage and the tomato-beef sausages found in Carlisle's covered market are amongst my favourites. Venison sausages continue to improve as the quality of British venison does. If you see some decent chunky *bratwurst* or

Toulouse sausages about, squirrel them away for later feasts of superior sausage and mash or for slicing into bean stews and the like.

Ordinary cooked bangers freeze perfectly well and make a good addition to soups, stews and pasta sauces. I also like to keep some decent Italian, Polish and French sausages if I have found them and have the space. The chewy Polish *mazurska* is the most useful, reheated simply by plunging into boiling water for a distinctive, extra-fat sausage in a roll; it is also my favourite for adding flavour and texture to *cassoulets* and otherwise disappointing stews of poultry, meat or game.

PEA SOUP WITH SAUSAGE

Serve this soup with hot Parmesan Muffins (page 125) or croûtons.

750 g (1½ lb) split peas
3 cloves
2 litres (3½ pints) cold water
125–175 g (4–6 oz) onion, chopped finely
3 celery sticks, chopped finely
2 large potatoes, peeled and cut into chunks
250 g (8 oz) smoked pork sausage, sliced thinly
a little onion stock or water if necessary
salt and freshly ground black pepper
To serve
croûtons

Serves 6

Put the peas and cloves into a large saucepan with the water and bring slowly to the boil. Remove any scum, reduce the heat, and cover and simmer for 1–1½ hours.

Remove the cloves and add the vegetables and some seasoning. Cover and simmer for a further 45–50 minutes until the vegetables are really tender.

Check the seasoning. Add the sliced sausage to heat through and, if necessary, dilute with a little onion stock or water. FREEZE or serve hot with *croûtons*.

To serve from frozen: Reheat the soup gently until piping hot.

SCALLOPS

Like all shellfish, scallops should be frozen on the same day that they are caught, so make sure you get your fresh scallops from a reliable supplier. If you buy them already frozen, make sure they are in their shells: suppliers tend to cut out and soak scallops to swell them to twice their size before freezing. If you can get fresh scallops, scrub the shells thoroughly and grill under a high heat or in a casserole over the heat for 1–2 minutes until the shells open. Take out the edible parts and trim away any gristly greyish-white membrane from around the central white cushion; then wipe and freeze. Use the same method for your frozen scallops once defrosted.

The delicate, rich and subtle flavour of scallops shouldn't be swamped by too strong a sauce.

see also
BERRIES (page 32)
SPINACH (page 186)
Fricassee of Seafood with Chervil Cream (page 91)
Lobster and Scallop Mousse (page 118)
Seafood Tartlets with Chervil Sauce (page 89)

S

SCALLOP AND CELERIAC SOUFFLÉS

The blend of elegant frag-rances and flavours in this dish gives unexpected combina-tions of luxurious textures to delight the palate. It can also be served as a stunning soufflé for two, in which case bake it for twenty-four minutes in the oven.

8 scallops out of their shells
150 ml (¼ pint) water or white wine
butter for greasing
142 ml (5 fl oz) carton of double cream
2 teaspoons Pernod
250 g (8 oz) celeriac, peeled and sliced thinly
3 eggs, separated, plus 1 extra egg white
salt and freshly ground black pepper

Serves 4

Rinse the scallops free of any remaining grit and cut the white part of each one horizontally into 2 or 3 slender discs, without damaging the bright arc of coral. Put the water or wine in a pan, bring to the boil, add the scallops and boil for 1 minute. Drain quickly, reserving the cooking liquid.

Generously butter four 9 cm (3½-inch) ramekins and place the scallops and corals evenly over the base of each one. Spoon 1 tablespoon of the cream into each one; then put ½ teaspoon of the Pernod around the scallops in each ramekin. Season lightly and leave in a cool place.

Add the remaining cream to the reserved cooking liquid and place in a pan. Cook the celeriac in the liquid until it is very tender. Remove the celeriac and purée it. Reduce the cooking liquid over the heat to about 3 tablespoons, add this to the celeriac purée, salt lightly and mix well.

Put the purée over a bowl of hot water and whisk in the egg yolks. Whisk all the egg whites until stiff and fold in. Divide the mixture evenly between the ramekins. FREEZE or stand the ramekins in a roasting tin. Pour boiling water into the tin to half the depth of the ramekins and bake in a pre-heated oven at Gas Mark 4/180°C/350°F for 10 minutes.

To serve from frozen: Thaw the soufflés for 20 minutes at room temperature and then bake as above.

© *Glynn Christian*

SEA BREAM

see FISH

SHALLOTS

One of the most misunderstood of all ingredients. Shallots are not any small onion; neither, as they insist in Australia, are they spring onions. The shallot is a special member of the onion family that has a gentler, sweeter flavour than the other members. Some think it con-tains a hint of garlic; indeed in some areas in France where it is used, garlic is added to onion but never to shallots. They make a very big difference for the better when making sauces, specially for fish. Thus a good stock of shallots, lightly blan-ched, is one of the most impor-tant things you will ever put into your freezer. After you have blanched them, open freeze them whole or chopped so you can eventually take out just the amount you need, and do make sure you wrap them well to pre-vent them flavouring other foods. A final warning: neither shallots nor onions taste the way they are supposed to taste if you simply toss them around over the heat for a few minutes. Long slow heating until they are really soft stimulates the gentle sweetness of flavour that is proper to good food; anything less is vulgar and your food would be better with none of it.

SHARK

see FISH

SHELLFISH

see individual headings

SLOES

see BERRIES

SMOKED FISH

see also
CROISSANTS (page 73)
PASTA (page 134)
PÂTÉS (page 144)
PISTACHIOS (page 154)
Buckwheat Blinis (page 39)
Potato and Parsley Galettes (page 159)
Smoked Salmon and Dill Ice Cream with Prawns (page 112)
Sole and Vodka Terrine (page 90)

Modern curing and smoking of fish is very much lighter than it used to be and so is more of a flavouring technique than a preserving process. Although I have frozen smoked fish that I have bought soft, a better texture and flavour is usually obtained if the manufacturers froze it in their bigger faster freezers. That said, freezing your own — well-wrapped to avoid it flavouring other frozen foods — is the way to ensure a regular supply of Manx or Craster kippers, decent smoked mackerel, smoked salmon or whatever. I buy the highest quality in some quantity when found and also store plenty of hot-smoked salmon and trout which I have made over tea leaves in my wok.

In a competition that I helped judge for *Taste* magazine, the outright winners were smoked scallops from Skye – perfectly wonderful. Another that is definitely worth freezer space is smoked eel, and the higher the fat content the better. Best in my experience, xenophobic though it may be, is New Zealand smoked eel. It is a classic first course or light supper to combine smoked eel and soft-curded scrambled egg on toast: I prefer to put the eel on the toast and cover it with buttery eggs, rather than the reverse. It is also the basis of the very best pâté, simply blended with at least half its weight of liquid, warm, unsalted butter, a modicum of lemon juice and some dry white vermouth or cognac: once the purée is cool but not set, fold it into quite a lot of lightly whipped cream – at least 300 ml (½ pint) to every 250 g (8 oz) of smoked eel. This technique also works wonderfully well with other smoked fish, particularly smoked salmon. It is the perfect filling for savoury choux buns, warm unsweetened brioches, blanched mangetout or *petites bouchées*, and a spectacular dip for *crudités*. Smoked eel, like most smoked things, also blends remarkably well with toasted walnuts: the two tossed in warm walnut oil, and quickly mixed into shapes of wholewheat pasta with coarsely chopped parsley and a breath of garlic, are exceptional. Smoked eel and melon salad, dressed with a mustardy vinaigrette, is a mixture that excites comment.

You might find smoking and freezing your own fish more than worthwhile. This ensures excellent quality and flavour and allows you to experiment with many different kinds of fish and shellfish. For this you will need a wok – which should include a steaming rack –

heavy-duty cooking foil and equal quantities of a grain (rice, barley, wheat or rye) and brown sugar (about 125 g/4 oz of each) and half that quantity of dry black tea leaves. Line the wok, including the inside of the lid, with the foil, spread over the ingredients and place the steaming rack on top. Place the fish to be smoked on the rack and seal the lid with damp tea towels. If the fish is already cooked, put the wok over a medium heat, leave for five minutes and then reduce the heat to low. Leave for ten minutes; then turn off the heat and leave for five minutes. You can add extra flavour to your food by adding herbs or spices to the smoking mixture. Experiment to find the best ones – I find rosemary and juniper good.

You will even find it possible to cook and smoke your fish at the same time, which is a revelation in flavour, moistness and texture. Make sure the fish is at room temperature for this and sprinkle it with lemon juice and sea salt, or marinate it beforehand. Smoke it for ten minutes over a medium heat, five over a low heat and ten off the heat. Don't use too many pieces of fish at a time or their juices will inhibit the smoking process, and put any extra flavouring next to the foil underneath the smoking mixture.

SMOKED FISH GRATIN WITH SAFFRON AND SMOKED MUSSELS

750 g (1½ lb) smoked haddock fillets
750 g (1½ lb) smoked cod fillets
150 ml (¼ pint) dry white wine
300 ml (½ pint) water
Sauce
250 ml (8 fl oz) dry white wine
250 ml (8 fl oz) fish stock
2 shallots, chopped
a pinch of grated nutmeg
50 g (2 oz) butter
50 g (2 oz) plain flour
a pinch of saffron, soaked in 1 tablespoon warm stock
284 ml (10 fl oz) carton of double cream
a squeeze of lemon juice
105 g (3½ oz) can of smoked mussels, drained
salt and freshly ground black pepper
Topping
175 (6 oz) fine white breadcrumbs
75 g (3 oz) freshly grated parmesan cheese

Serves 6

Cut the fish into 2 cm (1-inch) pieces. Bring the wine and water to the boil. Reduce the heat, add the fish and simmer for 2–3 minutes. Lift out the fish and spread it in a shallow *gratin* dish or individual cocottes. Cool and FREEZE or set aside.

For the sauce, bring the wine, fish stock, shallots and nutmeg slowly to the boil. Simmer until the liquid is reduced by half; then strain it. Melt the butter, stir in the flour and cook for 30 seconds. Gradually add the strained, reduced wine and bring slowly to the boil, stirring constantly to make a smooth sauce. Reduce the heat and stir in the saffron infusion, cream, lemon juice, well-drained mussels and seasoning. FREEZE or spoon this sauce over the fish.

Mix together the breadcrumbs and grated parmesan and

sprinkle this over the sauce. Bake in a preheated oven at Gas Mark 4/180°C/350°F for 25–30 minutes until the top is crisp and golden.

To serve from frozen: Thaw the fish overnight in the refrigerator. Reheat the sauce over a very gentle heat. Assemble and bake as above.

SMOKED TROUT AND COD'S ROE PÂTÉ WITH PISTACHIO BREAD

300 g (10 oz) smoked trout
125 g (4 oz) smoked cod's roe, skinned
125 g (4 oz) cream cheese
5 tablespoons double cream
lemon juice to taste
salt and freshly ground black pepper
Pistachio Bread
3 pitta breads
125 g (4 oz) unsalted butter
2 garlic cloves, chopped finely
3 tablespoons freshly chopped flat-leaf parsley, mint or basil
50 g (2 oz) shelled pistachio nuts, chopped roughly

Serves 6

Carefully remove the skin and bones from the trout and mash or pound the flesh with the cod's roe and cream cheese. Beat in the cream and season to taste with lemon juice and salt and pepper. Using two tablespoons as moulds, shape two small ovals of pâté for each serving. FREEZE or set aside while making the bread.

To make the pistachio bread, make a slit in the side of each pitta pocket. Beat the butter, garlic and herbs together. Add the nuts and spread this mixture over the inside of each pitta. FREEZE or grill the outsides of the breads until they are lightly browned. Open up the pitta breads, cut them into triangles and serve with the pâté.

To serve from frozen: Allow the pâté portions to thaw at room temperature for 40 minutes. Toast the pittas from frozen.

SMOKED SALMON AND SEVRUGA CUSHIONS

These are quick to prepare and equally effective if red caviare is used as a substitute for lavishly expensive sevruga caviare.

375 g (12 oz) smoked salmon, sliced thinly
3 tablespoons sevruga caviare
Garnish
sprigs of dill

Serves 6

Carefully cut 18 strips of smoked salmon measuring 9 × 2 cm (3½ × ¾ inches). Cover them and leave them to one side.

Chop the remaining salmon with a sharp knife into very thin slivers. Press the pieces together and shape into a sausage measuring 2 × 24 cm (¾ × 9½ inches) and wrap carefully in plastic wrap. Freeze until just firm; then unwrap and cut into 18 equal pieces.

Wrap each piece in a slice of the reserved smoked salmon. Rearrange the smoked salmon cushions end-to-end so that they are in the original sausage shape. Rewrap them tightly in plastic wrap and freeze until firm. Pack them into a polythene bag and FREEZE, or arrange three smoked salmon cushions on each plate and spoon sevruga caviare on to the tops. Garnish with sprigs of dill and serve with triangles of brown bread and butter.

To serve from frozen: Thaw the cushions in their wrappings in a cool room for 1 hour. Arrange them on plates, top with the caviare and serve as above.

SMOKED EEL AND TROUT SLICES

Smoked fish freezes well and this is just one simple way of making it into a tasty starter. Serve with soured or single cream flavoured with horseradish cream, or slices of fresh lemon or lime.

1 quantity of Puff Pastry (page 142)
  or 250 g (8 oz) flaky pastry
  1 egg yolk, beaten
142 ml (5 fl oz) carton of soured
  cream
  250 g (8 oz) cream cheese
2 teaspoons horseradish cream
  lemon juice to taste
200 g (7 oz) smoked eel fillets,
  separated into bite-size pieces
200 g (7 oz) smoked trout fillets,
  separated into bite-size pieces
salt and freshly ground black pepper

Serves 6

Roll the pastry into a thin sheet measuring about 20 × 30 cm (8 × 12 inches) and cut in half lengthways. Cut each rectangle across into six; then cut six of the pieces lengthways again. Lift the pastries on to baking trays, brush with the beaten egg yolk and bake in a preheated oven at Gas Mark 7/220°C/425°F for 10–12 minutes until well puffed and golden. Cool and FREEZE or set aside for filling.

Beat the soured cream into the cream cheese with the creamed horseradish, and a little lemon juice and seasoning if needed, to make a stiff piping consistency. FREEZE or pipe or spoon the cheese mixture in two parallel rows along each of the six larger pastries. Top one row with the eel pieces and the other with the trout pieces. Arrange two smaller rectangles of pastry at an angle on top of each row of filling.

To serve from frozen: Thaw the filling overnight in the refrigerator. Thaw the pastries in a preheated oven at Gas Mark 6/200° C /400°F for 5–6 minutes and assemble as above.

CHEESE ROULADE WITH SMOKED HADDOCK AND MUSSELS

A creamy fish filling made from fresh salmon and chopped dill makes an excellent alternative to haddock and mussels.

Cheese Roulade
50 g (2 oz) butter, plus extra for
  greasing
  25 g (1 oz) plain flour
  500 ml (18 fl oz) milk
1 teaspoon Dijon mustard
75 g (3 oz) Gruyère cheese, grated
  4 eggs, separated
salt and freshly ground black pepper
Filling
  1 tablespoon butter
  1 tablespoon plain flour
300 ml (½ pint) single cream or
  milk, plus extra if necessary
500 g (1 lb) smoked haddock,
  cooked and flaked
105 g (3½ oz) can of smoked
  mussels, drained well
2 tablespoons freshly chopped
  parsley
salt and freshly ground black pepper

Serves 6

To make the roulade, melt the butter in a saucepan, stir in the flour and gradually add the milk and mustard. Cook until thick and smooth, stirring continuously. Stir in the grated cheese and cook for 1 minute. Remove from the heat and cool for a minute before beating in the egg yolks, one at a time, and seasoning to taste. Whisk the egg whites until stiff and fold them into the cheese sauce.

Grease and line a 35 × 24 cm (14- × 9½-inch swiss roll tin with non-stick baking paper and spread the soufflé mixture evenly over the tin. Bake in a preheated oven at Gas Mark 3/160°C/325°F for 40 minutes or until golden-brown and set. Turn on to a sheet of non-stick baking paper and peel off the lining paper.

To make the filling, melt the butter in a pan, stir in the flour and cook gently for 30 seconds. Slowly add the cream or milk to make a smooth sauce which has the consistency of thick double cream, adding a little extra cream or milk if the mixture seems too thick. Season well and fold in the haddock, mussels and parsley. Cool slightly and spread over the roulade. Roll up lengthways and FREEZE or serve.

To serve from frozen: Thaw the roulade for 2–3 hours at room temperature, cover loosely with foil and reheat in a preheated oven at Gas Mark 4/180°C/350°F for 20–30 minutes until piping hot.

SMOKED SALMON AND PINK PEPPERCORN ROULADE WITH HERB CREAM

500 g (1 lb) smoked salmon, sliced
1½ teaspoons gelatine
3 tablespoons Armagnac
4 tablespoons single cream
1 teaspoon pink peppercorns
142 ml (5 fl oz) carton of double cream, whipped lightly
Herb Cream
6 tablespoons dry white wine
1 tablespoon freshly chopped dill
142 ml (5 fl oz) carton of single cream
salt and freshly ground black pepper

Serves 6

Lay three-quarters of the salmon in a single layer on a clingfilm covered tray measuring about 30 × 20 cm (12 × 8 inches).

Dissolve the gelatine in the Armagnac. Blend the remaining smoked salmon until smooth and add the single cream and peppercorns and the warm, dissolved gelatine. Fold in the lightly whipped double cream and spread this mousse over the layer of smoked salmon. Roll like a swiss roll from the widest side and FREEZE, or slice into 1 cm (½-inch) circles.

For the sauce, simmer the white wine in a pan to reduce it by half. Cool and stir in the dill. FREEZE or stir in the cream, check the seasoning and serve with the slices of roulade.

To serve from frozen: Thaw the roulade and the sauce in the refrigerator for 2–3 hours. Stir the cream into the sauce, slice the roulade and serve as above.

SMOKED SALMON AND DILL BLINTZES

Creamy baked blintzes make a delicious starter; if you prefer the more traditional version, fry them in hot oil until crisp.

125 g (4 oz) plain flour
2 eggs, beaten
350 ml (12 fl oz) water, plus extra if necessary
125 ml (4 fl oz) oil for frying
butter for greasing
salt
Filling
250 g (8 oz) smoked salmon, chopped finely
250 g (8 oz) garlic and herb cream cheese
2 teaspoons freshly chopped dill
lemon juice to taste
freshly ground black pepper
Topping
284 ml (10 fl oz) carton of single cream

Serves 6 (makes 12)

Sift the flour and a little salt into a bowl and slowly add the beaten eggs and water, stirring continuously to make a smooth batter which has the consistency of single cream. If the batter is too thick, add a little more water. Strain the batter.

Heat a little of the oil in a heavy-based frying pan and pour in a thin layer of batter. The pan must not be too hot as the blintz should set without browning. Cook on one side until the edges curl, turn on to a clean tea towel and continue to cook the remaining batter in the rest of the oil to make 11 more pancakes.

Combine all the filling ingredients and put a spoonful of the mixture on to the cooked side of each blintz. Fold the ends over the filling and roll them up into neat oblong parcels. FREEZE or place them side-by-side in a buttered ovenproof dish and pour over the single cream. Bake in a preheated oven at Gas Mark 6/200°C/400°F for 20 minutes until bubbly and golden.

To serve from frozen: Thaw the blintzes for 1 hour at room temperature, pour over the cream and bake as above.

SMOKED COD'S ROE SAUCE

This versatile sauce has great appeal for serving with a variety of dishes. Its smooth texture makes it perfect as part of an hors-d'oeuvre tray or as an accompaniment to poached or boiled quail's or hen's eggs. Made with a little less cream it is quite delicious enough to eat as a dish on its own with chunks of good bread.

**125 g (4 oz) smoked cod's roe
75 g (3 oz) garlic and herb cream cheese
juice of 1–2 lemons
142 ml (5 fl oz) carton of single cream
freshly ground black pepper**

Serves 6

Cut the roe in half, scoop out the inside with a teaspoon and discard the skin. Blend the roe and cheese together, and gradually beat in the juice of 1 lemon. Stir in the cream and a little pepper and add more lemon juice if necessary. FREEZE or serve.

To serve from frozen: Thaw the sauce in the refrigerator overnight. Beat it well and check the seasoning before serving.

SMOKED MEATS AND POULTRY

As with fish, it is not wise to rely on curing and smoking to be a true preservative process: better to rely on freezing to ensure goodness. Smoked hare and venison are generally good, as are smoked quail. But be very careful with smoked chickens, as they are invariably undercooked. I never eat them unless the flesh has been thoroughly reheated, perhaps in a sauce; that done, there is much to recommend them. I also like to freeze cooked meat that I have smoked over tea in my wok (page 174). But whatever you do, wrap your smoked meat well to prevent it flavouring food already in the freezer.

CARAMEL-CRUSTED BAKED SMOKED PORK LOIN

**1 kg (2 lb) smoked pork loin joint
125 g (4 oz) brown sugar
2 tablespoons Dijon mustard**

Serves 6

Centre the pork on a large square of foil. Sprinkle with half the sugar and wrap the meat loosely in the

see also
*CROISSANTS (page 73)
Avocado and Smoked Chicken Terrine (page 23)*

foil parcel with the join on top. Stand the parcel in a baking tray and bake in a preheated oven at Gas Mark 6/200°C/400°F for 40 minutes.

Open the foil parcel, spread the meat with mustard and press the remaining sugar firmly on top. Continue to bake for a further 20 minutes until the sugar has formed a crisp coating. Cool and FREEZE or serve.

To serve from frozen: Thaw the joint overnight in the refrigerator, slice and serve.

SNAILS

An excess of garlic is a relatively new flavouring for snails, introduced over the past few decades to disguise the fact that most snails sold in France or as French are actually imported under chillingly bad conditions from almost every other country in the world. Butter, parsley and the merest breath of garlic used to be right when snails had a naturally nutty flavour, induced by their diet in vineyards, but pesticides and the like have killed most of them off.

In Britain snails are now being farmed, and rather well. The results are sold frozen and make a good standby, providing you don't buy those which are in 'garlic butter', for they are so strongly flavoured you may as well be eating bread. The good news is that they also sell British snails in other flavours of butter, which let the gastropod's flavours come through. If you can get them, fresh snails, cleaned and ready-prepared, freeze successfully, with or without their shells, to use from frozen.

What I like to do is buy canned snails, crossing my fingers

see also
BUTTERS, FLAVOURED
(page 40)

that they will have some decency of flavour, and freeze them in my own butters: the vodka and black pepper version (page 41) is extra special. Or I freeze them in a cream and mushroom sauce for making into *feuilletés*. To do this I start by reconstituting a mixture of dried *girolles* and *cèpes* in very dry sherry, to which I sometimes also add a few fresh mushrooms tossed in butter. After this has sat around for a few hours I reheat it and add double cream, reduce that until thick and then add a can of snails with a little of their liquid. Once defrosted and reheated this is delicious served as a filling and sauce for hot filo or puff pastry squares.

SOLE

see FISH

S

SORBET

Another 'of course' but beware, for there is great silliness spoken of sorbets. Many make much of sneering at those ordering a pudding, and sit complacent and self-righteous behind a sorbet. Silly things, for virtually all sorbets rely upon heaps of sugar to give them their appeal and texture and are a far worse choice than many a slice of pie. It *is* possible, however, to make very good sorbets indeed, simply by freezing fruit purées, especially those of tropical fruit. Although I no longer do it, a really ripe mango can be simply puréed and frozen with no addition other than a little lime juice for sharpness or a whisked egg white for lightness. My favourite is the tamarillo, the scarlet-skinned egg-shaped fruit which is more and more available. When puréed, the orange flesh is turned a vivid scarlet by the pulp around the seeds, the unpuréed residue of which you may like to strain out. You will be rewarded with a perfectly balanced sweet-sour base to freeze as it is, with or without beaten egg whites. I have added a few drops of raspberry vinegar and crushed, toasted hazelnuts, to great effect. If you use very juicy fruits, like lemon and grapefruit, you may find that you need to add gelatine to stabilise the sorbet.

The texture and sweetness of canned fruits are perfect for making sorbets, particularly in an emergency. The best to look out for are lychees (page 119) and the *mountain, babaco* or *naranchi* varieties of papaya. Those to avoid are strawberries, kiwifruit and passion-fruit, none of which can well. The tech-

see also
BERRIES *(page 32)*
LYCHEES *(page 119)*
MANGOES *(page 121)*

181

nique is the same whichever canned fruit you use. Drain the fruit, liquidise and sieve carefully – you may need to do this several times to get maximum yield. Reduce the syrup over the heat to half its original volume, but do not let it caramelise. Mix the two together, chill and then freeze, stirring from time to time. Once the mixture is mushy in the middle but frozen at the edges, beat it quickly until smooth and even and then fold in the white of an egg. Let the sorbet soften slightly before serving or you will lose the subtleties of flavour. I recommend pears with Maraschino, Kirsch or Poire William and vanilla; apricots with orange rind or preserved ginger, a dash of Crème de Menthe and chopped fresh mint; peaches with chopped, toasted hazelnuts added after the initial freezing; Victoria plums with a squeeze of lemon juice; greenages with tiny chunks of dried apricot and a dash of Mirabelle; and apples flavoured the same way as Apple Strudel Ice Cream (page 109).

Professionals will say that a granita is a sorbet that does not contain Italian meringue. To home cooks it means making a sorbet with only a little sugar to produce a crunchy, granular texture. Slightly sweetened black coffee makes a coffee granita, for instance. Don't make a granita in a *sorbetière* for it will break down the crystals too much and give a smooth finish.

Savoury sorbets come in and out of vogue, but to stay savoury they must contain minimal sugar and thus are more likely to be a granita. These can be made from most things, and are often good served with seafood. Water ice is merely an alternative name for sorbet, although it is also used as a collective term for anything of that ilk.

ELDERFLOWER SORBET

This is a refreshing combination; add a couple of table-spoons of Cointreau if you have no elderflower.

**16 elderflower heads
250 g (8 oz) caster sugar
500 ml (18 fl oz) water, plus 3
tablespoons
rind and juice of 2 lemons
2 teaspoons gelatine
2 egg whites**

Serves 6

Wash the elderflower heads and shake them dry.

Heat the sugar in the 500 ml (18 fl oz) of water with the pared lemon rinds until the sugar dissolves. Add the flowers to the hot syrup and take off the heat. Cover and leave to infuse for 30 minutes. Strain and discard both flowers and lemon rind.

Dissolve the gelatine in the 3 tablespoons of water. Add to the warm syrup and stir well. Add the lemon juice and freeze until mushy.

Turn the sorbet into a chilled bowl and beat until it is light and snowy. Stiffly whisk the egg whites and whisk them into the sorbet; then return to the freezer and FREEZE.

To serve from frozen: Soften the sorbet for 15–20 minutes in the refrigerator before serving.

NECTARINE SORBET

**4 large nectarines
250 ml (8 fl oz) peach juice or water
4 tablespoons icing sugar or to taste
6 tablespoons lemon juice
3 tablespoons Mirabelle**

Serves 6

Peel and halve the nectarines and remove the pips. Chop the flesh into a food processor or blender with the peach juice or water, icing sugar to taste, lemon juice and eau-de-vie and process to a purée. Add more sugar if needed. Turn into a metal tray and freeze for about 30 minutes until just beginning to set.

Remove the sorbet, place in a chilled bowl and beat until smooth. Return to the freezer for a further 45–50 minutes. Repeat the process of beating 3 times; then FREEZE.

To serve from frozen: Soften the sorbet for 15–20 minutes in the refrigerator before serving.

SORBET DE BEAUMES DE VENISE

**175 g (6 oz) sugar
6 tablespoons water
juice of 2 lemons
650 ml (22 fl oz) Muscat de
Beaumes de Venise
2 egg whites**

Serves 6

Dissolve the sugar in the water. Add the lemon juice, bring to the boil and boil for 2 minutes. Stir in the wine and make up to 1 litre (1¾ pints) with cold water. Freeze until mushy.

Beat or whisk the semi-frozen sorbet to break down the ice crystals. Whisk the egg whites until soft peaks form; then whisk them into the half-frozen syrup and

S

FREEZE, stirring two or three times until the sorbet is solid.

To serve from frozen: Soften the sorbet for 15–20 minutes in the refrigerator before serving.

PEACH SORBET WITH CHAMPAGNE

100 g (3½ oz) sugar
125 ml (4 fl oz) water
5 large ripe peaches
juice of 1 lemon
1 large egg white (size 1 or 2)
To serve
champagne

Serves 6

Dissolve the sugar in the water over a gentle heat. Allow the syrup to cool.

Drop the peaches into a large pan of boiling water. Leave for 30 seconds until the skins are loose and rinse them under cold water. Remove all the skin, halve and remove the stones.

Purée the peach flesh and the syrup together until smooth. Add the lemon juice and freeze until solid at the edges.

Whisk the egg white until stiff. Beat the sorbet thoroughly and fold in the egg white. Return to the freezer and FREEZE.

To serve from frozen: Transfer the sorbet from the freezer to the refrigerator about 10 minutes before it is needed. Place a large scoop in each of six tall glasses and top up with champagne.

TEA SORBET

Tea sorbets are wonderfully refreshing and can be made with dozens of different flavours. Rose Pouchong, Earl Grey and Jasmine tea make the most elegant versions, and the wide variety of fruit-flavoured teas the most sensational flavours. You could also experiment with a mixture of half tea and half fruit juice – Ceylon tea with pineapple juice is good.

Match your sorbets to your menu – jasmine tea sorbet with lychee sorbet to follow Chinese food, for instance – and serve it with style. Perhaps as part of a carousel of tea ice creams (page 108) and sorbets served on top of a purée of fruit, or as the centrepiece of a colourful arrangement of exotic fruits that have been marinated separately in a suitable liqueur.

600 ml (1 pint) boiling water
25 g (1 oz) dry tea leaves
150 g (5 oz) sugar
lemon juice (optional)
1–2 egg whites

Serves 4–6

Pour the boiling water on to the tea leaves and leave to infuse for 5–7 minutes.

Strain the tea well and make it up to 600 ml (1 pint) with more water. Add most of the sugar, and a little lemon juice if you are using unperfumed tea. Leave to cool and then taste and add the rest of the sugar if necessary (it will taste much less sweet when frozen).

Pour the liquid into a suitable container and freeze until it is set at the edges and mushy in the centre. Beat it well until it is smooth and even. Whisk the egg white(s), fold them in and then FREEZE.

To serve from frozen: Soften the sorbet for 30 minutes in the refrigerator before serving.

© Glynn Christian

AVOCADO AND CUCUMBER SORBET

500 g (1 lb) soft, ripe avocado flesh
250 g (8 oz) peeled cucumber
4 tablespoons lime juice
1–3 tablespoons sugar
salt

Serves 4–6

Put the avocado into a blender or food processor, ensuring that you have scraped as much as possible of the dark-green lining of the skins into the mixture. Add the cucumber, lime juice and enough sugar to make it slightly sweeter than preferred (it will be less sweet when frozen). Add salt to taste and process until smooth.

Spoon the mixture into a suitable container and freeze until it is firm. Beat until it is smooth and even in texture and then FREEZE.

To serve from frozen: Soften the sorbet for 30 minutes in the refrigerator before serving.

© *Glynn Christian*

TOMATO AND ORANGE SORBET

2 medium–large oranges
1 medium–large lemon
1.2 litres (2 pints) tomato juice
2 teaspoons Worcestershire sauce
2 egg whites

Serves 4–6

Peel one of the oranges and reserve the peel. Chop both of the oranges and the lemon. Put them into the tomato juice in a pan and slowly bring to the boil; then simmer for about 5 minutes. Leave to cool.

Strain the liquid, squeeze the fruit and add the fruit juices to the liquid. Leave until cold; then stir in the Worcestershire sauce.

Freeze the liquid in a suitable container until it starts to set around the edges. Whisk it well until smooth and even. Repeat this process several times for an even texture. Whisk the egg whites until firm and fold them into the mixture; then FREEZE.

To serve from frozen: Soften the sorbet in the refrigerator for 30 minutes before serving. Cut the reserved orange rind into fine strips, blanch and use to garnish each serving.

© *Glynn Christian*

SOUP

A popular thing to buy frozen these days, and many of them are of high quality, but they do take space. Far better to cook down your vegetables in butter or oil in the usual way, purée and strain them, and then freeze them like that. Diluted with milk, stock or cooking liquids, perhaps even mixed one with another, they offer a much larger choice from very much smaller space. Of course if you do have space, tuck away a gourmet home-made soup or two, to reheat straight from the freezer for a quick and stylish meal.

S

If you have a warm kitchen, your spices will soon lose their vitality, or worse, their essential oils will oxidise and go off. Freezing spices for a couple of months, especially those which have already been ground, will prevent this happening, and they are easy to use straight from the freezer. Naturally the more rare or expensive a spice the more worthwhile it is to take care. Ground caradamom is perhaps the prime candidate; far more arcane is *ras-el-hanout*, the world's ultimate mixed spice. It is a speciality of Morocco and should have dozens of ingredients, including rosebuds, saffron, cloves, cumin, cubeb, ginger, mace, allspice, grains of paradise, bay and more. The authentic version often includes marijuana and cantharides, the Spanish fly, which turns out not to be so apocryphal after all.

I also find it more than useful to have a store of ice cubes flavoured with fresh ginger (page 103); these are invaluable for adding to hot dishes or cold drinks.

see also
BUTTERS, FLAVOURED
(page 40)
HERBS (page 103)
PASTRY (page 140)
POTATOES (page 158)
SMOKED FISH (page 174)

Sinfully sweet little Chinese pastries that look wonderful arranged in concentric circles on a round glass plate. Serve them with strong coffee or a well-chilled oriental fruit salad.

**250 g (8 oz) plain flour
a pinch of salt
1 teaspoon ground ginger
50 g (2 oz) butter, chilled and grated
sifted cornflour for rolling
oil for deep-frying
250 ml (8 fl oz) golden syrup
2 tablespoons water
3 tablespoons lemon juice**

Makes 80

Sieve the flour, salt and ground ginger together. Cut in the butter until the mixture is crumbly. Add cold water, a little at a time, stirring it with a round-bladed knife to form a smooth, firm dough. Chill for 30 minutes.

Roll the dough to a paper-thin sheet on a board covered with sifted cornflour and, using a sharp knife, cut the dough into 10 × 5 cm (4- × 2-inch) rectangles. Twist each rectangle in the middle to form a bow tie shape.

Heat the oil and deep-fry the pastries three or four at a time until they are golden. Lift them out and drain them while frying the remaining pastries.

FREEZE the pastries or mix together the syrup, water and lemon juice and heat gently. Dip the bow ties into the syrup one at a time; then leave them to drain on a rack over a tray. Allow them to cool completely and cover them well with an airtight wrapping until ready to serve.

To serve from frozen: Thaw the bow ties for 1—2 hours at room temperature, dip them in the warm syrup and continue as above.

SPINACH

Spinach is, of course, invaluable in the freezer. It is one of the few green vegetables that can be cooked completely before freezing as it keeps both its flavour and texture on reheating. One way I like to serve it is as a base for scallops that have been steamed (using wine as the steaming liquid) with chopped shallot, bay, lemon rind, garlic, parsley and saffron; this is surrounded by a sauce made from the steaming liquid, strained greek yogurt and butter.

If you want to freeze spinach in made-up dishes, particularly any that involve the use of pastry, it is a good idea to drain it of all its moisture first. To do this successfully, tear the spinach into pieces, layer it with salt in a colander and leave for a couple of hours. Once it has been rinsed and squeezed it won't produce any further moisture.

see also
POTATOES (page 158)
SANDWICHES (page 171)
Lentil and Spinach Lasagne (page 137)

SPINACH AND PINE KERNEL ROULADE

1 quantity of Herb Roulade mixture (page 104)
250 g (8 oz) cooked spinach
25 g (1 oz) butter
300 g (10 oz) garlic and herb cream cheese
25 g (1 oz) pine kernels, toasted
1 teaspoon lemon juice
salt and freshly ground black pepper

Serves 6

Make up the herb roulade mixture, bake and turn out as directed on page 104. Peel off the lining paper.

Meanwhile, stir-fry the spinach and butter over a moderate heat until all the liquid has evaporated and the butter is absorbed. Cool slightly and stir in the rest of the ingredients.

Spread the spinach mixture over the roulade and roll up along the longest edge. FREEZE or reheat the roulade in the oven at Gas Mark 4/180°C/350°F for 10–15 minutes or until piping hot. Serve with a fresh tomato sauce or Red Pepper Sauce (page 152).

To serve from frozen: Thaw the roulade at room temperature for 1 hour and reheat as above.

SPINACH SOUFFLÉ(S) WITH BLUE CHEESE AND WALNUTS

You can make a cauliflower soufflé in the same way: use one small cauliflower broken into sprigs and cook it in a little boiling, salted water until quite soft.

175 g (6 oz) spinach, chopped
50 g (2 oz) walnuts, chopped finely
125–150 g (4–5 oz) Stilton cheese, cut into 1 cm (½-inch) cubes
50 g (2 oz) butter, plus extra for frying and greasing
3 tablespoons plain flour
375 ml (13 fl oz) milk, heated
4 eggs, separated, plus 1 extra egg white
50 g (2 oz) grated Cheddar cheese
salt and freshly ground black pepper

Serves 2 as a main dish or 6–8 as a starter

Wash and dry the spinach well; then stir-fry in a knob of butter until it has softened and all the moisture has evaporated.

Generously butter a 1-litre (1¾-pint) soufflé dish or six to eight small ones and sprinkle with the chopped nuts. Place the cubes of cheese in the bottom of the dish or dishes.

Melt the butter, stir in the flour

and gradually stir in the hot milk, stirring continuously to make a smooth, thick sauce. Take off the heat and beat in the egg yolks, one at a time. Add the grated cheese, spinach and seasoning to taste. Whisk all the egg whites with a pinch of salt until stiff and fold them into the spinach mixture. Turn into the prepared dish or dishes and FREEZE, or bake in a preheated oven at Gas Mark 6/200°C/400°F for 35–40 minutes until firm on the outside(s) but still soft and creamy in the centre(s).

To serve from frozen: Thaw the soufflé(s) for 20 minutes at room temperature; then bake as above.

SQUASH

see PUMPKIN

SQUID

Of the family of cephalopods it is only the squid and cuttlefish about which you need bother; octopus requires far too much time and effort if you can't buy it ready prepared, and you usually can't.

Squid is often sold frozen and thus can be stored like that. Otherwise it must be frozen within two to three hours of catching or once cooked. Either way you almost certainly have to prepare it yourself.

First you remove the tentacles, beak and innards in one, by grabbing behind the knob which holds the eyes and pulling gently. Whatever else is left inside must also be removed, including the squid's long transparent quill or the cuttlefish's thicker backbone; the latter may be dried and handed on

to any cage bird of your acquaintance. Then you cut the tentacles free just where they all join together and rinse the tube well. You can remove the purplish outer skin as well if you want.

Squid and cuttlefish cook very quickly indeed and they can be cooked from frozen, but they will shrink and weep if you cook them past the proper stage. A quick fry-up in garlic flavoured olive oil suits thickly cut rings or slices of small ones; bigger ones might have the rings or pieces dipped in batter for deep-frying, but I think this disguises the flavour. Perhaps better is to use the rings of fresh squid to finish soups and the sort of quick cream or tomato sauce which you would ladle upon pasta.

SWEETBREADS

Lamb's sweetbreads are smaller, cheaper and far more easily available frozen than the more admired calves' sweetbreads. The defrosting process can be combined with the soaking which is necessary to ensure all blood has been dissolved away. Incidentally, the usual advice to remove all membranes after the initial blanching is a waste of time. Certainly, get rid of any grey knots of fat or gristle, but the transparent membranes help keep the sweetbreads in shape and so have an important part to play. Calves' sweetbreads may require more care but I leave them to restaurants; the preparation is much more complex and they are hard to find.

Sweetbreads make a wonderful salad, and here your store of blanched pepper strips (page 150) are invaluable. I

see also
Pâté of Lamb's Sweetbreads and Pernod (page 147)
Venison Pâté (page 197)

warm through cooked sweetbreads in double cream and vermouth, at which stage they can be frozen as they are, and serve them in their sauce sprinkled with chopped parsley and grated lemon rind and surrounded by strips of red, green, white and yellow pepper.

SWEETBREADS WITH CHESTNUTS AND MUSHROOMS

Accompany this dish with an undressed salad of very young spinach leaves and curly endive. It can be served in smaller portions to serve six to eight as a starter.

500 g (1 lb) lamb's sweetbreads
50 g (2 oz) dried mushrooms
50 g (2 oz) dried chestnuts
lemon juice
25 g (1 oz) butter
2 shallots, chopped finely
1 tablespoon plain flour
150 ml (¼ pint) dry white vermouth
142 ml (5 fl oz) carton of double cream
salt and freshly ground black pepper

Serves 4

Soak the sweetbreads in 3 or 4 changes of water for at least 4 hours. Add a little salt to the water as it gets clearer to draw out any remaining blood.

Rinse the dried mushrooms and then put them into a pan with the chestnuts. Cover with warm water and allow them to soak for 30 minutes.

Bring the mushrooms and chestnuts slowly to the boil and simmer gently for 20–30 minutes until they are tender and only a little liquid remains. Leave to cool.

Put the sweetbreads into a pan with water and a squeeze of lemon juice. Bring slowly to the boil, simmer for 3 minutes and then drain and cool under running cold water. Remove any large lumps of membrane, leaving on the thin coating that holds the sweetbreads in shape. Drain and sprinkle with lemon juice.

Melt the butter in a pan and cook the shallot until softened but not brown. Add the flour, cook for 2 minutes and then stir in the vermouth. Bring to the boil, stirring, until thick and smooth. Add the mushrooms and chestnuts with any remaining liquid, the cream and seasoning. Cook for 2–3 minutes; then stir in the sweetbreads. FREEZE or lower the heat and simmer to warm through gently.

To serve from frozen: Thaw overnight in the refrigerator and reheat gently.

© *Glynn Christian*

SWEETBREADS WITH MUSTARD AND TARRAGON

1.25 – 1.5 kg (3–3½ lb) lamb's
sweetbreads
½ teaspoon salt
75 g (3 oz) unsalted butter
Sauce
125 g (4 oz) butter
1 tablespoon freshly chopped
tarragon
2 teaspoons plain flour
300 ml (½ pint) vegetable or
chicken stock
2 tablespoons coarse-grain mustard
150 ml (¼ pint) dry white wine
284 ml (10 fl oz) carton of double
cream
1 yellow pepper, grilled, peeled and
sliced thinly
salt and freshly ground black pepper

Serves 6

Soak the sweetbreads for up to 2 hours in plenty of water to which the salt has been added.

Drain the sweetbreads, transfer them to a saucepan of clean water and bring slowly to the boil. Hold them just below boiling for 30 seconds; then plunge the sweetbreads into cold water. Pull off any thicker membranes and gristle but not the fine skin that holds the sweetbreads together. Dry them thoroughly.

Heat the unsalted butter in a large frying pan until really hot. Add the sweetbreads and sauté them quickly over a high heat until they are just beginning to colour and are lightly cooked. Drain them well. FREEZE or keep them warm while making the sauce.

To make the sauce, add the butter to the frying pan and stir in the tarragon; cover and let it sweat over a very low heat for about 30 seconds. Stir in the flour and cook for a further 30 seconds before gradually adding the stock. Bring slowly to the boil, stirring constantly, to make a smooth sauce. Add the mustard, wine and salt and pepper and simmer together for 1–2 minutes. Add the cream and pepper strips and FREEZE, or stir in the sweetbreads and reheat until the dish is piping hot.

To serve from frozen: Thaw the sweetbreads at room temperature for 45 minutes. Gently reheat the sauce, whisk it well and check the seasoning. Add the sweetbreads and heat through until piping hot.

SWEET POTATOES

Only bother with the more seasonal orange-fleshed ones, for their appearance makes any trouble worthwhile. They generally take less time to cook than ordinary potatoes: store them mashed so you can add rum, cream, butter and spices and then serve them hot like that, or souffléed.

SWORDFISH

see FISH

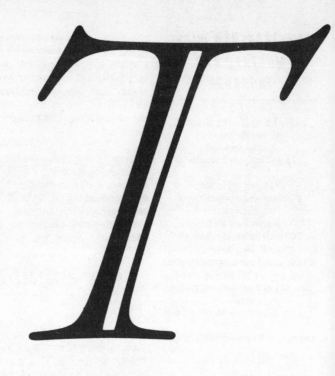

Tea
Tomatoes
Truffles
Turnips

TAYBERRIES

see BERRIES

TEA

I keep my most expensive teas, such as Formosa Oolongs, Yunnans and the finest Darjeelings, in the refrigerator. For the freezer I make fabulous sorbets (page 183) and ice creams (page 108) with tea, but don't be misled by other recipes which don't use enough. You need a good 25 g (1 oz) of tea leaves or tea bags per 600 ml (1 pint) of liquid to make a flavour worth eating.

see also
ICE CREAM (page 107)
SMOKED FISH (page 174)
SMOKED MEATS AND POULTRY (page 179)
Custard-based Ice Cream (page 108)
Tea Sorbet (page 183)

TOMATOES

Only freeze them if you grow them or buy them really cheaply, and then only if you cook them down and reduce the flesh to a concentrated, strained purée and store that in small amounts, for adding to soups and stews, sauces and doughs; quite the best and proper thing to use on top of pizza too. If I freeze tomato purée I add no flavourings of any kind, so I can use it more flexibly. But flavoured tomato sauces of all kinds are invaluable in the freezer, and they can be reheated from frozen.

see also
BUTTERS, FLAVOURED (page 40)
COURGETTES (page 64)
PASTA (page 134)
PEPPERCORNS, FRESH (page 149)
PUMPKIN (page 160)
Tomato and Orange Sorbet (page 184)
Tomato and Sherry Sauce (page 21)
Tomato Cream (page 155)

TOMATO COULIS

This is the ideal sauce to accompany grilled foods or to use as a base for poached eggs or fish. If you like a spicier mixture, cook a de-seeded chilli with it. If you prefer a more delicate result, sieve the

sauce and thin it with equal quantities of single cream. For a richer sauce, boil hard with some olive oil until the mixture emulsifies.

1 kg (2 lb) ripe tomatoes, peeled, de-seeded and chopped
1 tablespoon tomato purée (optional)
1–2 garlic cloves, chopped finely
a pinch of sugar
salt and freshly ground black pepper

Serves 6

Simmer all the ingredients together over a gentle heat for 15–20 minutes until most of the liquid has evaporated. FREEZE or serve.

To serve from frozen: Reheat the sauce gently in a saucepan until piping hot.

TOMATO AND CORIANDER SAUCE

Use whatever tomatoes are ripest, reddest and bursting with flavour to make this richly coloured sauce. Serve it hot with grilled meat or fish, hot poultry, pasta or risotto.

75 g (3 oz) butter
3 shallots, chopped finely
3 garlic cloves, chopped finely
1 teaspoon coarsely crushed coriander seeds
6 tomatoes, chopped roughly
1½ tablespoons tomato purée
5 tablespoons sherry vinegar
175 ml (6 fl oz) dry white wine
450 ml (¾ pint) water
3 tablespoons soy sauce

Serves 6

Heat the butter in a pan and gently sauté the chopped shallots, garlic and crushed coriander until the onion is soft. Add the tomatoes and tomato purée and stir well. Add the vinegar and simmer together for 3–4 minutes; then add the wine and water. Cover and cook gently for 20 minutes.

Sieve the sauce and stir in the soy sauce to taste. FREEZE or serve at once.

To serve from frozen: Thaw the sauce over a gentle heat until piping hot.

VEGETABLE CREAM SAUCE

This is perfect with pasta, grilled meats or fish.

2 tablespoons oil
30 g (1¼ oz) butter
250–275 g (8–10 oz) onion, chopped finely
4 celery sticks, chopped
2 garlic cloves, chopped finely
3 carrots, chopped finely
750 g (1½ lb) ripe tomatoes, peeled and de-seeded
2 tablespoons tomato purée
200 ml (7 fl oz) dry white wine
2 tablespoons freshly chopped parsley
a pinch of sugar
142 ml (5 fl oz) carton of double cream
salt and freshly ground black pepper

Serves 6

Heat the oil and butter in a pan and soften the onion, celery, garlic and carrots over a gentle heat, stirring frequently. Add the tomatoes, tomato purée, wine, parsley, sugar and seasoning. Stir well and simmer gently, uncovered, for 1 hour.

Check the seasoning and then purée the sauce. Sieve and stir in the cream. FREEZE or reheat and serve.

To serve from frozen: Thaw the sauce over a gentle heat until piping hot.

TROUT

see FISH

TRUFFLES

Purists might sniff, but they shouldn't. If ever you get a fresh truffle, freezing is quite the best way to preserve its mysterious flavour and aroma, some of which is lost when they are bottled or canned. I learned the trick from an eighty-year-old couple in a Provençal hill-top village, who had been collecting and preparing truffles most of their lives. If they say it is the best way to keep truffles, that is good enough for me. There is sometimes an escape of juice when the truffle defrosts, and their advice was thus always to defrost the truffle in a bath of good, but not powerful, olive oil. You can add them to hot dishes frozen, although you won't get their full benefit.

In case you don't know, slicing truffle and using it to decorate food is a load of old cobblers, unless the truffle has sat with that or other food for a good period of time. Truffle has little flavour of its own, but magically stimulates other foods into flavours they did not know they had. When truffles were much more common, truffled turkey was made by stuffing a turkey with a pound or more of them, wrapping the turkey in a damp sack and burying that in the garden for some days. The dark dankness spurred the truffles into fulsomeness, and the time allowed the truffle and turkey to create something quite new. Now we have fewer and they are so much more expensive, but we would do well to follow that basic pattern. Even if you have but one truffle to flav-

T

our a turkey or chicken, and that has come from a bottle, take time to do it properly: push the slices of truffle between the flesh and the skin, wrap in damp greaseproof paper and then in foil, and keep in the refrigerator for at least three days before cooking.

CHAMPAGNE AND TRUFFLE PATTIES WITH CHAMPAGNE SAUCE

1 kg (2 lb) boneless, rindless
shoulder of pork
250 g (8 oz) unsmoked back bacon
fat
2 teaspoons coarsely crushed
coriander seeds
1 ½ teaspoons freshly chopped
thyme
1 tablespoon freshly chopped
parsley
½ teaspoon coarsely crushed black
peppercorns
1 large egg (size 1 or 2), beaten
lightly
150 ml (¼ pint) dry champagne
25 g (1 oz) truffles, diced
butter for frying
salt
Champagne Sauce
75 g (3 oz) unsalted butter
a sprig of fresh thyme
1 shallot, chopped
2 teaspoons plain flour
250 ml (8 fl oz) champagne
250 ml (8 fl oz) chicken stock
284 ml (10 fl oz) carton of double
cream
1 truffle, cut into thin strips
(optional)
salt and freshly ground white pepper

Serves 6

Mince the pork and bacon fat together using a medium-gauge mincing blade. Mix in the coriander, thyme, parsley, peppercorns, a little salt and the lightly beaten egg. Gradually stir in the champagne and fold in the diced truffle. Shape into small 'burgers' and chill for 2–3 hours. FREEZE or

sauté in butter until golden on both sides and cooked through.

To make the sauce, melt the butter in a saucepan and gently sauté the thyme and shallot until the shallot is tender. Stir in the flour. Cook gently for 30 seconds; then gradually stir in the champagne and stock. Bring to the boil and reduce the liquid by half. Strain, stir in the cream and seasoning and FREEZE, or reheat until piping hot. Add the strips of truffle, if used, and pour the sauce on to six warm plates. Top with the patties and serve with *pommes frites allumettes*.

To serve from frozen: Sauté the patties in butter until golden; then bake for 25–30 minutes in a preheated oven at Gas Mark 4/180°C/350°F. Reheat the sauce over a gentle heat, add the truffle, if used, and serve as above.

TUNA

see FISH

TURNIPS

It is worth giving freezer space only to one type of turnip, the tiny, purple-blushed variety which can be boiled or steamed whole. If you have some, look in Middle Eastern and Eastern Mediterranean cookery books for interesting ways to use them. My favourite way is to turn them with a little chopped onion in a mixture of olive oil and butter, cover with orange juice and simmer without a lid until a syrup is formed, which takes the same amount of time as the turnips do to cook. Then add fresh dates which have been halved and stoned, warm them through and serve with a dash of cinnamon and coarsely chopped parsley.

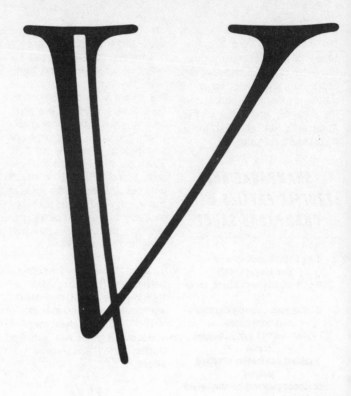

Veal
Venison
Vine Leaves

VEAL

Good quality veal, which should be moist, very pale pink in colour and have finely grained flesh, is worth freezing. It will need careful cooking on thawing to avoid it drying out. Moist cooking methods – covered frying, braising, stewing, casseroling or baking in pies – are preferable for this reason. Its delicate flavour is perfectly complemented by butter and cream.

see also
CITRUS FRUITS (page 62)

BAKED TARRAGON VEAL

4 tablespoons olive oil
finely grated rind and juice of 1 lime
18 thin slices of stewing veal
2 garlic cloves, chopped finely
4 tablespoons freshly chopped tarragon
1 tablespoon freshly chopped parsley
300 ml (½ pint) dry white wine
250 g (8 oz) Jarlsberg cheese, grated
salt and freshly ground black pepper

Serves 6

Mix together half the oil and the lime rind and juice and brush the mixture over the meat. Leave for 1 hour at room temperature.

Mix the remaining oil with the garlic, tarragon and parsley and spread over the meat slices. Lay them, overlapping each other, in a large, shallow, ovenproof dish. Pour round the marinade and wine. Cover and bake in a preheated oven at Gas Mark 3/160°C/325°F for 1 hour. Cool and FREEZE or continue to bake for 10–15 minutes until the veal is tender. Uncover the meat, season, sprinkle it with the grated cheese and serve.

To serve from frozen: Reheat the meat and continue cooking in a preheated oven at Gas Mark 3/160°C/325°F for around 45 minutes. Uncover and continue as above.

STRIPS OF VEAL WITH ARTICHOKES IN A TOMATO SAUCE

1.25 kg (3 lb) stewing veal
4 tablespoons olive oil
25 g (1 oz) butter
400 g (13 oz) cooked artichoke hearts
175–250 g (6–8 oz) onion, chopped finely
2 garlic cloves, chopped finely
1 kg (2 lb) tomatoes, peeled, de-seeded and chopped
2 tablespoons tomato purée
1 teaspoon dried oregano
125 ml (4 fl oz) chicken stock
250 ml (8 fl oz) dry white wine
40 g (1½ oz) freshly grated parmesan cheese
3 tablespoons freshly chopped parsley
salt and freshly ground black pepper

Serves 6

Cut the veal across the grain into strips about the size of a little finger. Heat a little of the oil and butter together in a large frying pan and stir-fry the meat in six to eight batches over a brisk heat until lightly browned. Remove and set aside.

Thickly slice the artichoke hearts and stir-fry them in a little more of the oil and butter for 30 seconds. Add them to the meat.

Add the onion to the frying pan with the rest of the oil and butter, and sauté it until soft. Add the garlic, tomatoes, tomato purée, oregano, stock and seasoning. Simmer together for about 10 minutes. Add the wine and cook for a further 15 minutes.

Return the meat and artichokes to the sauce and simmer over a gentle heat for 30 minutes. FREEZE or continue to cook for a further 15 minutes until tender.

Sprinkle with the cheese and parsley and serve with risotto.

To serve from frozen: Reheat over a very gentle heat until piping hot. Add the cheese and parsley and serve.

VENISON

see also
SMOKED MEATS AND
POULTRY (page 179)

Modern farmed venison freezes outstandingly well for at least twelve months, and indeed in some areas is only available like that. Otherwise it is best to get your butcher to joint it; and wrap it well before freezing, protecting the bones with extra foil. Anyone with the slightest interest in being healthy or modern, or both, should have worked out by now that venison is the world's healthiest red meat. No longer a rank gamy meat riddled with the flavours of unidentifiable wild fodder and shot full of fear-induced chemical during the hunt, farmed venison has flesh as delicate and silken as the best fillet steak, closely grained and well-behaved in the kitchen.

Generally you treat farmed venison exactly the same as you would any excellent beef cut, but with even more care. The most popular cuts are those suited to grilling or frying: steaks, chops and escalopes should be cooked under or over the heat until pink, and then left to one side of the heat until they reach the desired state. If this is done out of the pan you will have every opportunity to make extraordinarily good pan sauces, particularly if you have cooked in unsalted butter. My favourite starts with dried *cèpes*, more easily available from Italy as *porcini*. These are reconstituted by simmering in sherry, madeira or red wine for 10–20 minutes; then the mushrooms are removed and the liquid reduced furiously until it is little more than a few teaspoonfuls. This is whisked into voluptuousness with knobs of chilled butter before the mushrooms are returned.

Joints of venison which have virtually no fat should never be left in the oven beyond a state of pinkness or they will desiccate. Roasting for 10–15 minutes per 500 g (1 lb) (according to the temperature of the meat when put into the oven and its thickness) at Gas Mark 7/220°C/425°F followed by a 15–45 minutes rest to complete the cooking, is the recommended method. The slower method of cooking, at about Gas Mark 4/180°C/350°F, is felt by some to be more reliable, but if the joint is boneless it requires 30–45 minutes per 500 g (1 lb) in the oven, plus an equally long rest before carving. This sitting time continues the cooking without any chance of drying out.

Most of all, modern farmed venison should not be put into strongly flavoured marinades. These were formerly used with wild venison both to tenderise the flesh and to reduce the rankness of flavour; if you were to do this to farmed venison you would ambush its flavour altogether. However, a little marinating never hurt anything, so if you do marinate it, don't use onion and use a minimum of any acid, including wine and other alcohols, and no more of any liquid than is needed to coat rather than cover the meat.

PEPPERED VENISON WITH ORANGE

A splendid dish for cold weather eating.

2 tablespoons vegetable oil
175 g (6 oz) back bacon rashers,
chopped roughly
8 shallots, chopped finely
3 tablespoons tomato purée
500 ml (18 fl oz) dry white wine
750 ml (1 ¼ pints) beef stock
2 garlic cloves, crushed
1 tablespoon juniper berries,
crushed
a *bouquet garni*
grated rind of 1 lemon
grated rind and segmented flesh of 3
oranges
2 kg (4½ lb) boneless shoulder of
venison, cut into 4 cm (1½-inch)
cubes
2 tablespoons coarsely crushed
black peppercorns
2 teaspoons plain flour
salt

Serves 6

Heat 1 tablespoon of the oil in a heavy-based casserole and gently sauté the bacon and shallots for about 8 minutes. Stir in the tomato purée; then gradually add the wine, half the stock, the garlic, juniper, *bouquet garni*, lemon and orange rind and salt. Bring to the boil, stirring frequently, and then simmer for 15 minutes.

Roll the venison in the crushed peppercorns. Heat the remaining oil in a frying pan and sear the cubes, a batch at a time. Add the venison to the casserole. Sprinkle the flour over the frying pan and cook for 20 seconds. Slowly whisk in the rest of the stock and then add this gravy to the casserole.

Cover the casserole and cook in a preheated oven at Gas Mark 6/200°C/400°F for about 1 hour or until the meat is just tender. FREEZE or add the orange pieces, check the seasoning and continue to cook, uncovered, for 15–20 minutes before serving.

To serve from frozen: Thaw the casserole for 1–2 hours at room temperature; then reheat in a preheated oven at Gas Mark 6/200°C/400°F for 30–40 minutes until piping hot and continue as above.

VENISON PÂTÉ

This pâté is perfect for any momentous occasion. Serve it in thin slices with a variety of sharp jellies and mustards; perhaps with a jelly of rowan-berries, a few raspberries and a creamy horseradish sauce.

Because of the long cooking time, extra flavour must be added to the venison, so here the rules are broken and a robust marinade is used.

500 g (1 lb) lean stewing venison,
cubed
300 ml (½ pint) strong red wine
125 g (4 oz) onion
2–4 garlic cloves, chopped
125 g (4 oz) orange, de-pipped and
cut into pieces
8 juniper berries
12 black peppercorns
3 bay leaves
2 blades of mace
2 teaspoons ground cinnamon
½ teaspoon grated nutmeg
500 g (1 lb) lamb's sweetbreads
whisky or brandy for marinating
375 g (12 oz) streaky bacon
½ teaspoon freshly ground rosemary
1 teaspoon dried thyme
500 g (1 lb) chicken livers
250 g (8 oz) belly of pork, chopped
2 tablespoons whisky
50 g (2 oz) ground almonds
25 g (1 oz) shelled pistachio nuts,
skins removed
fresh or preserved vine leaves for
wrapping
oil for greasing

Makes about 1.25 kg (3 lb)

Place the cubed venison in a bowl and add the wine, onion, garlic, orange pieces, juniper, peppercorns, bay, mace, cinnamon and nutmeg. Leave to marinate for 24 hours.

Soak the sweetbreads in at least 3 changes of water for 3–4 hours to draw out any blood. Blanch them for a few minutes in boiling water and then carefully remove any traces of fat, gristle or membrane, but keeping them whole. Leave them to marinate in a little whisky or brandy.

Cut the bacon into strips or cubes and add it to the venison mixture. Put the mixture in a pan, cover and cook gently until the venison is tender and the bacon has started to melt. Drain the liquid into another pan, add the rosemary and thyme and reduce it over a gentle heat to just under 150 ml (¼ pint).

Liquidise the venison mixture, keeping some texture. Purée the trimmed chicken livers and fold them into the venison mixture, with the pork. Stir in the reduced liquid with the whisky, almonds and pistachios.

Soak or wilt some preserved or fresh vine leaves in hot water for 5 minutes and use to line a large oiled loaf tin, keeping the shiny side outwards. Carefully put two-thirds of the venison pâté in the tin; then arrange the sweetbreads in parallel lines along the length of the tin. Sprinkle on any remaining alcohol from the sweetbreads and cover with the rest of the venison pâté. Cover with more vine leaves and fold over those from the sides of the tin.

Cover the tin with a dome of aluminium foil, sealing tightly around the edges and leaving 7–10 cm (3–4 inches) space above the mixture. Stand the tin in a tray of boiling water and bake in a preheated oven at Gas Mark 4/180°C/350°F for 1¼ hours. Leave the pâté for at least 24 hours; then FREEZE or chill, turn out and serve.

To serve from frozen: Thaw the pâté overnight in the refrigerator.

© Glynn Christian

VINE LEAVES

Vine leaves are wonderful for lining any pale coloured pâté or terrine instead of foil. Their colour will brilliantly enhance that of chicken or vegetable mixtures. In the same way use them instead of foil to poach, grill or barbecue delicate fish. They should be blanched for half a minute before freezing, and they can be used straight from the freezer. If you freeze pickled or canned leaves, thaw and rinse them before using.

VINE LEAF DOLMADES

When freshly picked, tender young vine leaves are not available, use preserved ones, rinsing them well in cold water first.

18–20 fresh or preserved vine leaves
125 g (4 oz) brown or green continental lentils
4 tablespoons olive oil
175–250 g (6–8 oz) onion, chopped finely
2 garlic cloves, chopped finely
50 g (2 oz) pine kernels
50 g (2 oz) rice
1 teaspoon dried mint
125 g (4 oz) pre-soaked dried apricots, slivered
250 ml (8 fl oz) chicken stock
12 long chives (optional)
lemon juice for sprinkling
150 ml (¼ pint) water
salt and freshly ground black pepper
To serve
1 quantity of Smoked Cod's Roe Sauce (page 179)

Serves 6

If using fresh vine leaves, plunge them into a bowl of boiling water and leave them for 1 minute until they are limp and soft. Drain and pat dry. If using preserved vine

198

V

leaves, rinse them and pat them dry.

Cover the lentils with cold water. Bring them slowly to the boil and simmer for 10 minutes. Drain.

Heat the oil in a pan and sauté the onion and garlic until soft. Add the pine kernels, rice, lentils, mint and apricots. Stir well and pour in the stock. Season, cover, and simmer for 15–20 minutes until the rice is tender.

Place 12 vine leaves, veined sides up, on a work surface. Place a spoonful of rice filling on the stem end of each leaf. Fold the stem end over the filling. Fold in both sides of the leaves and roll them up firmly. Tie each one up with a long chive stem if liked.

Line the bottom of a large shallow saucepan with the remaining vine leaves. Pack the stuffed rolls inside, seam side down. Sprinkle the dolmades with lemon juice and add the water. Put a small plate on top of the dolmades to prevent them from moving and simmer over a very low heat for 2 hours. FREEZE or serve hot or cold with the sauce.

To serve from frozen: Thaw the stuffed vine leaves overnight in the refrigerator or for 2 hours at room temperature. If serving them hot, reheat them gently in 150 ml (¼ pint) of chicken stock. Serve with the sauce.

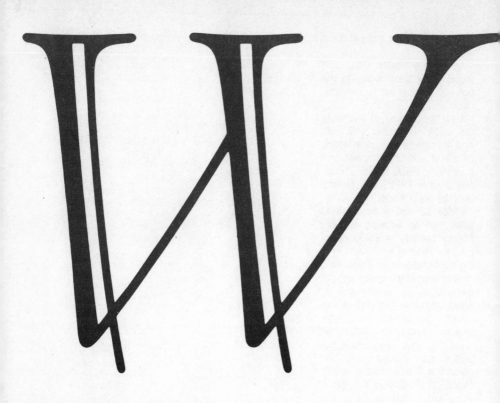

Waffles
Walnuts
Wild Mushrooms

WAFFLES

A long slow bore to make but a long slow deliciousness to eat when you are in the mood. I serve them for breakfast when lunch is likely to be non-existent and dinner late, as on Christmas Day when I dine in the evening. Wonderfully, even savoury waffles with bacon and eggs, are very much better for lashings of butter, and even better with hot syrups of fruit or of maple. Warm waffles are also a great way of making the equivalent of fruit shortcakes, layering them with fresh berries and cream or ice cream.

If you do make your own you should bake them without overbrowning before freezing. Frozen waffles only need heating through under the grill or in a moderate oven for ten minutes or so.

WALNUTS

Now we know that they help reduce cholesterol levels we should none of us be without a stock of walnuts, and they certainly keep better in a freezer. They can be used in their frozen state.

see also
BUTTERS, FLAVOURED (page 40)
SMOKED FISH (page 174)

BRANDIED WALNUT AND FIG MOULDS

500 g (1 lb) dried figs
150 ml (¼ pint) brandy
250 g (8 oz) cream cheese
250 g (8 oz) skimmed milk soft cheese
142 ml (5 fl oz) carton of single cream
3 tablespoons clear honey
50 g (2 oz) walnuts, chopped

Serves 6

Soak the figs in the brandy for at least 1 hour.

Drain the figs and reserve the brandy. Carefully cut the figs open and press them flat. Use the figs to line six individual dariole moulds or soufflé dishes, skin side outside, pressing them firmly into the base and sides of each mould.

Beat the two cheeses with the cream, reserved brandy and honey to taste. Stir in the walnuts. Spoon the mixture into the fig-lined moulds, pressing the filling down firmly. Fold any fig ends neatly over the cheese filling. FREEZE or chill and serve.

To serve from frozen: Thaw the moulds overnight in the refrigerator and then at room temperature for 1 hour before serving.

WATER ICE

see SORBET

WHITEBAIT

see FISH

WILD MUSHROOMS

The increasing interest in mushroom eating is reflected in the publication of several excellent books devoted to the subject, plus a similarly focused television series. There is a splendid earthiness in first finding wild mushrooms and fungi and then preparing and eating them as soon as you return, but this is not something vouchsafed to many of us. Of course the rarity of finding wild produce in shops might induce something of the same euphoria if they were also found to be relatively fresh, worth eating and at something per pound less than the national debt. Even worse is cultivated produce masquerading financially as wild – oyster mushrooms are all farmed, whatever the label says.

You will need to consult specialist books about preparation as each variety behaves differently: the gorgeous chanterelle loses lots of moisture when heated, yet the snow white puffball absorbs even more oil than aubergines, for instance. In broad terms it is best to use such wild produce as an accent rather than a main ingredient, so they go further more often: perhaps to top a pasta sauce for one or two, or as a final layer on a steak and kidney pie before the pastry. Frankly, you may find it simpler to keep a selection of dried ones and to freeze the resulting dishes.

CHANTERELLE PASTRY SANDWICHES

Button, open or oyster mushrooms are equally good for filling the 'sandwiches', as is a mixture of lightly cooked baby vegetables tossed in a hot cream and herb sauce.

1 quantity of Puff Pastry (page 142)
beaten egg to glaze
Filling
50 g (2 oz) butter
500 g (1 lb) chanterelles
2 teaspoons plain flour
142 ml (5 fl oz) carton of soured cream
4 tablespoons dry white wine
2 tablespons freshly chopped chervil or flat-leaf parsley
salt and freshly ground black pepper

Serves 6

Roll the pastry to a rectangle approximately 15 × 23 cm (6 × 9 inches) and cut it into six squares. Place the squares on a baking tray, brush the tops with beaten egg and make 8–10 shallow cuts across the top of each one. Bake in a preheated oven at Gas Mark 6/200°C/400°F for 15–20 minutes or until golden. Cool and split each square in half. FREEZE or set aside while making the filling.

To make the filling, heat the butter in a saucepan and sauté the chanterelles for 1–2 minutes. Stir in the flour. Slowly add the cream and wine, stirring all the time, until the sauce has thickened. Season with salt and pepper and add the herbs. FREEZE or put the bottom half of each pastry on to a plate, spoon on the chanterelle filling and top with the remaining pastry squares.

To serve from frozen: Thaw the chanterelle mixture at room temperature for 1–2 hours; then reheat gently until piping hot. Meanwhile, thaw the pastries in a preheated oven at Gas Mark 6/200°C/400°F for 5–6 minutes, and finish as above.

To serve from frozen: Thaw the chanterelle mixture at room temperature for 1 hour; then gently reheat it with the cream. Reheat the pastries in a preheated oven at Gas Mark 6/200°C/400°F for 5–6 minutes. Fill the hot pastries with the chanterelle mixture and serve.

CHANTERELLES EN CHOUX

2 quantities of Savoury Choux Pastry (page 141)
a little beaten egg
grated parmesan cheese
Filling
75 g (3 oz) butter
1 garlic clove, chopped finely
500 g (1 lb) chanterelles, washed and dried
1 teaspoon plain flour
100 ml (3½ fl oz) white Bordeaux wine
284 ml (10 fl oz) carton of double cream
salt and freshly ground black pepper

Serves 6

Pipe or spoon the choux pastry into six large 'buns' on a dampened baking tray. Brush the top of each 'bun' with a little beaten egg and dust with grated parmesan cheese. Bake in a preheated oven at Gas Mark 6/200°C/400°F for 25 minutes. Take out of the oven and make a long slit in the side of each one and, if necessary, pop them back into the oven for 5 minutes to dry out the centres. FREEZE or fill.

Meanwhile, make the filling. Heat the butter in a saucepan and sauté the garlic for 10 seconds. Add the chanterelles and continue to cook over a high heat for 1–2 minutes until soft and tender. Sprinkle with the flour. Stir well and gradually add the wine and seasoning to taste. Cool and FREEZE, or add the cream, reheat gently and use to fill the hot pastries.

Yeast
Yogurt

Fresh compressed yeast freezes extremely well and is invaluable in the freezer for those who bake their own bread, particularly if fresh yeast is difficult to obtain regularly. It should keep well for up to three months or more.

Pack yeast in sensible amounts – 15 g (½ oz) or 25 g (1 oz) amounts – in individual parcels of foil. Store these in a sealed polythene bag and, when eventually used, allow to thaw slowly before dissolving in lukewarm liquid in the usual way.

Experts tend to disagree about freezing yogurt. I find that it freezes quite well; even if it sep- arates on thawing you can stir the excess liquid back in or pour it off. You may find the greek types of yogurt the most useful, and these are very good substitutes for cream. Of course yogurt will freeze in many made-up dishes and you can always stabilise it by gently heating it with a little cornflour. But never boil yogurt – it should be added to dishes at the last minute and *very* gently warmed through.

Of course frozen yogurt is a wonderful alternative to ice cream, only needing the addi- tion of fruit purée and a little sugar. Otherwise, for every 600 ml (1 pint) of natural yog- urt, blend in 300 ml (½ pint) of fruit purée, a little juice, grated lemon rind and sugar, and fold in a stiffly beaten egg white before freezing. For a light and refreshing variation, beat a couple of egg yolks that have been beaten with 40 g (1½ oz) of sugar into 250 g (½ lb) of greek yogurt; beat in 300 ml (½ pint) of purée and a little lemon juice, and fold in a couple of stiffly beaten egg whites before freezing. You may need to whisk these several times during the freezing process to avoid crystallisation.

APPENDIX

INDEX

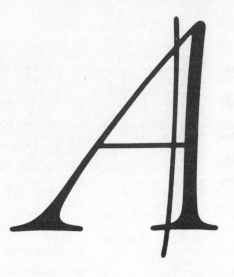

This index includes references to recipes, ingredients and information on preparing, freezing and cooking each ingredient. Recipe titles within entries are in roman (upright) type. Other information within entries is in *italic* type.

E

F